LIBRARY BUILDINGS AND EQUIPMENT INSTITUTE, University of Maryland, 1959 .959

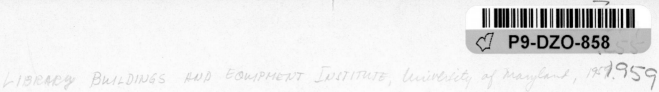

Guidelines for library planners

proceedings of the

LIBRARY BUILDINGS

AND EQUIPMENT INSTITUTE

Sponsored by the Buildings and Equipment Section
Library Administration Division
of the American Library Association

June 18-20, 1959
The McKeldin Library, University of Maryland
College Park, Maryland

To which is added

To remodel or not to remodel

Papers presented at the Washington A.L.A. Conference

Edited by KEITH DOMS and HOWARD ROVELSTAD

Chicago 1960
AMERICAN LIBRARY ASSOCIATION

FOREWORD

The Proceedings which follow reflect the content of the first major Institute organized and operated by the Section on Buildings and Equipment of the Library Administration Division.

General sessions were included which would be of common interest to anyone who might be contemplating a library building program. These open meetings were supplemented by group meetings which were planned to meet needs according to type of library and interest. Discussion thus included all phases of building from the general to the specific.

It is interesting to note that for the first time equipment was treated as a subject of general interest. This subject was discussed in considerable detail at one of the School Libraries Section meetings.

Program participants consistently emphasized the principles of good planning in both the general and the section meetings. In addition to being lively, discussions of specific building plans were always constructive. To place one's preliminary plans on the "firing line" can prove to be extremely beneficial to participants and audience alike.

The Institute was attended by more than 350 librarians, architects, consultants, trustees, and interested persons; the names of representatives of ten countries appear on the roster.

Committees that helped to plan the program and conduct meetings included the Architecture Committee for Public Libraries, Raymond E. Williams, chairman; Buildings Committee for College and University Libraries, Edwin T. Coman, Jr., chairman; Equipment Committee, Howard M. Rowe, chairman; and the Planning School Library Quarters Committee, M. Bernice Wiese, chairman. Harold L. Roth, vice-chairman of the Section, also served as a member of the planning group.

Much of the success of the Institute can be attributed to the splendid facilities and services provided

3

by the University of Maryland and the University Libraries. Howard Rovelstad, director of the University of Maryland Libraries, acted as local arrangements chairman and served with me as co-editor of the Proceedings of the Institute.

A collection of photographs, plans, color slides, program statements, dedication programs, specifications, and other material on recently constructed libraries of all types was available to participants during the Institute. The collection was prepared and manned by Mrs. Dorothy K. Smith, consultant, Library Administration Division.

Finally, I wish to acknowledge the outstanding co-operation and assistance provided by Miss Hazel B. Timmerman, executive secretary, Library Administration Division, and Mrs. Smith. This debt of gratitude is expressed in behalf of the entire membership of the Section on Buildings and Equipment.

Keith Doms, Chairman

Section on Buildings and Equipment
Library Administration Division

CONTENTS

SCHOOL LIBRARIES AND EQUIPMENT

WRITING SPECIFICATIONS FOR LIBRARY EQUIPMENT

APPENDIX

To Remodel or Not To Remodel

THE SPACES IN BETWEEN

PAUL SCHWEIKHER
Head, Department of Architecture
Carnegie Institute of Technology
Pittsburgh, Pennsylvania

In the next two days you will hear about and talk about library planning and equipment. You will discuss the special problems of light, heat, ventilation, floors and other items, and the costs and maintenance of these. I understand, too, that you may review some preliminary plans and budgets for new libraries. These are important elements and they are to be presented by competent people, many of them experts. I think that a synopsis by me in anticipation of the program as a whole or defining the many parts of it would not be useful to you. Instead, I have been permitted to say something less exact about architecture. Perhaps it is un-architecture. I shall keep in mind libraries and the planning and equipping of them, but most of what I say will be about buildings generally and how we may regard them.

Josef Albers[1] says of art, "An art exists because there is something which cannot be said in words, not in dancing, not in music...." I think that this is so for architecture, too, and that although architecture exists partly because of the utilitarian need of shelter, it exists also because there is something which cannot be said in any other way. Utilitarian needs did not compel men to build stone piles as great as the pyramids or temples as perfect as the Parthenon. The delicate balance of stone and glass in a French medieval church, the elegance of a Florentine palace, are remote from the need of them as shelter. And I doubt that the skyscrapers in Dallas, Texas, are there because of the scarcity of land or the pressure of people on it. If there isn't something else, if utility is our one objective, we'll do better in the days ahead to go underground.

Philosophies of Architecture

It is significant that very little has been uncovered of principles or philosophies of architecture written before the middle of the fifteenth century. When it was written, as in Alberti's *De Re Aedificatoria*, it was concerned with "new procedures in musical harmony and mathematical technique to produce a perfection of proportion in plan, elevation and the interrelationship of parts."[2] Vitruvius, before Alberti, and Palladio, after him, acknowledged a few utilitarian justifications but gave most of their attention to form. And so do architects, critics, and historians of the twentieth century. *Constructivism* is an abstraction in line and plane, of forms suggested by construction rather than construction itself. *Neo-classicism* refers to Palladian adaptations to plan and to façade in concrete and in steel; it does not imply new perfections in equipment. *Romantic realism* is a mildly derogatory way of referring to organic architecture; and *new brutalism* is a kind of accusation hurled at those who are trying to "integrate" ducts and pipes and "take material as it comes." The "isms" are unimportant, but they attempt to describe ideas, people, and work that have been important to architecture.

All of these philosophies or trial philosophies are involved in problems of order and proportion, form and space. These may be called the *constants* of architecture. They are visible, perceptible. Words suggest them but cannot define them.

The utilitarian functions of a building are the *variables* of architecture; they change as materials, methods, and equipment change.

The comparative values of the two components, constant and variable (useless and useful), may appear in an abbreviated definition of a building and its function.

Functions of a Building

A building is made up of walls or frames that rest on the ground and support the floors and the roof. Its first function is to resist the forces, both internal and external, that tend to overturn or collapse it: wind and snow on the roof, people and equipment on the floors.

Its second function is that of acting as a selective filter by keeping out rain and snow, and letting in daylight—sometimes sunlight—and air in limited quantities.

The third function, comparatively recent in development and increasingly complicated, is the me-

1. Chairman Emeritus of the School of Design, Yale University; known best for his paintings, "Homage to the Square."

2. *Encyclopaedia Britannica* (Chicago: Encyclopaedia Britannica, Inc., 1958), 1:527.

chanical one of controlled temperatures, artificial light, and other automata.

Fourth is the building's suitability to its use. This, in a sense, is its program. The diagram of it is to be seen in the partitioned subdivisions of the plan.

There are many minor functions, but these are the main ones. The order in which functions have been given is the order in which a building is built, and it is the order of importance in the functioning of it.

Again, a building must have structural stability; it must be weathertight; it must be equipped to control light, air, and temperature; and it must be planned to fit its use.

The Order of Parts of a Building

Yet, a building may have these functions—or the proper counterparts of them—and still be incomplete, for they are in themselves merely quantitative fragments of a whole. It is the order of them that completes the building, gives it form: structural and mechanical order certainly, but more importantly, visual order. (The architect's first responsibility is order; not, as some believe, co-ordination.)

The juncture of beam and column; the way in which a wall turns a corner; the care given to the installation of a pipe, duct, or electric outlet; the precision with which partitions are placed and with which doors are located in them; the placement of the building on the site are all aspects of this order. A building takes its form from the order of these things and from the spaces in between them, not from the things themselves. And now, since I have mentioned space, this should be said of it: that it costs less than things and means more—it is a measure, a distance, a dimension of all directions. It gives unity to things in it and that contain it. It gives form to things and is formed by them. Here is a quotation from *The Way and Its Power*, a translation of the Tao Tê Ching by Arthur Waley:

"We put thirty spokes together and call it a wheel;
But it is on the space where there is nothing that
    the usefulness of the wheel depends.
We turn clay to make a vessel;
But it is on the space where there is nothing that
    the usefulness of the vessel depends.
We pierce doors and windows to make a house;
And it is on these spaces where there is nothing that
    the usefulness of the house depends.
Therefore just as we take advantage of what is, we
    should recognize the usefulness of what is not."[3]

It is difficult to persuade ourselves that there is a usefulness to what is not immediately and apparently useful to us. We are curious but uncertain that space in between things can have meaning or value. This is a difficulty with most building committees and many architects who think and talk of space as so many square feet per person or per something, and use cubes only as alternatives of unit costs.

Chapter 21 of *Revelations* gives the measure of a city: "...And he that talked with me had a golden reed to measure the city, and the gates thereof, and the wall thereof. And the city lieth foursquare, and the length is as large as the breadth: and he measured the city with the reed, twelve thousand furlongs. The length, and the breadth and the height of it are equal." Leland Hazard in a recent talk to students at Carnegie pointed out that "this made heaven a cube of one and one-half miles."

Three-dimensional Extension

We are familiar with two-dimensional extension into space: the Moebius curve is a topological example—it can be observed with critical disinterest. But three-dimensional extension affects and involves all of our senses, thoughts, and actions at every moment of our lives. It is necessary constantly to resolve the differences between psychological effect and physical fact. Architecture as a three-dimensional extension of and into space affects and involves us in this way. The experiments begun by Adelbert Ames, Jr., at Princeton and continued by Hadley Cantril and Warren J. Wittreich reveal the manner in which we perceive the sizes and shapes of spaces, and of one another in them. The settings for the experiments are architectural ones: distorted rooms in false perspective. Seeing them, moving in them produced surprising reactions. Professor Wittreich writes: "...Out of his past experience with the cues provided by perspective, the viewer has assembled a set of assumptions that he brings to the occasion and applies to the immediate experience.

"Ames built one of these rooms large enough for people to walk about in it. A surprising thing now happens. When the viewer sees another person walk across the room, he typically observes an extraordinary alteration in that person's size. Depending on the direction the person walks, he appears to grow or shrink...."[4]

These are spatial, visual perceptions. The recession of the walls in space, the tilted floor, change the perception. The experience brought to the experiment by the observer is acted upon by what he sees and the distortions occur.

Referring to the normal experience, Wittreich writes: "When we watch a person walk away from us, his image shrinks in size. But since we know for a fact that he is not shrinking, we make an un-

3. Published by Allen & Unwin, Ltd., London. Used by permission of The Macmillan Company.

4. Warren J. Wittreich, "Visual Perception and Personality," *Scientific American*, 200, no. 4:56 (April, 1959).

conscious correction and 'see' him as retaining his full stature. Past experience tells us what his true stature is with respect to our own. Any sane and dependable expectation of the future requires that he have the same true stature when we next encounter him. Our perspective is thus a prediction; it embraces the past and the future as well as the present.

"From such considerations psychology has taught us all by now that perception is not a simple act. We do not merely see what is 'out there' in the here and now. Perception is an ongoing process that involves our image of our own self, our needs, values and purposes, as fully as it involves the image of the object perceived."[5]

The Architect Applies Order

The architect is not working with space and things in it to deceive, but he is working with this "ongoing process." And he is working with space, knowing that it acts upon us, our intellects, our emotions, and is effective. He will apply to space, therefore, all that he knows of order: scale, proportion, rhythm, balance, and symmetry just as he would apply these to the building.

There are many noteworthy examples of this: the Greek agora, the Roman forum, the piazzas of Italy, the squares of London, and the courtyards of Paris.

The spaces of the squares, courtyards, and piazzas are defined in width and breadth, of course, but especially—and this is what gives the piazza at San Marco its distinction—they are defined by the roofs of the buildings that surround them. It is the relation of the heights of these roofs to the width and length of the piazza that is so remarkably successful. And one must see it to know how the eye is carried vertically beyond the limit of the roofs by the Campanile and to know the way in which the large space is extended and given scale by the smaller square of the Doge's palace, and the entrance and boundary marked by the lions and the Grand Canal.

Usefulness of What Is Not

An excellent, modern example in this country is that of the Seagram Building on Park Avenue in New York. The simple device of leaving space where buildings have always been before provides a setting for the building that gives it and the space around it more importance than anything else along the avenue. Seen from a distance the empty space leads to anticipation, realized upon arrival in the beauty and perfection of the building itself—the usefulness of what is not.

The parks and squares of our own cities and towns are spaces in between. They vary in size and

5. *Ibid.*

in effect, but all serve to compose the buildings, streets, and boulevards which define them—or did, until many were reduced to parking lots. These, too, are spaces in between, but they are spaces used rather than useful; convenient but not composed. They are disorderly, gross, and ugly. Parenthetically, there are too many parking lots, too many streets full of automobiles, noise, and dirt. Open spaces should be for people, not for their automobiles. The automobiles may be stored away from the centers of towns and cities, preferably below ground.

Spaces in Buildings

I have been talking so far mostly about space outside the building. What I have said applies just as well to space within the building. Here again we have our historic prototypes: the great naves of the French cathedrals, the lofty interiors of the Duomo in Florence or of Hagia Sofia in Istanbul, and a thousand others.

Spaces do not need to be as mysterious or awe-inspiring as these, or as monumental even as those in modern railway stations. But in their own scale and in their own place and meaning, they can have importance; they need not be mean.

The structural elements and the interior subdivisions of buildings respond to space, affecting it and being affected by it in exactly the same manner that has been described for the exteriors of buildings and spaces around them and exterior to them. The depths of beams and the sizes and cross sections of walls—all these are directly affected by the spaces in between.

When walls support the floor and the roof, then the spaces between the supporting walls are important, in height and in width. They are important to see and experience, but they are important also in determining the material of which the walls and floors are made. Walls must vary in thickness according to their height, or they will not be stable: wind can push them over; superimposed loads can crush them or make them twist about their own axes.

Columns and beams react to the spaces between them in a similar way. Their capacity for carrying loads affects the spaces between them, and, in turn, the spaces affect their sizes (the cross sections—widths and depths, heights and lengths).

These effects are not limited to rectilinear, labial constructions, but apply just as well to the use of thin shells and folded forms in concrete, wood, and steel: hyperbolic parabolas, tetrahedrons, "pinked" edges, and other exotic shapes. For if these are not called into existence by the requirements of space, they should not be used.

The psychologists tell us that our dominant sensory field is vision. We must train ourselves to use it. We can be told what there is to see, but it is better to see for ourselves.

See for Yourselves

To those responsible for existing library buildings or for planning new ones, it is good to talk about planning and about materials and equipment or to read about these things. It will be better to see for yourselves. Look at buildings, not just libraries, and look to see, learn to see, the spaces in between them—in between buildings as well as in between the elements of them; see what they do or fail to do. Having done this yourselves, you may insist that those you work with—committees, engineers, architects—do the same.

Require of yourselves and of those you work with at least two things in buildings: (1) to see and to know the value of spaces, the usefulness of what is not, and (2) perfection of detail in structure and in the enclosing fabric, for this is a good sign of durability and a low cost in maintenance. See these qualities in existing buildings and look for them on the drawings made for new buildings. By the way, learn to read drawings. Do not look for the impressive or the expressive. Just look for what is *good*, as you might look for good in writing. In a building it will be form, made up by the ordering of space and building elements. It may be remembered that in architecture it is how a thing is done rather than what is done that is important. A building may be good or bad depending upon the care given to putting it together by the owner, the architect, and others.

Above all, learn to *see*, and to care for what you see. Ruskin has written: "...I find this conclusion impressed upon me that the greatest a human soul ever does in this world is to see something and tell what it saw in a plain way. Hundreds of people can talk for one who can think, but thousands can think for one who can see. To see clearly is poetry, prophecy and religion all in one."

LAYOUT PLANS AND LIBRARY INTERIORS

MARTIN VAN BUREN
Interior Planning Consultant
Charlotte, North Carolina

Not long ago I met a man who had just visited for the first time a new modern public library. "But it doesn't *look* like a library," the man exclaimed.

Such a reaction to the many contemporary innovations in library design and construction is not unusual, but it raises the logical question: What *should* a library look like? Or, more generally, what *is* a library? This apparently superficial question needs no answer to most professional librarians, who are constantly aware of the scope of library services and their increasingly complex demands. But the original question did not concern library services; it concerned the building which houses such services. What is there about today's successful library building that differs from its Carnegie predecessor? Are these gleaming metal and glass structures which are springing up in so many communities across the land truly an improvement over the older concepts of a generation ago? To what advantage are the spacious open interiors with their relaxed settings of informal furniture, their cheerful colors, their friendly atmosphere? Should we of today's mad pace frown on these obvious attempts at merchandising?

Such revisions in our approach to library planning are not only advantageous, they are essential as well. They are *advantageous* because the spirit of hospitality thus created brings an unquestionable increase in community interest and use of the library, which in turn communicates the further spread of knowledge, heightens understanding among mankind, engenders a more enlightened society. They are *essential* because they not only make use of modern-day technologies for more efficient service, but, in addition, they fulfill one of the true requirements of the library building and its equipment—that it must stand as an outstanding symbol of cultural advancement and leadership within the community. To those who question the wisdom of current-day thought on library planning, reference can be made to the phenomenal increase in patronage of those new buildings already in existence.

The Planning Team

With this general observation in mind, let us consider the problems and responsibilities involved in planning such a library building, more specifically its interior and equipment.

From beginning to end, the planning of such a complex structure requires the close co-operation of certain specialists. This group of specialists we call the Planning Team. Each member of the Planning Team bears distinct responsibilities which must be carefully integrated into the concept of the whole. The basic core of this team is comprised of three members:

1. The Government Authority, whose primary duties are legal, appointive, and financial.

2. The Librarian, who is generally the co-ordinator (or, you might say, the moderator) of the Planning Team during all phases of planning, constructing, and equipping the building, involving an endless maze of notes, budgets, schedules, check lists, decisions, and plans, which terminate only when occupancy of the finished building is accomplished. In addition, the Librarian is the logical author of the written program—that vital outline which is the basic key to a successful library.

3. The third core member of the Planning Team is the Architect, whose duties include advice on site selection (its location, orientation, size, slope, drainage, etc.), preparation of initial size and cost requirements, preparation of preliminary plans and sketches, execution of working drawings and specifications, and finally supervision of construction.

There are two additional members of the Planning Team who can contribute invaluably to the success of the building. One is the Library Building Consultant. He is generally an expert thoroughly versed in both library practice and in architectural procedures; thus he offers an experienced liaison between the librarian, who perhaps has never before faced a building project, and the architect, who may possess a limited background in the architectural needs peculiar to library function and operation.

Last but (I am inclined to add) not least is the Interior Planning Consultant. He is assigned the task of developing the furniture and equipment budget; preparing furniture and equipment layouts for the building; selection of interior colors in collaboration with the Architect; evaluation of available equipment; and preparation of detailed construction specifications for the above-listed items. Often the Interior Planning Consultant will evolve special designs for equipment which meet certain needs peculiar to the project at hand. Finally, it is his responsibility to make final inspection of the installation and recommend acceptance or rejection of each item of equipment.

Thus we have, briefly described, the members of our all-important Planning Team. Since each member's duties are so interrelated with those of other members, it is necessary that the entire Planning Team be mentioned even though our primary concern here is with interior planning and equipment layout and evaluation.

The Building Program

Before any interior planning can be accomplished, a schedule of equipment requirements must be pre-

pared as a basic guide to such planning. This is normally accomplished in the written program and is broken down area by area, clarifying such needs as book storage requirements, seating capacities, work stations or desks, special equipment needs such as card catalogs, atlas stands, and so forth. Descriptive pointers in the program as to aesthetic desires, or atmosphere, are of help not only to the architect but to the interior planner as well.

In brief, then, the written program is the basic guide from which the interior planning consultant proceeds. In view of the obvious importance of such a program, it is expedient here to submit a precise definition of the program as a whole:

"The programme is a written statement prepared by the librarian or other competent authority describing the purpose, scope, and function of the library building. It should state as comprehensively as possible the specific needs of the library and should outline in detail the areas, their requirements, relationships, and functions within the building. In addition, it should define the aesthetic character of the building and chart generally the type and nature of furnishings and equipment."

The above definition was developed by Mr. Galvin and myself for inclusion in the UNESCO book, *The Small Public Library Building.*[1]

Interior Planning and Layouts

A logical question concerning the interior planning of a library building is: When does it commence? At what stage in the over-all building program does the problem of interior planning first arise? The answer is: During the development of the initial architectural plans. It is during this early stage that changes in building plans can readily be made, and it is therefore only logical that spatial requirements for equipment, seating needs, and the like should be determined as a check against area allowances within the building itself. Often a slight shifting of partitions, relocation of a door, adjustment of a window, can solve an interior furnishing problem which otherwise might pose a serious restriction to library operation or interior beauty. Without question, the architectural matter of telephone and electrical outlet locations must relate to interior furnishings; therefore these should be considered jointly.

This relationship of interior planning to early architectural concepts is too often ignored, and results in unfortunate and awkward compromises in equipping the building. Parenthetically, it might be added that early interior planning adds nothing to planning fees since most interior planning consultants work on either a percentage or a flat fee basis

1. Hoyt R. Galvin and Martin Van Buren, *The Small Public Library Building* (Paris: UNESCO, 1959), p.29.

regardless of work-hours consumed, and an efficient marriage of architectural and interior plans can often result in economical solutions through the use of standard mass-produced equipment.

During this early stage in planning, considerable emphasis must be placed on the functional relationship of areas within the building, for it is from this important stage that an efficient interior plan becomes possible. Here, not only the librarian and the architect render valuable service, but the interior consultant as well. It is his task to work closely with the librarian and the architect to interpret the program needs in terms of actual space requirements, control factors, and traffic flow. If certain areas are not adequate, for example, to contain the designated equipment—or seating, or book shelving—such facts should be brought out and corrected. If certain areas obviously lack supervision from exposed work stations, the basic plan must be altered or the librarian must determine if additional personnel can be afforded for this purpose. If disturbing traffic cuts directly through quiet reading areas, the defect in plan must be studied and corrected. If insufficient space is allocated to card catalogs, they must either be relocated or the plan altered. If orientation and plan are such that harsh sunlight will disturb patrons or staff-work areas, provision must be made for sun control, either by architectural means or in the interior plan. And so on.

The question might be asked: lacking a final interior plan at this stage, how can the adequacy of space allowances be determined? Actually, a very rough equipment sketch-plan is evolved, sufficient to determine sizes, traffic possibilities, and other space requirements. Scaled to the architect's preliminary plans, equipment needs as set forth in the written program are roughed in sufficiently to determine if a solution is possible. As an aid in accomplishing this, various formulae have been developed which offer general standards; these can be found in such publications as Wheeler and Githens, *The American Public Library Building*,[2] or *The Small Public Library Building*, which Mr. Galvin and I wrote for UNESCO.

Equipment and Furnishings Budget

Concurrently with the above initial stage of interior planning, basic cost data should be assembled for interior furnishings and equipment. Normally a building project is confined to a fixed over-all sum which encompasses procurement of site, construction of the building, and furnishings and equipment. This over-all sum must be broken down into component allowances for the accomplishment of these various

requirements. Therefore, a fairly accurate breakdown budget for furnishings and equipment should be made at this stage. This budget can then be balanced against site and construction estimates to make certain all budget allowances are in line with the over-all building fund. Once a site is procured and a building contract let, further adjustments in equipment allowances become possible.

Often during initial budget considerations certain "average" figures for furniture and equipment are used. These are obtained from other recently completed projects of similar nature. In recent years these "average" figures range from $2 to $3 per square foot. Another rough guide is the "average" figure of 10 to 15 per cent of the over-all building cost. It should be noted that such figures not only vary with time, but they also vary from one geographical area to another.

Whereas such general cost figures are sufficient for preliminary budget allowances, they should be used only as a guide, with more detailed computations made before architectural plans proceed to any detailed degree. To accomplish this, reference is again made to the written program. From this program a complete cost list of equipment, shelving requirements, seating capacities, etc. should be made. To this list should be added contemplated allowances for such items as draperies, carpeting and the like; interior consultant fees; miscellaneous requirements such as janitorial equipment, office machines, waste receptacles, umbrella stands, coat racks, ash trays, etc. To determine budget allowances item by item, two sources are available: other libraries which have recently acquired similar equipment and manufacturers themselves. The assembly of the list itself might appear to be a monumental task. Actually it is not so formidable as it seems. If the librarian and the interior planning consultant review the plan of the building area by area, and function by function, it will be found that requirements materialize quite naturally.

A word of caution: preconceptions of equipment as to type, style, or particular manufacturer should be avoided during the compilation of the budget list. Such preconceptions will invariably hamper future creative design of the library interior. Even lacking specific manufacturers' models in the list, one experienced in market costs generally will be able to assign reasonable allowances for each item included. In the final analysis it will be found that certain items will be higher in cost, certain items lower, than originally anticipated because of variances in types and materials finally selected. But a fair *over-all* allowance is the goal—a figure toward which the interior planning consultant can work.

Final Layout Development

Once an architectural plan is finalized and an over-all furnishing budget figure determined, detailed interior planning can commence. It is ad-

2. J. L. Wheeler and A. M. Githens, *The American Public Library Building* (Chicago: A.L.A., 1941).

visable as a first step to "block in" accurately the shelving requirements of the various areas since these requirements are generally inflexible, are normally qualified precisely in the written program, and will by architectural necessity be already considered in some detail.

Next, other fixed equipment should be indicated and placed on the plan. This includes such items as the lending desk, card catalog, information and reference equipment, and the like. The librarian should review extensively the location of equipment located thus far, and study its relationship to pertinent areas with particular reference to its use in actual operation by both patrons and staff. Accessibility of equipment to those who frequently make use of it is a vital element of efficient library operation; this point cannot be overstressed.

With the placement of shelving and basic fixed equipment, applied carefully to scale on the architect's plan, additional study should be made of traffic flow and space allowances immediately adjacent to such equipment. Does the bookstack arrangement permit the 3-foot minimum aisle space required? Is there adequate circulation space around the more heavily used centers such as the lending desk and the card catalog? Here, future traffic jams can be a serious bottleneck. Although this matter of traffic and circulation space has already been considered during the architectural development, it must be constantly rechecked during the placement and location of furnishings and equipment.

Most contemporary library buildings follow a concept of "open planning" with a minimum of permanent partitions, thus offering a feeling of spaciousness, of friendly invitation as one's glance embraces the easy flow of one area into another. Such open planning also permits great flexibility as future needs of the library alter and change by season or by growth. Into this plan has been located fixed or permanent equipment, and various areas labeled according to previous decision. The matter of visual or psychological separation of certain areas may be approached by means of movable equipment such as freestanding book shelves, bulletin boards, display racks, or movable partitions. Often the arrangement of furniture groupings can create psychological separation. Again, the subject of traffic flow will determine the placement of such divisions. As each area is considered, the question should be asked: where is the most logical and least disturbing point of traffic entry and exit? Proper placement of divider units permits patrons to be subtly routed into the desired area, where they will have immediate access to its material with as little disturbance of readers as possible.

There has been—and still is—some debate as to the practicality of such open planning, of the use of low, psychological area divisions. In the case of public libraries this is particularly true with regard to the children's area and the young adults' area. Many librarians are of the opinion that these two areas should be completely isolated by solid partitions. There is valid argument to this viewpoint, but it must be pointed out that one of the most crucial difficulties in library operation today is sufficient personnel, since salary budgets in most libraries are woefully inadequate and experienced personnel difficult to find. Personnel costs are absorbing an ever increasing proportion of library operating budgets, and enclosure of any areas requiring constant supervision may thus increase staff requirements. Glass partitions may partially solve the problem. Some librarians believe that discipline in open areas is just as effectively controlled under the firm and wary eye of a nearby staff member, who perhaps serves a dual function at the lending desk.

We come to the question of lounge seating versus table seating. In recent years there has been an increase in the proportion of lounge seating, which is an encouraging trend so long as it does not lead to overemphasis. Attractive, informal lounge areas add much to a library's atmosphere of hospitality. Where an open façade at street level is planned, attractive lounge groups can be so located as to be pleasantly visible from the exterior. In plan, this arrangement is logical, for the more informal browsing areas need not be secluded but can be left open to public view. The more serious study and research areas, which offer primarily table-reader facilities, should be located away from heavy traffic and circulation, i.e., away from the main entry and related traffic.

To maintain a sense of orderliness, seats should be arranged in groupings. A haphazard scramble of chairs and tables creates an immediate impression of chaos. To discourage patrons from shuffling chairs about, and as a guide for janitors who straighten up, area rugs of a durable material are sometimes employed as a definition of each group location. In addition, the placement of a heavy central piece, such as a coffee table which is not easily moved, will serve as an "anchor" around which lounge chairs may be placed. Although the use of sofas is discouraged because readers invariably prefer separate chairs, their immobility also serves to "anchor" a grouping. Furthermore, in a very spacious reading area a certain amount of visual bulk is desired to balance the scale of furnishings with that of the surrounding area.

The amount of table-reader seating should be indicated in the written program. Naturally a college or reference library will require a preponderance of such seating, whereas a public library's requirements will vary according to the amount of student and research activity anticipated. Individual study units should be incorporated, either as separate tables or in the form of carrels. A recent study of a typical college library made by the writer indicated that standard 36-inch wide reader tables were inadequate to serve the surface-area requirements for student work. Consequently 48-inch tables were specified and the difficulty alleviated. This observation is not an original one, but it points out the careful thought which must be applied to every aspect of library planning.

Before an over-all furnishing plan has been finalized, it should again be checked against the requirements set forth in the program. Quite often there develops a certain amount of give-and-take, of compromise, that is unavoidable. It is unrealistic to assume that an absolute ideal exists, and here the program must be considered as a goal rather than a precise dictate. Whatever compromise appears necessary should be judged carefully and discussed among members of the planning team. If the discrepancy between the program requirements and actual conditions does not seriously impair the efficiency of the library, it is probably expedient to accept the compromise; if, on the other hand, the actual plan requirement poses a serious concession, the furnishing plan must be reworked, if necessary from the very beginning.

Selection of Items of Equipment— Function, Durability, and Beauty

However, let us not be pessimistic. Assuming that a workable plan has been completed, the actual selection of furnishings and equipment must be undertaken. This involves extensive evaluation, of judging and weighing the relative merits of materials, styles, finishes, colors, construction standards, and the like. When one considers the seemingly endless variety of equipment to be specified, from the more obvious chairs and tables to such items as upholstery fabrics and display racks, one is tempted to give up in despair. How does one go about this task? There are two obvious avenues of approach: (1) experience and (2) investigation. For purposes of this discussion let us assume that *experience*, in the above sense, is lacking.

Investigation of equipment in all its phases is a time-consuming but important task. Let us first consider the three basic attributes which apply to the selection of all library furnishings and equipment. They are function, durability, and beauty. If we examine these three elements in order, we find that the task of evaluation is greatly simplified. First, function—which encompasses comfort, convenience, efficiency, simplicity of operation, economy of maintenance, and so forth. For example, what is the most comfortable table-top height and color for readers? The most convenient lending desk height? The most comfortable type chair? The most efficient desk arrangement as to drawer and typewriter arrangement? The most workable arrangement of lending desk components?

As a concrete example, during the planning of the public library for Charlotte, North Carolina, we questioned the 24-inch table height which was a proposed standard for children. This standard was apparently based on the old maxim of a 10-inch differential between chair seat and table height, since children's chairs are normally 14 inches from floor to seat. Upon investigation we discovered that this 10-inch differential, although quite acceptable for adults, was uncomfortable for children. Further investigation indicated a table height of 22 inches as a more acceptable—and functional—solution, based upon the utilization of apronless tables.

From the question of function we progress to the matter of durability. It is an obvious fact that a substantial expenditure for furnishings and equipment cannot be duplicated every few years; that replacement within a short time is normally out of the question. Therefore, great care must be exercised in specifying furnishings which will resist public abuse day after day, year after year. One might ask now an intelligent investigation can be carried out by a layman who is unfamiliar with construction technologies? One method is to consult unbiased authorities who do possess such background and knowledge. Another is to make exhaustive inquiry regarding the past performance of identical equipment—to determine where it has been previously installed, for how long, and under how severe abuse. Inquiry can then be made as to its durability under test conditions.

It might be said that a piece of furniture or equipment is only as strong as its weakest joint. To this might be added such factors as the strength of its component parts, durability of finish, and ruggedness of upholstery materials. It is accepted practice among manufacturers to submit samples of materials, finishes, joint construction, and so forth, which can be subjected to rigorous tests. Such tests are informative but not conclusive, for it is the combination of all structural features which determine over-all strength.

A significant misconception regarding durability is that bulk and weight are synonymous with strength. Particularly with regard to today's technologies, materials and construction systems permit lightweight forms and shapes, which are stronger than anything dreamed of a generation ago.

Finally, be wary of manufacturers' claims. Even the most reputable are not infallible, and there is no such thing as a single manufacturer who is unquestionably superior to all others. Simple logic indicates that the tools and machinery necessary to produce top caliber equipment can be procured by any manufacturer with the means and initiative to do so, and with such tools there is an optimum standard that can be attained.

Standards of beauty are regrettably often left in the wake of the more practical standards of function and durability. Cost, some say, is the restrictive factor. Others claim that a choice must be made between beauty, and function and durability; that it is impossible to achieve all three. Nothing could be more fallacious. Through the ages many examples of furniture have been created which prove the possibility of this combination of qualities.

In the library world, possibly more than in any other, honest pioneering into the realm of beauty has been deplorable. In a recent German publication, *Public Library Building,* the author's extensive study of American public libraries led to the conclusion that, although we are established leaders in the development of such public service, the United States "has reached a great measure of standardization which seems today to have led to a partial stagnation in this field."[3] True, a few manufacturers have made feeble attempts at streamlining, or styling—to use the commercial connotation—but there is a certain smugness which, if one digs beneath the surface, appears strongly allied to comfortable profits. It is an irony that the library, at least in America, is confined to such limitations of attractiveness when it should be, above all other buildings, the accepted model of cultural beauty.

To evaluate furnishings and equipment with regard to beauty is a difficult task. Good taste is not a birthright enjoyed by a chosen few, but it is rather a matter of education. The subtle balance of form and line, of proportion, of color harmony—all enter into the picture.

Whereas it is a simple matter to write letters asking whether a certain chair has proven its structure under the rigors of public abuse, it is impossible to ask if this same chair has proved its aesthetic beauty of design. The simplest answer, I think, to this search for honest judgment of beauty lies in our present-day wealth of visual communication, particularly photographic publications. Most outstanding libraries today are published pictorially with professional comments as to beauty as well as other aspects. Even though members of the planning team are unable to visit such outstanding examples, they can study them in detail by this means. The point is, each example should be studied objectively and minutely, with the question constantly in mind: "Wherein lies its beauty?"

Perhaps the only way to become specific regarding this subject is to cite an example. One of the most unattractive items of library equipment is the card catalog. At the same time its bulk is unavoidable, and its prominent location mandatory. There it squats, a veritable miniature fortress amidst its more refined companion equipment. What can be done to make this necessary monster more pleasing to look at? Some libraries have managed their plans in such a way that the cases are recessed into a wall, thus concealing their bulk. In the Charlotte public library, this was not feasible. Therefore, an open metal base was designed which gave the cases a lighter "floating" appearance, and the cases themselves were made of a richer dark wood with an oil finish. It is gratifying to note that this light, open-

base innovation is now being offered as standard equipment by a prominent manufacturer.

Specification Writing

Returning to the broader subject of library interior planning, we find ourselves faced with the task of interpreting our furniture and equipment selections, their function, durability, and beauty, in the form of written specifications. There are two basic objectives in preparing such specifications for bidders:

1. To describe and qualify each item of equipment as to size, construction, material, design, and quality.

2. To prescribe minimum standards in sufficient detail as to eliminate the participation of unqualified bidders, or the submittal of unacceptable merchandise or services.

The written specifications should also contain a section, normally titled "General Conditions," in which are included various forms of legal protection for the library, and general contractual terms under which the contractor and the library agree to work. Many governmental agencies have standardized these general conditions as they relate to all such bidding procedures; these are readily obtainable and can be used as a guide to library equipment specifications. It is important that legal protective clauses be thorough and comprehensive—a matter which should be reviewed in writing by the library's legal counsel.

The problem of writing detailed specifications which satisfy the qualities of design and construction outlined above is not a simple one. For reasons of practicality it must be conceded that specific items of manufacture must necessarily be chosen during the planning stage; otherwise budget allowances and design concepts become an almost impossible task. Therefore, it is common practice to prescribe an exact item, by manufacturer and catalog number, as the chosen standard. This definition is commonly followed by the phrase, "or equal." And herein lies a great danger, for the term "or equal" opens infinite avenues for compromise, dissension, political shenanigans, and even the possible loss of carefully developed design and construction standards. It is thus vital that evaluation and judgment of alternate proposals be done with as much experience and care as were the original selections.

On the other hand, the "or equal" phrase is an invaluable aid in procuring advantageous bids, for bidders who are aware of keen competition will react accordingly.

Specific manufacturers' selections having been made, it will be found that these manufacturers are more than eager to furnish detailed construction and design data which can be included in the specifica-

3. Werner Mevissen, *Büchereibau* (Public Library Building) (Essen: Ernst Heyer, 1958), p.11.

tions. One inherent weakness in most specifications is the lack of design definitions. It has been mentioned previously that beauty of equipment is an important element to an attractive and successful library building, and it is assumed that this quality has been carefully considered in selecting items to be specified. Yet, if design qualities are not described in the specifications, a low bid is conceivable which meets all structural standards but simply does not satisfy the design standards wanted. If standards of beauty or design are not included in the specifications, this presents a moral and legal question as to the award of bid. Who can state in legal terms which is acceptable design and which is not? The argument is abstract and therefore indefinable.

The answer lies in the writing of the General Conditions. In order to allay such a possibility, two insertions are relevant. One should state as follows: "In consideration of alternate proposals, quality of design shall bear equal weight with that of construction." The second clause, which is commonly used, states: "The Owner reserves the right to waive informalities and to accept or reject any or all bids." With the added comment that the decision of the Owner is final, the library achieves the legal protection it requires. These are not unfair inclusions; the basic premise is to plan and equip the best possible library building in all respects, and a planning team devoted to this end must remain firm, at the risk of appearing dogmatic.

Bids

Receiving and opening bids, which is normally a formal affair performed at a previously stated time and date, requires only two comments.

First, a responsible party must be assigned the task of keeping records of all proceedings, from the list of those requesting and receiving specifications and any subsequent addenda, to preparation of a tabulation sheet which records the compilation of bids received. Such records circumvent argument among bidders, questions of procedure, and objections as to final awards.

Second, from the moment bids are opened and publicly announced, all arguments and protestations from interested parties must be avoided. It is only human for a defeated bidder to want to plead his case; however, one accepted plea can only result in rebuttal, and confusion soon results, occasionally to the point where the responsible parties become too involved to assess bids on a fair and equal basis. This comment appears trivial, but the condition described does happen in public bid-openings—and often.

Summary

In summing up, it is perhaps expedient to take the librarian's viewpoint. In this regard there are three extremely critical stages during the planning of a library in which the librarian assumes vital and unavoidable responsibility.

First is the written program. This document is the key to any successful library building project. And the librarian, whether he actually writes the program or not, must assume responsibility for its correctness and for its completeness.

Second is the architectural floor plan. The adequacy of spaces and areas within the building, as well as their interrelationship for efficient function, fall to the librarian for final analysis and judgment.

Third, the final list of furnishings and equipment is subject to review and approval by the librarian. Although this may be prepared by other members of the planning team, it is the librarian who must live and work with this equipment. Decisions of function, durability, and beauty can rest in the hands of others perhaps, but the list itself must be complete, encompassing the myriad items that will be required. Only the librarian can determine this appraisal.

Taking all these items into consideration, we find that a library building project consists of a series of logical procedures, each integrated with the others, each approached in its own way, all building up to a final goal—the conception and realization of a successful library building.

RESILIENT FLOORINGS
FOR LIBRARY BUILDINGS

L. E. FOSTER
Marketing Manager, Floor Division
Armstrong Cork Company

I understand that you are interested in such subjects about flooring as: cost, composition, flooring types, recommended uses, wear properties, and maintenance. I shall attempt to touch on all of these bases. I shall consider such things as cost, what the various products will and will not do, their recommended applications, and I shall make some comments about maintenance.

Choosing the *right* floor for *each* area is critically important. Each area has different requirements and each basic type of material has different physical characteristics. Also, floorings differ greatly in their maintenance costs. Thus a floor that you might choose because of low initial cost might be the most expensive floor for the long pull.

Presentation of Floorings
Arranged by Cost

Asphalt tile

I'll start at the bottom of the price scale and work up, appraising each product as we go along. First is asphalt tile. One-half-inch gauge asphalt tile is the lowest-priced permanent floor in the industry, costing about 15 to 25 cents a square foot installed. The darker colors cost slightly less than the lighter ones. One of the great attributes of asphalt tile is that it can be installed directly to concrete that is on grade or below grade, in other words, at ground level or below ground level. Most flooring types deteriorate when subjected to the alkaline moisture normally found in grade and below-grade slabs, but asphalt is virtually unaffected.

In passing, perhaps I should mention that grade and below-grade floors can be sufficiently waterproofed to receive other types of flooring, but the process is tedious and costly. Asphalt tile has good, but not outstanding, maintenance properties. Throughout this discussion we will rate each product as being superior, excellent, good, or fair in terms of maintenance cost. Asphalt is next to the bottom on this count, being scored as good.

The most serious limitation of asphalt tile is its susceptibility to indenting. A static weight load of 25 pounds per square inch will indent this product. You can imagine what happens when your bride and mine walk through with their stiletto-type heels, which impose a load of something like 1500 pounds per square inch. Asphalt has another limitation you should know about. It has poor resistance to oils and greases. For a lunchroom or any areas where foods are likely to be spilled, we definitely would not recommend asphalt tile. But, all things considered, asphalt gives a lot of floor for the money. It is a good economical buy.

Vinyl asbestos—1/16-inch

As we move up the price scale to 30 cents a foot, the next product is 1/16-inch vinyl asbestos. Our trade name for such a product is Excelon. Like asphalt tile this product can be used on or below grade. One of its shortcomings is that it indents with a static load of 25 pounds per square inch. This product has superior maintenance characteristics; it has much clearer and sharper colors than those found in asphalt tile. It has high resistance to chemicals, oils, and greases, and is fire retardant. For library installations we think vinyl asbestos has real merit, but the 1/16-inch gauge is too light for heavy duty areas. It should serve well, though, in light to moderate traffic areas.

Linoleum standard gauge

Standard linoleum falls just above Excelon at 35-45 cents. Generally, we regard the standard gauge as a residential floor; however, it should suffice for light traffic areas. One appealing feature of linoleum is that the field material can be flashed right up the wall to form a streamlined conjuncture between floor and wall. This is true of all sheet goods items. This treatment is called *flash cove base*, a very practical treatment that facilitates cleaning and produces a handsome baseboard trim. We will talk more about linoleum when we encounter heavy-gauge linoleum a bit higher on the price scale.

Vinyl asbestos—1/8-inch

Moving on to the 35-50 cent a foot range, we find the 1/8-inch gauge of vinyl asbestos. As we mentioned earlier, this product can claim superior maintenance characteristics. It can be installed on or below grade. It has high resistance to oils and greases. It is a very durable floor. Its one serious shortcoming is its vulnerability to indentation. A static load of 25 pounds per square inch will indent vinyl asbestos.

Thin sheet goods

Moving on to the 55 cent a foot bracket, we find .070-inch-gauge sheet vinyl offered in a number of design effects. Though this product is homogeneous vinyl and is rugged, we would not recommend a gauge this thin for heavy duty areas. For light traffic areas sheet vinyl has much to commend it— virtually no seams, exceptionally good color clarity and permanence, superior maintenance properties, and good indentation resistance. In short, it is a fine floor but not for heavily traveled rooms.

Vinyl asbestos—through grain

In the next price bracket at 65 cents a square foot we find another member of the vinyl asbestos family—this one with a through grain. This product, which we call Imperial Excelon, has the same physical properties as our other vinyl asbestos, but its graining goes all the way through to the back. Incidentally, that is an important consideration in choosing a floor. When you ask, "How long will a material wear?" what you really want to know is how long it will wear before the pattern portions become unsightly. This product is superior on that count.

Linoleum

At this price range—a 55-cent range—is one of the well-known, time-proved, old reliables—1/8-inch linoleum. The indentation characteristics of linoleum are quite good, three times as good as asphalt tile or vinyl asbestos. It is considerably more resilient than either asphalt tile or vinyl asbestos. It is quieter. Its durability, grease resistance, surface alkali resistance, and ease of maintenance are excellent. Despite the advent of some of the newer or more glamorous types of floors, linoleum is still being used extensively in institutional construction. It has many friends who have tried all of the new products and have decided that linoleum is still a fine economic buy.

Cork tile

Also in the 65 cent a foot bracket is 1/8-inch cork tile. This gauge is the minimum gauge we would recommend for general use in libraries. Cork is a fine library floor. It is the quietest floor we make and is also the most resilient. It has good indentation resistance—75 pounds. It rates well on durability. On the unfavorable side of the ledger cork has relatively poor resistance to oils and greases, but normally that is not important in libraries. Another limitation is that cork, being cellular in nature, is more susceptible to dirt retention than some of the more dense floors. We suggest you not use cork immediately adjacent to outside entrances where dirt, grit, salt, etc., will be tracked on it.

Rubber tile

Just above cork tile at 85 cents a foot is 1/8-inch rubber, which also is superior in terms of quietness and resilience. Rubber is also superior in indentation resistance with eight times the resistance of asphalt tile. Rubber has a very high gloss and comes in clear, rich colors. On durability we would call it excellent, but on the other counts—grease resistance, alkali resistance, and ease of maintenance—we would be obliged to give it a lower rating.

Sheet vinyl

At 90 cents, we find three products that are used extensively in library installation. The first is Tessera Corlon, which is a heavy-gauge sheet vinyl—90/1000 over-all. This product has a Hydrocord back which permits its installation on grade or below grade. It is one of the few sheet-type materials that can be installed on a slab in direct contact with the ground. As far as indentation is concerned, this product has the same rating as linoleum and other sheet vinyls—75 pounds per square inch. We would rate it about the same as linoleum on resilience and quietness. We can rate it as excellent on durability, grease resistance, surface alkali resistance, and ease of maintenance.

Tessera has one significant advantage over other types of vinyls: it has an embossed surface. One of the real, characteristic problems of vinyls is that high gloss materials tend to show imperfections in subfloors. When the mason leaves a score mark, a scuff, or a scratch, a high gloss vinyl material is inclined to reflect that subfloor imperfection. Tessera does a good job of concealing these subfloor flaws. Tessera should give good service in most library areas.

Homogeneous vinyl

Just above Tessera at 90 cents to $1 we find the 3/32-inch homogeneous vinyl tiles. Let me say here that vinyl tiles vary all over the lot in price, and some of the low-priced ones vary all over the lot so far as dimensional stability is concerned. One of the real bugaboos in the vinyl tile field has been shrinkage—not immediate, but about two years after installation. Our suggestion to you is to buy a vinyl tile for which the manufacturer will guarantee dimensional stability.

Custom Corlon is a splendid floor for libraries. However, for heavy traffic areas, we would recommend the 1/8-inch gauge instead of the 3/32-inch. This material is superior so far as resilience, quietness, indentation resistance, and ease of maintenance are concerned. We rate it as good on the other resistance factors.

Linotile

Also, at this price of 90 cents-$1, there is Linotile, which we would recommend highly for general library use. It has the best ease of maintenance record of any product we make. It also is the longest wearing. Linotile is also tops in resistance to oils and greases and in resistance to indentation. It would rate only fair in resistance to surface alkali, and it should not be used on or below grade.

As far as long-range costs are concerned—as distinguished from initial costs—many people tell us that Linotile is the lowest-cost floor one can buy. We would rate it as outstanding for library use.

Solid vinyl

At the top end of the price scale is Opalesq Vinyl Tile at about $2.50 a square foot installed. At this price we would not normally expect you to do your major areas in this type of product; however, you may elect to use this in some of your areas where elegance is a desirable characteristic. This product has a satin finish. It is a solid vinyl tile consisting of a combination of translucent and metallic vinyl colorings mixed together and suspended in solid clear vinyl plastic to create a high-style dimensional texture. Like Custom Corlon, this product has a 200-pound per square inch static load resistance, superior durability, superior ease of maintenance characteristics, and is excellent in terms of grease resistance and surface alkali.

Maintenance of Floors

Thus far we have only touched on maintenance. Now let's consider in a little more detail the object of maintenance. This subject can be a rather involved one if we choose to talk about what you do when you spill Mercurochrome, shellac, nail polish, hydrochloric acid, etc., on these floors. Suppose we just comment on the most common maintenance subjects. Incidentally, the booklet *Armstrong Floors, Walls and Countertops, Technical Data, 1959* presents a rather complete story on maintenance.[1]

Generalizing a bit, we would recommend that library floors be given a pretty thorough scrubbing, waxing, and buffing about every seven or eight weeks. The reason for this periodical wax removal is that wax tends to build up. The deeper it gets, the more dirt it holds. Naturally, weather conditions and traffic volume may alter this. We suggest that you damp mop the floor every two weeks or thereabouts with clear water and then apply a very thin coat of wax, followed by a buffing with a sheepskin pad.

We have observed that there are more floors that are washed away than are worn away. The tendency is to use too much soap and detergent. This practice can cause the face of a material to crack and craze, and may cause others to fade and soften. Generally, a damp mopping with clear water every couple of weeks does a tolerably good job of cleaning. If you then apply a very thin coat of wax and buff it, you will have good-looking floors.

An exception to this biweekly damp mopping are corridors, which should be *buffed* at least once a week. For these particular areas, we would recommend a No. 1 steel wool pad attached to a floor machine. This loosens the dirt, which can then be easily removed with a hair-type push broom. After that, we suggest a thin coat of wax, followed by buffing.

1. This 52p. booklet is available without cost from the Floor Division, Armstrong Cork Company, Lancaster, Pa.

Undoubtedly some of you will ask, "What do you think of the so-called miracle finishes that require no further waxing?" Frankly, we have found nothing that does that job. I can assure you that our research people have given a great deal of thought and ingenuity to the development of such a product, but to be entirely honest, we are not close to it, nor is anyone else, as far as we know. The problem with most of these miracle-type preservatives is that they do a good job of preserving where there is no heavy traffic, but they tend to wear away in the traffic areas, thus causing a lightening in color value of those areas. A retouching with the preservative does not seem to bring these areas back to the color of the floor areas adjacent, and what usually results is that you have lighter- or darker-colored traffic lanes.

Much as we would like to tell you that there is a *floor* that never needs any maintenance or that there is a preservative for floors that precludes any maintenance, we cannot, as there just isn't any such floor or product as far as we know.

One of the questions we're frequently asked is, "What do you do when you get chewing gum or candle wax or grease or tar on a floor?" On all floors other than asphalt, vinyl asbestos, or rubber, we would recommend the removal of the gum or other foreign matter with a putty knife; then apply a solvent wax (one of the paste waxes such as Johnson or Simoniz) to a rag or to zero steel wool and rub the spotted area. Then wipe clean before the wax dries completely, and when the spot is dry, buff it.

The procedure that we have just specified for linoleum or Linotile would be damaging to asphalt tile, vinyl asbestos, or rubber because a solvent tends to soften these products. For these three products we would recommend again removing the excess foreign material with a putty knife; but instead of using a solvent type wax, use Armstrong Cleaner, full strength, combining with it a mild abrasive cleaner (such as Dutch Cleanser or Spic and Span), and rub with a zero steel wool pad. Rinse well and allow to dry. Then wax and buff. I should like to underline that you should never use a solvent type cleaner, such as naphtha, or any solvent type wax on asphalt, vinyl asbestos, or rubber. They will discolor and cause premature wearing of the material.

Another problem that we frequently hear about is rubber heel marks. These are particularly characteristic of high gloss floors. The procedure for removing rubber heel marks is exactly the same as for removing chewing gum, tar, asphalt, etc.

We can throw into one hopper the following items: cigarette burns, rust stains, mildew, dye, blood stains, and grass stains. On all of our basic types of materials, we suggest that you rub the spot with zero steel wool dipped in Armstrong Cleaner full strength and rinse it well. Otherwise, you will have a milky film on top. If the stain remains, try again with a mild household abrasive cleanser and rub with zero steel wool dipped in full strength cleaner. Rinse well again and wax when dry.

Rather than try to cover all of the many things that can happen to a floor, we will just refer you to the *Technical Data* booklet.

For light duty areas such as offices we suggest you first sweep the floor to remove loose dirt, then dampen with plain water, which will remove most of the dust that is left after the broom sweeping. Then use Wax Clean, a dual purpose product which does a moderate job of cleaning and, at the same time, provides a *preservative* surface. Wax Clean will remove considerable dirt and will also remove some stains. Using the same mop that was used to apply the Wax Clean, wipe up the excess Wax Clean and let the floor dry. The remaining film will give you a good protective coating. If you desire a higher gloss, allow the wax to dry about twenty minutes, and then buff it with a sheepskin buffer.

Some of the other subjects we might cover today are light reflectivity, radiant heated slabs, the effect of air conditioning on resilient floors, resilient floors over lift and tilt-type slabs, preparation of subfloors, selecting the right type of underlayments, choosing the proper adhesive, and how to inspect a resilient floor installation; but since these subjects are fairly technical and involved, we will merely mention them here, and tell you that they are covered in some detail in the *Technical Data* booklet.

EQUIPMENT EVALUATION AND SPECIFICATION WRITING— A PANEL DISCUSSION

Moderator:
HOYT R. GALVIN
Director, Public Library of Charlotte and Mecklenburg County
Charlotte, North Carolina

Panel Members:
DONALD C. DAVIDSON
Librarian, University of California at Santa Barbara Library
Santa Barbara, California

FRAZER G. POOLE
Director, Library Technology Project
American Library Association
Chicago, Illinois

MARTIN VAN BUREN
Interior Planning Consultant
Charlotte, North Carolina

HOWARD M. ROWE
Librarian, Free Public Library
San Bernardino, California

CHAIRMAN GALVIN: The first question is addressed to Mr. Van Buren. "Mr. Van Buren: Wouldn't beauty first, simplify the problem of selecting equipment also functional and durable?"

MR. VAN BUREN: I presume he means to consider the matter of beauty before any other consideration is taken into account. Actually, I would think that all three would have to be taken into account almost simultaneously. In my talk this morning, I did not intend to put one necessarily in front of another.

CHAIRMAN GALVIN: "How essential and important is humidity control for storage of microfilm?"

MR. POOLE: This is something I hope we will investigate. If necessary, we will do some testing, if we do not find it has already been done.

CHAIRMAN GALVIN: Dr. Davidson, are you informed on that subject?

DR. DAVIDSON: I live in a naturally air-conditioned area, which is ideal for the use of all types of material. I do think I remember that 40 to 60 per cent humidity is good for the average microfilm.

CHAIRMAN GALVIN: The next question is in two parts.

Question 1: "How does one make contact with a building consultant?" A.L.A., I suppose, is the only standard answer for that. Mrs. Dorothy Smith in the A.L.A. Headquarters office does have a list of building consultants. State libraries would no doubt be another source.

Question 2: "On a college library planning team, who would be the 'Governing Authority': the president, the business manager, or a board member appointed by the board?"

DR. DAVIDSON: In some cases, the governing authority might be a building committee. I think this would be the most usual. The building committee might have representatives of business management. In cases such as the University of California, the administration would be represented in a large, responsible way by employees of the university's office of architects and engineers.

I do not think there is any one answer. It could be the regular library committee if authority is vested in it. It could be the president; in some cases, it might be even the dean. It depends, I think, on your local structure of government.

MR. VAN BUREN: The only addition I want to make is to back up Dr. Davidson's statement, because we have served as planning consultants on several college libraries. From my experience I know of one where the president was the ruling authority. I know two other cases where the president was not interested; the business manager had the authority. I recall another institution where there was a committee.

CHAIRMAN GALVIN: "How do you select an architect? Local school libraries by a local architect have been most sad. Trustees do not want to go out of town to select an architect."

MR. ROWE: I would like to say that, if the local school authorities are the ones who are going to select the architect, let them be responsible for what the building looks like; but, I think, in the selection of an architect there should be a great deal of care. I would like to indicate a possible procedure: you should, by all means, invite all interested architects to appear before your governmental agency, whether it be a board of library trustees or your mayor and council.

But I would advise two things: First, that you have a standard list of questions which would embody those things you are most interested in to ask the architects. Are they capable of building a library? Are they capable of building it within your budget? What are their ideas about the development of a particular site area you may have in mind? And what are their particular theories of construction? The standard questions, then, can be more or less analyzed so that you get a clear picture of the thinking.

We used a tape recorder for every architect who came in, had the answers typed and sent back to him for corrections. By reviewing these typed reports, we were then able to select an architect who best suited our particular needs.

DR. DAVIDSON: My answer to this problem may be a bit radical. There may be two main questions: First, does he listen? Second, can he read? I would ask these two questions primarily, and would not be particularly concerned with whether the man had built a library building before. As a matter of fact, if he had built two, I would be in-

clined to be a bit suspicious of him, because one or two buildings are not enough to make a man an expert; it really takes six or eight to make him have something special to offer.

CHAIRMAN GALVIN: "When the architect asks the librarian for a cost estimate for furniture and equipment (at an early stage in planning), is there some guide to help make such an estimated cost? We have no interior planning consultant."

MR. VAN BUREN: I think some research has been done—I thought you did some, Hoyt—on average building costs and breakdowns. Wasn't it published?

CHAIRMAN GALVIN: That was limited to the Southeast. It appeared in the *Southeastern Librarian.*

MR. VAN BUREN: There are certain averages which can be taken from other building projects. I mentioned some very general figures in my talk this morning. One was the figure per square foot; the other was a percentage of the over-all building costs. Also, I mentioned that my percentages and figures were very general, and that they would vary from one geographical area to another.

I think some investigation could be made among libraries in your area to find out how much it cost to construct the building and how much to furnish and equip it. With a number of such examples tabulated and averaged, I think you can come up with a reasonable estimate.

DR. DAVIDSON: Some of the firms which deal in equipment would be only too glad to help in this process; I do not think you should be reluctant to ask one of them for advice.

CHAIRMAN GALVIN: My study in the Southeast, the results of which appeared in the Summer, 1958, issue of the *Southeastern Librarian,* set the figure at $2.19 per square foot.[1] I had to do a little guessing to interpret what some of them meant. In some instances, they had incorporated old furniture with new, making the tabulation somewhat inaccurate.

MR. VAN BUREN: I would like to do one at $4 sometime.

CHAIRMAN GALVIN: Here is one question addressed to Mr. Van Buren: "How do you make friends with your purchasing agent in order to get the furniture and equipment you want? Also, is it unwise to buy nonstandard furniture, because of replacing it or adding to it?"

MR. VAN BUREN: Let's take these one at a time.

I would like to cite an incident which happened only a week or two ago in which we took bids on furniture and equipment for a certain public building. We got into an unusual situation in which the low bidder was bidding all alternate proposals. This morning I mentioned that it is

1. Hoyt R. Galvin, "Post War Public Libraries in the Southeast," *Southeastern Librarian,* 8:55 (Summer, 1958).

the prerogative of the owner to handle such bids in any way he sees fit.

The alternate proposals were for a line of a manufacture which is known; the line is durable. But it did not fit into the building. The attitude of the owner was this: It is foolish to hire a doctor if you do not take his medicine. When I recommended that the specifications for that low bid be thrown out, they followed my recommendation, simply because they had paid my fee for just such advice.

The second question reads: "Is it unwise to buy nonstandard furniture, because of replacing it or adding to it?" I presume the meaning here is custom furniture or locally manufactured furniture.

There is a point to the question which would have to be considered, of course; but some locally manufactured products are easily duplicated. Usually, we keep in our files any detailed drawings of special items which we have designed for certain conditions. If it is necessary to add to these at some later date, we will dig out those same drawings and put them out for bid again.

MR. COMAN: I was thinking of standard library chairs, for example, that you purchase in large quantities; I do not mean the special items such as lounge chairs.

MR. VAN BUREN: For that matter, there is always the danger of a standard brand of a manufacturer being discontinued. We run into that all the time. With fabrics especially it is a nuisance.

DR. DAVIDSON: I would like to invent a rule of thumb. I would like to say that for a building which is costing a total of less than a million dollars, it is normally desirable to purchase standard equipment, unless you have the benefit of an architect who wants to design the furniture professionally, an interior consultant, or perhaps even an industrial designer such as was employed by the Air Force Academy. I would be willing to have people argue with me on this point.

CHAIRMAN GALVIN: I think Mr. Van Buren is ready.

MR. VAN BUREN: We had a case on a relatively small remodeled library in Gaston County. I think I showed a colored slide of the old lending desk which we had redone. But, in addition, we designed the special reading tables, which cost us approximately half the cost of standard tables. This explanation is not in any way to criticize standard library tables. It would not cost the library a premium if it wanted to order some more at a future date.

MR. ROWE: I would think the answer would depend upon the situation in the local area for which the furniture is being purchased. If you have a reliable cabinetmaker in the area, I am sure your custom-made furniture would cost less than standard.

MR. POOLE: I would like to add to what Howard said that you must write specifications with great care so that you do get quality.

MR. ROWE: From a local builder you can demand good quality. It is when your order goes across the country that you may have trouble.

CHAIRMAN GALVIN: "How valid is it for a library to have a supplier write specifications, thus restricting bids to nonstandard, special-order material?"

MR. ROWE: I would say, first of all, it would probably depend on what you want. If you want a particular piece of equipment, you should specify that. If there are other bidders, let them come up to this standard. This is a standard you have set for your library.

MR. POOLE: I would second that. I am thinking of specifications we wrote for some stacks. We did not let the supplier write them; we used specifications based on one supplier's specifications, because we wanted a quality product. As it turned out, we got a low bid from another firm that supplied what we asked for. We did not make these specifications so restrictive that only the one firm could bid, but we did try to write specifications for quality stacks.

DR. DAVIDSON: I would think that in stack specifications you are not faced with the problem that you might face in furniture specifications, because one stack manufacturer can compete with another quite successfully, as Frazer indicated.

MR. VAN BUREN: I think there are two elements here. If you are talking about a specification for a fairly standard item, such as perhaps a chair or table, I do not know of a situation which would not conceivably permit alternates to be bid.

I would like to mention just one thing about this word "beauty." Beauty in a piece of furniture is always relative to the building and the other furniture it is to go with. Therefore, we have sometimes discarded a specification or, let's say, an alternate proposal, not because that alternate was ugly or not functional or not durable, but because it did not go at all with the other equipment and furniture or with the building. That is one reason for rejecting. On the other hand, many times I have accepted alternate proposals.

The second point: If you are talking about a very specialized piece of equipment, and if it is very doubtful that anyone can even bid an equal, the librarian or the owner leaves it to our judgment as to whether the price of the item is fair. We must keep up constantly with production costs so that we are able to determine or estimate about what an item should cost.

CHAIRMAN GALVIN: "Is it better to have building plans prior to a bond issue or after approval of the bond issue?"

MR. ROWE: I would say, from my personal experience, it is somewhat dangerous to have plans drawn before a bond issue. We had plans before a bond issue; we lost three bond issues. As soon as we threw out the plans, we passed the bond issue.

However, there are some communities that probably would like to see what they are buying. You must know your community pretty well.

CHAIRMAN GALVIN: As the panel moderator, I want to jump into this one. I think it is very important that the program be written because from the written program it is possible to show that you need so many square feet for the children's area and so many for each other area of the building, and you can get a pretty good estimate of what the building is goint to cost. Without an idea of what it is going to cost, how do you know what to ask for in the bond issue?

Although I am involved now as a consultant on a building for which the preliminary plans were done before a request was made for the bond issue, I am not at all certain it is necessary; but I do recommend that the program be thoroughly prepared and that the architect be selected. Let him help in estimating the cost.

If you make a plan, you are going to have a few people vote against it because they do not particularly like the façade. The average voter is not going to care about the inside, anyway. He likes or dislikes the façade the architect has drawn up.

CHAIRMAN GALVIN: "Should fees for a library building and interior planning consultant be included in an architect's fee of 8 per cent, or over and above this fee?"

I would have to start off by saying that the architects in my part of the country would think they were ready to retire if they got an 8 per cent fee; but the California architects seem to have been in the habit of getting fees like that.

Don, do you care to speak to that?

DR. DAVIDSON: First, what is the architect's fee in your part of the world?

CHAIRMAN GALVIN: Well, we normally talk about 6 per cent; but, if it is a big enough building, it will go down to $4\frac{1}{2}$.

DR. DAVIDSON: If you are going to ask the architect in California, where the residential fee is 10 per cent and 8 per cent is low, to provide special services of consultants, you should raise his fee above 8 per cent. I may be wrong in this; but that is my initial answer.

MR. ROWE: Of course, this is something which should be discussed when you are interviewing an architect. It may be that he has in his own firm consultants who may be brought into the picture under the same 8 per cent fee. Or, if you want a color consultant or an interior consultant, you can negotiate this on a percentage of cost basis or on a flat fee basis.

MR. VAN BUREN: The only other point I might make is that if you are interested in retaining the architect for the interior planning as well, you

should determine quite definitely how capable he is in this field. I have found the majority of architects are not interested in doing interior planning themselves.

CHAIRMAN GALVIN: "Please mention some good turntables for phonograph records."

MR. POOLE: We like the Califone, for one; but this certainly is not the only one. I notice that Mr. Rovelstad has some Thorens here; they have certainly been successful. In California, we have also used Rec-o-cut. The Garrard has been used with satisfactory results.

The Califone, first of all, is not just a turntable; it is a complete unit. We made some tests four or five years ago to determine which one we thought was the best on the market to suit our particular purposes. We decided at that time that the Califone was a particularly good model; we purchased a number of them. They stood up well, but we did find some bugs. Being close to the manufacturer, who happens to be in Los Angeles, we were able to talk with him about some of the difficulties. When the new models came out, a number of them were rectified on the basis of our recommendations. For a complete unit with a speaker, amplifier, and turntable combined, we liked it very much.

CHAIRMAN GALVIN: Since the point of testing has been raised, perhaps Mr. Poole would tell us of his work as Director of the Library Technology Project at A.L.A.

MR. POOLE: Let me give you what I think is the basic purpose of the program, then a few of the specific tasks we see which lie ahead of us.

The basic purpose is to provide librarians with accurate, technical information which will enable them to use library equipment and supplies on the most efficient and economical basis.

We have two or three specific tasks ahead of us. At the last meeting of the Advisory Committee for the project, it was decided that the first task of the project was to collect all of the existing standards and specifications which may relate to library equipment and library supplies and to develop from these the minimum quality standards for these items of equipment and supplies, and then to publish the results.

Secondly, we hope to provide in the near future, but not for several months, a referral service for equipment problems related to standards; in other words, we would like to be able to furnish reference service on problems related to equipment and supplies.

To begin with, we have to make ourselves experts in this field; we are not yet, by any means. Some of us have some background in one or two fields; but, certainly, we do not have the necessary experience to cover all fields.

Thirdly, we expect eventually to develop certain areas of research which we hope will result in new or revised equipment or systems.

We have already received requests in the three or four weeks we have been operating. I might cite a couple of examples of the questions. We have had a request for the development of a better card-holding platen for typewriters. I think a good many catalogers will probably say there isn't a really good one on the market. We have also had a request that we work with the typewriter manufacturers in developing a standard library keyboard.

We have also had a request that we work with the publishers in establishing a minimum standard margin and signature thickness for children's books so that the prebinders can do a better job of binding.

How much we are able to produce, and how useful we are able to make this project to the profession, will depend in part on you in the field. We will welcome your questions and suggestions.

CHAIRMAN GALVIN: Back to the questions. "In a remodeling job, should the librarian hold out for capital improvement money to do a good building job, or try to program expenditures out of current operating budget?"

MR. ROWE: If you think it is going to be a long-term situation trying to program this out of current operating funds, it might be better to try for capital improvement money.

I found that the methods of raising capital money differs throughout the country: bond issues, special legislation, sales tax, etc. I would not know just how to answer this question unless I knew more about the local situation.

CHAIRMAN GALVIN: "Is it a reflection on the chief librarian of a college library and his staff when the writing of the specifications for furnishings must be done by the business manager, because the chief librarian and his staff are unable to do so?"

MR. VAN BUREN: When you say the librarian is unable to do so, I am not quite clear on that point. Are you talking about capabilities or time? It is no insult to a librarian to be completely unfamiliar with the problems of a building project, writing the specifications, and so on. Building a library involves many problems which a librarian may never have faced, studied, or even seen.

As to the business manager, I have yet to see one who could write specifications either, although business managers express quite a bit more self-confidence in that field than most librarians. I think the librarian should be able to have the opportunity to work with the business manager.

I think the person asking the question should seek out an expert to talk with at the buildings booth during A.L.A. Conference next week in Washington. At the booth appointments can be made with any consultant he would choose to give him help along this line.

CHAIRMAN GALVIN: "For an addition to an old building is it possible to ask all architects to submit plans and select the one most suitable?"

MR. ROWE: That is how Carnegie buildings were selected, by competition. Our architect opposes this; he says that architects are professional people and the better architects would not enter into competition. I personally do not think that competition is a very good approach to the problem. If you have a program, I think you should call all the architects in and explain to them what you want. Then let them tell you how they would solve your problem of remodeling. On the basis of their solutions, select your architect.

MR. VAN BUREN: I think it is fair enough to start working with one architect; but to expect all of them to do drawings is unfair. It takes more time, I think, than the layman realizes, even to produce a reasonable, preliminary sketch or drawing.

CHAIRMAN GALVIN: There are a number of fine architects here at this meeting. I would like to hear some of their opinions on this subject.

UNIDENTIFIED: There are some competitions which are approved by the A.I.A.; others would not be.

CHAIRMAN GALVIN: Could you define what A.I.A. approves for competition?

UNIDENTIFIED: No, I cannot. There are very few approvals.

VOICE: I think I can amplify somewhat by saying that any competition which is approved by the A.I.A. is run by the American Institute of Architects. A board of judges, made up mostly of professional architects of recognized standing, selects the best plan, so that even you, as its owner, would have to accept the decision of a board.

VOICE: Calling in a group of architects and having each of them prepare preliminary plans for an addition to a library may be compared with a magazine firm, say the *Saturday Evening Post*, calling in six authors to try their hands at writing an article on a particular subject. Each author would perhaps be required to write a chapter or two to see how he would do it.

MR. W. B. FLACK (architect, Baltimore, Maryland): I would say that an architect actually doesn't mind competition, in this sense: every building we design, we feel, is in competition architecturally with all the others designed by the other architects. So, if you want competition, in a sense, you examine what a firm has been doing. If it has been doing what you consider good architecture—whether it has been doing libraries, schools, churches, or whatever—it will do a good job for you; the results will be good architecture. If what you see is poor and shoddy and not what you have in mind, you should not consider that firm until such time as it does prove itself.

The one exception would be young architects who probably need their first commission. These people you could judge by talking to them.

MR. WILLIAM F. BERNBROCK (Moline, Illinois): I would simply like to add that I subscribe to everything these other architects have said here. I would like to add that it is pretty much like selecting your doctor and lawyer, who are also professional people.

MRS. LEE B. GORSUCH (Enoch Pratt Free Library, Baltimore, Maryland): Suppose we have the building we want and the equipment we want; we have maintained it according to all the instructions. But, after a certain number of years, it is beginning to look shabby. Is there any figure based on a percentage of your investment which could be used in an operating budget for refurbishing at certain times so that you would always be assured that your building would look all right?

CHAIRMAN GALVIN: If I understand correctly, you are talking about something similar to what an industry does when it allows for depreciation of plant and equipment.

MR. ALFRED RAWLINSON (McKissick Memorial Library, West Columbia, South Carolina): One guide might be the depreciation allowed for federal income tax purposes.

MR. VAN BUREN: I think one of the problems or complications is the great variance in types of buildings and materials and equipment which go into them. If a building is constructed with marble walls, for example, you probably will have no maintenance cost. If plaster and paint are used, you are going to have to repaint, etc.

CHAIRMAN GALVIN: Are there any libraries represented here which have some type of depreciation allowance set up for replacements and refurbishing?

MR. DAVID H. R. SHEARER (Free Library of Philadelphia, Pennsylvania): The Free Library of Philadelphia allows for a new building five years without any maintenance costs. Then 1.43 per cent annually for seventy-five years is allowed.

MR. KEYES D. METCALF (Belmont, Massachusetts): Harvard University, for each of its buildings, puts into a special fund a sum, every year, to keep the buildings in good shape, going on the basis that its buildings must never deteriorate, but must always be as good as they ever were. The old East Building, which is now 239 years old, is a better building than it was 239 years ago. A different percentage is used for each building; but, after very careful study, that money is set aside.

It is set aside immediately, beginning with the first year. Funds are accumulated so that if the roof blows off in a hurricane, money will be available. It does not have to be spent at any particular time. During the Second World War, no painting was done at Harvard. When the war was over, the university hired 350 painters for two years to put buildings in good shape. The money was available to take care of things. I think the same procedure is followed in some other institutions.

CHAIRMAN GALVIN: Here is another question: "Has anyone here experienced using a fund-raising firm to raise money for a new building? I would like to talk with him."

MISS LENA B. NOFCIER (Public Library, Lima, Ohio): We have had an amateur group raising funds for our library. We formed a nonprofit corporation; members of the corporation have sold library bonds to people throughout the community, bonds which will pay 3 per cent and mature in five to ten years, and will be paid off by rent from our operating fund.

CHAIRMAN GALVIN: I have another question here: "Are there any areas of specification writing which are strictly the responsibility of the architect rather than of the librarian and his consultants?"

MR. ROWE: Yes; there are some areas. For example, in our building, the air-conditioning return ducts are in the wall. The architect insisted that he be given the responsibility of designing the wall shelving in that particular area in order that the return ducts would be properly placed and the shelving be something which would be usable. You will find that in certain areas there are cabinets which would be part of the architect's specifications because of space limitation.

MR. VAN BUREN: I would say, to generalize, the responsibility of the architect, as to both plans and specifications, has to do with the building and everything which is fastened to or becomes a part of the building. In libraries shelving is sometimes one, sometimes another. Shelving can be set up without being fastened down or it can be fastened down. An agreement is usually reached at an early stage.

MR. POOLE: It seems to me that writing a whole specification document is a teamwork job which should be done by the librarian and the architect together. The architect is usually more qualified to write the legal part involved, instructions to bidders, etc.

DR. DAVIDSON: I would like to suggest that the architect is often the most logical co-ordinator of all the various requirements, including color and the design of furniture. The more opinions you get which are on a coequal basis in the area of aesthetics, I believe, the more trouble you are in. You have to accept in certain areas of aesthetics the opinion of an architect in whom you have faith.

LIBRARY LIGHTING

ROBERT L. ZAHOUR
Manager, Application Engineering
Headquarters Commercial Engineering Department
Westinghouse Lamp Division
Bloomfield, New Jersey

In order to do any job, adequate facilities must be made available. You wouldn't expect to carry a 5-ton load with a $\frac{1}{4}$-ton truck. Likewise, when an interior is to be air conditioned, the engineer measures the volume of air to be handled and computes for the size of air-conditioning unit to provide comfortable air temperatures and humidity.

Library lighting is designed on a scientific basis in accordance with basic fundamental principles to provide good lighting for eye comfort and ease of seeing. The library, in a sense, is a warehouse of knowledge (current and historical) published in books, manuscripts, and on parchments. This knowledge is transmitted through the process of reading to students of all walks of life. In the library, therefore, the job is a seeing task, and to see and read easily and comfortably, good illumination is essential.

Books are printed in various sizes of type on different grades of paper. Furthermore, historical volumes, parchments, and transcripts may be faded in one way or another and therefore difficult to read unless the lighting is adequate. Then, too, young eyes can see more easily than old eyes, even with the aid of glasses. Good lighting helps both.

Since the major task in the library is seeing to read, good lighting is very important. According to results of years of research by the I.E.S. Research Institute sponsored by the Illuminating Engineering Society, the recommended minimum illumination level for libraries is 70 foot-candles. As a comparison, on a sunny day the illumination on the campus measures as high as 10,000 foot-candles while in the shade of a tree, the daylight is about 1000 foot-candles. However, the seeing tasks outdoors are not as severe as those in a library reading room. We should not skimp on lighting in libraries where reading and learning is the important task.

Color and Finishes

Now, a lighting system involves a little more than just lamps and fixtures. The color of the ceilings, walls, floors, table and desk tops—all contribute in some measure to redistribute light around the room and provide an atmosphere conducive to eye comfort.

To avoid direct glare from the light sources, fixtures must be selected that have a low brightness surface. Furthermore, ceilings and walls should be light in color and of a nonglossy finish, so that light received at these surfaces will be efficiently reflected back into the room. Dark finishes absorb this useful light.

Table and desk tops should be finished with a fairly light, diffusing surface to provide a comfortable brightness ratio between the white pages of a book and the immediate surroundings. Avoid glossy finished or glass-covered table or desk tops, because these specular surfaces reflect images of overhead light sources and cause reflected glare. For comfortable, balanced brightness ratios the following reflection factors of room surfaces are recommended by the Illuminating Engineering Society:

Recommended Classroom Reflectances[1]

Ceiling	85%	(70-90%)
Walls	60%	(50-70%)
Furniture	35%	(25-40%)
Table and desk tops	40%	(35-50%)
Floors	30%	(20-50%)
Window walls	80%	(75-85%)
Door trim	40%	(30-60%)

Types of Lighting Equipment

Various types of efficient lighting equipment are available for library lighting. Where the ceilings are low, continuous rows of fluorescent troffers with low brightness bottom covers are one type that is recommended. Another type is the low brightness, plastic bottom square- or rectangular-shaped flat fixture equipped with fluorescent lamps that can be mounted to the ceiling. These fixtures are made in sizes 1 foot square, 1 by 2 feet, or 2 by 4 feet, and may be installed in groups to form artistic arrangements of large area lighting. Wall-to-wall luminous plastic ceilings may be used if desired. In rooms with ceilings 12 to 16 feet, continuous rows of suspension type louver-bottom fluorescent fixtures may be used. Cool white fluorescent tubes seem most popular in libraries, classrooms, and offices.

Where high ceilings are involved, a more concentrated light source is needed to direct the light downward to the table tops. Deluxe color-corrected mercury lamps have proved highly desirable for such applications. One noteworthy installation is that in Butler Library of Columbia University in New York, where the ceiling is 37 feet high. The former installation consisted of 300-watt incandescent lamps with reflectors recessed in the border of a beautiful classical architectural ceiling design. The resulting level of illumination on the tables was 6 foot-candles. Without changing the outlet locations, the incandescent lamps were replaced with 400-watt deluxe color-corrected mercury lamps in aluminum reflectors fitted with prismatic lenses. With the new system, the illumination on the tables was increased from 6 to 70 foot-candles, which meets the I.E.S. Recommended Practice.

1. Illuminating Engineering Society, *IES Lighting Handbook: The Standard Lighting Guide* (3rd ed.; New York: The Society, 1959), p.11-24.

Incandescent, Fluorescent, and Mercury Lamps

Now just a word about light sources. Incandescent lamps for general lighting purposes have an average life of 1000 burning hours. Fluorescent lamps have a useful life of 7500 to 10,000 hours, are more efficient in light output than incandescent lamps, and operate much cooler. Mercury lamps, which are also much more efficient than incandescent types, have a useful life of 10,000 hours, although they may burn several thousand hours beyond that point. Because of the long life and high efficiency characteristics of fluorescent and mercury lamps, they have become more popular in providing higher levels of light at lowest cost for maintenance.

Furthermore, fluorescent and mercury lamps maintain their light output efficiency during their period of long useful life with a very low mortality rate. Consequently, group relamping, which has proved more economical than random lamp replacement, can be scheduled once every 2 years if lamps are used 8 hours per day; every 18 months if lamps burn 16 hours per day; and once a year if lamps operate 24 hours per day. Accordingly, for most libraries, the 18-month group lamping schedule would be most economical. While fixtures should be cleaned periodically to maintain their efficiency, in libraries (many of which are being air conditioned) this fixture cleaning can be done at the same time with the group relamping operation.

HEATING AND VENTILATING

CHESTER H. HOSMER
Chief, Air Conditioning, Ventilating,
*   and Heating Section*
Government Services Division
Washington, D.C.

There are a good many things that you should know about heating and ventilating systems if you are involved in the construction or remodeling of a library. Even if the best engineer available is to do the actual design work, there will be numerous decisions that you must make. One of the first will be concerned with the primary function of the system. Is it to provide optimum conditions for the preservation of valuable, perhaps irreplaceable, documents, or is it for the comfort of the occupants?

Complete Air Conditioning

If the purpose of the system is the preservation of documents, it will be necessary, in almost any part of the United States, to provide a complete air-conditioning system. The system will have to be designed to achieve the closest possible control of both temperature and humidity. If comfort of the occupants is the principal consideration, which is probably true of a majority of libraries, heat and ventilation may be considered the basic necessities, although summer cooling is rapidly acquiring that status. While cooling in office buildings can be justified on the basis of increased employee efficiency, in a library, where a majority of the occupants are not employees, it is probably a policy matter related to the type and quality of service to be rendered to the users.

A complete air-conditioning system will cost from $2.50 to $6 per square foot of net floor area depending on climate, size of building, and type of equipment used. A heating and ventilating system will cost from $1 to $2.50 per square foot of net floor area, depending, again, on climate and, to a lesser extent, on type of system and size of building.

There should be no difficulty in deciding the temperature required in the library. A temperature in the range of 72^0 to 76^0 should be satisfactory to a majority of people. The optimum temperature for the storage of paper also falls in this range. Don't be alarmed, however, if you find that the heating system is being designed on the basis of 70^0 inside when the outside temperature is about 15^0 above the lowest temperature ever recorded in the vicinity. The latter temperature, known as the design outside temperature, probably will not be reached more than once a year on the average, and at other times the system will be able to produce any required temperature in the range mentioned. To increase the size of the system further would add to the expense with a far from commensurate return.

Humidity Control

Humidity is more of a problem. Humidification has been widely advocated as a means of reducing heating cost, because, for a given feeling of warmth, the temperature can be reduced somewhat if the humidity is raised. The temperature reduction results in a decreased heat loss through the walls and windows and a corresponding saving in heating cost. This is fine as far as it goes, but one point is overlooked. Any building occupied by people must have some ventilation. Air brought in for this purpose in cold weather contains very little moisture, and moisture must be added continuously to maintain the desired humidity. Heat is required to evaporate this moisture—more heat, in fact, than is saved by the reduction in temperature. Humidification will therefore increase, rather than decrease, the over-all heating and ventilating cost.

High humidities are undesirable in very cold weather because moisture will condense on windows unless they are double glazed. It may also condense or freeze within the walls unless an effective vapor barrier is provided. Persons wearing glasses are annoyed by having them steam up immediately upon entering the building in cold weather. Odors are generally more noticeable in a humid environment. While a few persons find higher humidities helpful in some respiratory disorders, I believe that a majority of people do not find them an advantage. They are actually detrimental in many cases. High humidities do have some effect in suppressing static sparks generated by a person's walking over certain floor coverings, but such sparks probably can be overcome at less cost by suitable selection of floor coverings.

In general, I believe that humidification should be avoided except in those areas where it is necessary for the preservation of documents. For this, a relative humidity of 50 per cent is required, controlled within 3 per cent, plus or minus. Windows should be double glazed, and walls should be well insulated and sealed against moisture penetration.

Selection of Fuel

The selection of fuel should be based primarily on total annual cost. The actual fuel cost is relatively easy to estimate, after your engineer has calculated the probable consumption and applied local prices per ton, gallon, etc. Other factors may be more difficult to evaluate but should be reduced to dollars and cents if at all possible. Items that should be included are: interest on first cost, depreciation, value of fuel storage space, annual maintenance and labor costs directly related to fuel handling, and firing and general building cleaning costs that can be attributed fairly to the fuel used. The last item may be the one most difficult to evaluate. Where gas is the primary fuel, and service may be interrupted during periods of peak demand,

fixed charges on stand-by fuel equipment should be added to the above.

Local prices for available fuels vary so much that no general statement can be made as to over-all costs. It will be found in a good many cases that a fuel that is cheapest on a price per heat unit basis is not cheapest when suitable consideration is given to the cost of operating labor and such items as equipment required for smokeless operation. And, incidentally, let me say that coal is not the only fuel that is subject to smoke nuisance. Oil, particularly the cheaper and heavier grades, can produce a lot of smoke unless the firing equipment is properly selected and maintained in good adjustment.

Selection of Heating System

With some of the basic requirements covered, we may now consider some factors affecting the selection of the type of heating system. Again, cost should be the principal factor. This does not mean the cost of the heating equipment alone, however. The cost of the building structure may be affected by necessary provisions for the heating system, and all this, as well as the interrelation of the heating and the ventilating systems, must be taken into account. On the other hand, a building arrangement based on library functions alone, or on an architectural style suitable to the location, may severely limit the selection of the heating system. There may even be cases when it is better to select the system that your designer is most familiar with rather than the one that may otherwise appear to be ideal for your building. It is probably more important that the system be well designed than that it be of a particular type.

In general, I believe that any type of system that would be suitable for an office building will be suitable for a library. Systems for very small libraries may come closer to being residential in character. The principal types to consider are steam, hot water, and warm air. There are a number of variations of each type.

Steam systems

One-pipe steam systems are adapted to small buildings only, say those having no more than 10,000 square feet of net floor space. They are generally low in cost but lack the flexibility of other systems. The supply of heat cannot be modulated in accordance with the weather but must be turned on and off intermittently. It is difficult to divide the system into zones so that individual rooms or different exposures can be controlled separately. One-pipe systems are apt to be noisy due to errors in design or installation, and even a perfectly designed system can become exceedingly noisy if radiator valves are carelessly left in a partly open position.

Two-pipe steam systems are superior to one-pipe systems and are adaptable to buildings of any size. Pipe sizes are smaller and may be more readily concealed. Two-pipe systems can be controlled by modulating the steam flow continuously to match the heat requirements. They can be arranged to provide separate control of individual rooms or groups of rooms as desired. They are also somewhat more expensive than one-pipe systems.

Two-pipe systems are generally quieter than one-pipe systems, but noise can result from incorrect sloping of pipes and inadequate sizes. Orifices placed in radiator valves to regulate the steam flow also generate noise. These orifices are used frequently in office buildings to prevent steam waste and to insure even heat distribution to the various rooms. The subdued hiss of these orifices is not loud enough to be disturbing in an ordinary office but might be considered excessive in rooms where other background noises are low.

Hot-water systems

Hot-water systems are adaptable to buildings of all sizes. The so-called one-pipe system is suitable for small buildings, and the two-pipe system is suitable for buildings of any size. The disadvantages associated with hot-water systems of the old gravity flow type—such as large pipe sizes, slow heating up, and large radiators—do not exist in a well-designed modern system employing relatively trouble-free, quiet operating pumps. The possibility of freezing under some conditions still exists, but with good design and modern controls, capable of furnishing adequate heat during nights and weekends, is generally considered negligible. The possibility of water damage is probably not much greater than in a steam system, although the hot-water system does contain a greater amount of water initially.

The principal advantages of hot-water systems over steam systems are the ability to regulate the heat supply by a simple adjustment of the water temperature, in addition to modulating the water flow, and the fact that radiators may be placed below the flow and return mains. Hot-water systems are thus particularly adapted to heating rooms with floors placed directly on the ground, since no pipe trenches will be required below the floor, as would be the case with steam systems.

The cost of two-pipe steam and hot-water systems will generally be about the same. Differences will be due more frequently to peculiarities of a particular building layout than to basic differences in systems.

Both steam and hot-water systems deliver heat to the rooms by means of radiators. The placement of these radiators is important if uniform heating is to be secured. Radiators should be placed as near as possible to the surfaces through which the heat loss from the room takes place. The outside walls and windows will account for most of the heat loss from a room, and radiators should be placed close

to them. Most, if not all, of the radiation should be below the windows to offset the cold draft that will otherwise flow downward across the glass. This will also produce the most uniform temperature throughout the room. If radiators are placed at inside partitions having no heat loss, the heat will have to travel across the room to reach the outside walls and windows. Room temperatures will then be too high for comfort near the inside partitions and too low near the outside walls and windows. I have seen rooms in which temperature differences in excess of 10° existed due to improper placement of radiators. This should be kept in mind during the functional planning stages so that adequate space may be available for radiators at the proper locations.

Warm-air systems

Warm-air heating systems have, in the past, been considered suitable only for small buildings. At the present time, however, a good many large buildings are being heated by warm air. Such systems are advantageous primarily in those cases where a ventilating system must be installed or where cooling is to be provided, either as part of the original system or at a later date. The modifications required to permit a ventilating or a cooling system to function as a heating system will frequently cost less than the addition of a separate heating system.

Warm-air heating is also advantageous in those cases in which humidification is required. It is more satisfactory to introduce the moisture for humidification into an air-duct system at a central point than it is to introduce it directly into the air in the rooms themselves. The apparatus required for the latter method would be unsightly, probably would be noisy, and almost certainly would deliver a good many large water droplets that would not evaporate completely before reaching walls, floors, or objects in the room. While this is accepted industrial practice, it is hardly suitable for a library.

Warm-air systems for very small buildings may be similar to residential systems in which a fan blows the air across the combustion chamber of the furnace and through the ducts to the various rooms. The fan, as well as the burner, is operated intermittently to control the supply of heat. This system is relatively cheap if the duct system is short and control from a single thermostat is acceptable. It is not suitable where a constant flow of air is required for ventilation, and it is not very well adapted to situations where independent control of a number of rooms is required.

Warm-air systems for larger buildings will usually be of the indirect type, employing a boiler which supplies steam or hot water to so-called "coils" which, in turn, heat the air drawn across them by the fans. In this type of system one boiler can supply several coils, each furnishing warm air to a different part of the building. Such systems can be designed so that independent, continuously modulated control is provided for as many rooms or areas as may be desired.

In warm-air systems, as in systems employing radiators, the point at which the heat is delivered into the room is important in achieving uniform temperatures. Correct location is also important in avoiding drafts. The ideal arrangement is to deliver the air under the windows in an upward direction. Unfortunately, this sometimes requires more duct work than other schemes and therefore is more expensive.

A cheaper arrangement is to deliver air through grilles above head level in the interior walls, the air being directed toward the outside walls and windows. With this scheme ducts may be shorter and cheaper. It is necessary, however, to use higher rates of air flow and lower air temperatures than in conventional residential warm-air systems, the air temperature being from 100^0 to 110^0 instead of 140^0. This arrangement is not adapted to rooms in which the depth—that is, the distance from the outside wall to the inside wall—exceeds the ceiling height by more than about $2\frac{1}{2}$ to 1, although this ratio may be increased somewhat with higher than average ceilings. A third possible arrangement is to deliver the air through ceiling diffusers designed to distribute the air radially across the ceiling. This system probably is not much cheaper than the arrangement under the window. It does not deliver all of the warm air directly toward the outside wall and windows, and therefore may fail to provide maximum uniformity of temperature. Ceiling diffusers are generally better for distributing cool air than warm air.

A fourth warm-air heating scheme, commonly used in residential systems, delivers the air at low velocity through grilles placed on inside walls just above the floor. Return air grilles are often placed below the windows in an effort to draw in cold air descending from the windows before it spreads across the floor. This scheme has only one advantage. It is cheap, particularly in a single-story building with a basement. It does not, as a rule, produce reasonably uniform temperatures. Warm air tends to stratify in the upper part of the room and cooler air in the lower part. Temperatures near outside walls and windows are noticeably lower than those near the inside walls. In my opinion, such a scheme should not be used in a library unless it is absolutely necessary to have the cheapest system regardless of quality.

All of the foregoing schemes for introducing warm air into a room, except the last, are similar to those used for introducing cold air in air-conditioning systems. This does not mean, however, that all warm-air systems so arranged can be converted into cooling systems without difficulty. Cooling will, as a rule, require greater rates of air flow than heating. Unless the system has been designed initially for cooling as well as heating, it may be found that the grilles and ducts are too small to handle these larger flow rates. In view of the increasing public demand for air conditioning, I believe that it would be very shortsighted to install a warm-air heating system that could not be used for cooling without extensive alterations to the air-distributing system.

Ventilation

Ventilation is required, in any enclosure occupied by people, to supply oxygen and remove air contaminants. Oxygen supply will be more than amply provided for if other requirements are met. Of the many air contaminants that might be considered, the ones that will generally determine the ventilation rate are those lumped together under the term "odors." While it is impracticable to remove odors and other contaminants entirely, they can be held to tolerable levels by continuously diluting the air in the room with outside air and exhausting a corresponding amount of contaminated air from the room. The rate of flow required is variable, depending on the socioeconomic status and the aesthetic sensibilities of the persons directly concerned. Commonly accepted rates are 15 cubic feet of air per minute per person, or $\frac{1}{4}$ cubic foot of air per minute per square foot of floor area.

Ventilation may also be used to remove heat. The flow rates required for this are high, possibly from ten to forty times the rates just mentioned. In a residence, where only a simple propeller fan and a few open windows are required, the results obtained from these high rates of flow are quite worth while. In a library, drawing large amounts of dust-laden air through windows would be unacceptable, and the cost of providing filters and ducts for cleaning and distributing the air would be out of proportion to the results obtainable. Any proposed increase in ventilating system capacity, for the purpose of removing heat, should be studied carefully to determine whether the expected improvement is worth the cost and whether air conditioning may not produce far better results at little additional cost.

Air filters

Of the various components of a ventilating system with which you may be concerned, the most important, perhaps, will be the filters for removing dust from the incoming air, which includes not only the air taken in from outside but any air recirculated from inside the building.

The installation of filters must be justified on the basis that it is cheaper to remove dust by filtering the incoming air than it is to remove it after it has settled on books and equipment. Extremely fine dust may be impossible to remove, and the cost of air filtration must be compared with the cost of refinishing, replacement, etc.

Filters are available in many types, differing in

first cost, operating cost, and efficiency in removing dust particles of various sizes. It is unfortunate that many years of effort on the part of the filter industry and professional societies have not yet resulted in acceptance of a uniform standard for testing and rating all types of filters. It is, therefore, difficult to evaluate the conflicting claims of filter manufacturers.

For the average library, I believe that the most suitable filter will be one of the types employing a renewable medium that is removed and discarded after it has become clogged with dust. Cleanable filters are less desirable, because tests have shown that, as a class, their efficiencies are somewhat lower than those of renewable medium filters. The labor cost of cleaning and recoating cleanable filters is difficult to determine and may exceed the cost of replacing media in the renewable type. The efficiency of cleanable filters may be impaired seriously by careless cleaning and improper application of the adhesive coating.

Among the renewable medium filters, there are a few that have efficiencies considerably higher than those generally used in commercial applications. These filters, in addition to costing more initially, require greater fan horsepower to draw the air through them and consequently cost more to operate. Before such a filter is selected for a library in preference to those more commonly used, it is necessary to consider the over-all effect of this increased efficiency. Extreme cleanliness in the incoming air may not result in a corresponding improvement in room cleanliness if dust enters the room by other routes, such as open doors, window cracks, clothing of occupants, etc.

The electrostatic filter is another type that has a higher efficiency than those of other filters in common use, particularly in removing extremely fine particles, such as smoke. It is one of the highest in first cost, but it is not expensive to operate, since excessive fan horsepower is not required. The electric power required to charge the ionizing and collecting elements is comparatively small. This filter does, however, require continuous electric current supply and a higher than average quality of maintenance. Indifferent attention to periodic inspection and cleaning, neglect of broken wires, and frequent interruptions to the charging current will result in loss of filtering efficiency. Both the overall effect of the higher efficiency and the probability of adequate maintenance should be considered thoroughly before this type of filter is selected.

Sound attenuation

Another element in ventilating system design which is worth some attention is sound attenuation. The modern trend in air system design is to use small ducts and consequently high air velocities and system pressures. This, in turn, results in greater noise generation by fans and other system components. Fans should be isolated from rooms in which low noise levels are essential, either by distance or by heavy floor and wall construction. Ducts should be provided with sound attenuation devices where they pass through fan room walls. Air outlets should be selected for their acoustic properties as well as for their ability to distribute air in the required pattern. In critical cases it will be highly desirable to have the ventilating system design reviewed by an acoustical expert, in order to eliminate errors that may be expensive to correct after the installation is completed.

GETTING THE MOST FOR YOUR MONEY FROM THE POINT OF VIEW OF THE LIBRARIAN

RALPH A. ULVELING
Director, Detroit Public Library
Detroit, Michigan

Some years ago the Sunday supplements of nearly all newspapers carried a familiar ad: "Learn to play the piano in 20 easy lessons." My assignment tonight is analogous: "How to get the most for your money," complete in twenty minutes. For obvious reasons I will confine my talk to some over-all principles, and then, to the extent that time permits, I will add illustrative examples of how a well-planned investment can be made to yield a higher than normal return.

Creating a Planning Team

Nearly twenty years ago Wheeler and Githens, in their well-known volume on building said: "The planning of a library is an intricate matter. It is too much to expect anyone in the few months while a library plan takes shape to master the intricacies of a complex and rapidly developing subject in which only a few architects and librarians are fairly competent after a lifetime of study and practice."[1]

The planning of a new building is a project of such dimensions that the institutional investment it involves will not likely be repeated for half a century or more. Most librarians who are confronted with such a problem have had no actual experience to prepare them for it, though all will probably have heard a few lectures on building planning given as part of an administration course in library school years before. Sometimes these lectures create a false sense of security in librarians and their governing boards alike, though these same people would quickly recognize the folly of allowing someone with such a very meager background to catalog the library's books even though cataloging errors would lend themselves to easy economical correction in a way that a building error would not.

On the other hand, other librarians and boards recognize that successful administration of a library's service does not by that fact include experience in planning buildings; so they engage library building consultants to help them, just as school administrators turn to school consultants, and hospital administrations to hospital consultants. I have spoken briefly on this point only because some librarians who deeply feel the need of help in planning are fearful of saying so lest they be thought

inadequate for the positions they hold. Wheeler and Githens, however, met the issue in these words: "Most business men agree that technical advisers are well worth the cost. It is an evidence of good judgment and no reflection on the intelligence of trustees to call in an experienced adviser before starting sketch plans, thus preventing unnecessary expense, inefficient service, and lasting regret."[2] To this they add in a later paragraph, "Consultants or advisers are particularly important at the earliest stage."

Since the term consultant has many applications, a few words on the selection of a building consultant may not be amiss. Eminence in the library profession is not synonymous with experience in planning buildings. Similarly the consultants from the state library who periodically tour the state are for the most part service and operational advisers, not building experts. They fill a very important function, but it must be recognized for what it is. In selecting a building consultant, begin by getting a list of the projects he has planned. Analyze the extent and variety of his experience. If possible, go and see some of the buildings he guided, but—a word of caution—do not allow your liking or your dislike of the architecture to influence your judgment of the layout and plan. A library building consultant has nothing to say about architectural treatment. That is the full responsibility of the architect.

Also obtain, either in person or by mail, a confidential report on the consultant's ingenuity in solving problems, his ability to work harmoniously with the librarian, and—what is quite as important—his skill in working harmoniously with the architects. A planning team must do teamwork, and your library building consultant will, by virtue of his place on the planning team, be a key factor in interpreting the library's needs to the architect, and structural limitations to the librarian. Finally, check on his care in looking after the small details that become so important in obtaining convenience and flexibility in the finished building. Weigh all these factors and then make your selection of a consultant.

I have given this point top priority in my talk because there is no single item which will go so far toward giving you the most for your money as the use of an experienced building consultant. He will often, through the wise use of space, achieve significant savings in the amount of floor area required and, therefore, in construction costs. But even more important, he can usually develop a plan which will effect savings in operating costs. If he is successful, through able work in layout, to reduce by one position what had seemed to be the minimum staff required to operate the library, he will in a short time bring about savings in excess of his fees, and from that time on the savings will continue year in and year out as long as the building is used. Further, he will be a safeguard against the omission of

1. J. L. Wheeler and A. M. Githens, *The American Public Library Building* (Chicago: A.L.A., 1941), p.59.

2. *Ibid.*

building features which neither the architect nor the librarian who is inexperienced in building planning might detect, but which would be costly to add later. Finally, because of his familiarity with blueprints, he is able to see the project in three dimensions and can thus detect possible difficulties in supervision or appearance which might not be caught by the librarian who sees the plan only in a flat plane.

Modernizing Procedures before Planning a Building

Libraries, in common with progressive businesses and institutions, are generally moving toward greater simplification of records and procedures. In public libraries the enormous dual registration files formerly maintained—that is, the name file and a number file—are being virtually eliminated. Likewise the cumbersome lending desks of old are no longer necessary where modern simplified and efficient charging systems have been installed. The old-time practice of maintaining a separate lending desk for the children's rooms, which is still amazingly widespread in older libraries, is a heritage of a bygone era. Substantial reductions in space can be effected if these and other procedures are revised before rather than two years after the new structure is planned. This is the second area of importance in seeking to get the most for your money.

Planning for Dual Use of Facilities

Great economy can develop from the placing of certain facilities so strategically that each may conveniently serve dual needs instead of duplicating the facility. Though every library's site as well as its program and size are likely to make it a unique problem, I shall suggest several specific items which may have applicability in many libraries.

1. In this day, when much of the travel to libraries is by motorcar, a parking lot is desirable, if not mandatory by city ordinance. This creates a need for two major entrances to the library—one from the street and another from a point convenient to the parking area. With ingenuity buildings, except the very large ones, usually can be planned so that a single lending desk will control both entrances. This is not always easy or even possible to achieve, but where it can be done, the savings that result from staffing one instead of two desks at all hours of the day, while providing a maximum of patron convenience, are significant.

2. Public toilets for men and women are essential, but they can be sources of great concern and trouble when placed in basements or other unsupervised areas. It is not impossible—in fact, it is usually quite feasible—to locate them where they are under supervision and readily accessible to

reading room patrons and yet are equally accessible to the meeting room during "after hours" programs when the library proper is closed to the public, even to those attending the lecture or discussion. This kind of planning is an excellent example of how money can be saved with sacrifice of convenience.

3. A story-hour room that is readily available from the children's department is a must item in all public libraries. There is no economic justification, however, for building a room large enough to accommodate 75 to 150 children if it can be used only one hour a week. With a little study it can be located where it will double for children's and adult gatherings without inconvenience to either age group using it, thus saving thousands of dollars.

4. The inexperienced planner of a library building too often thinks in terms of walls to separate different activities, i.e., the children's department must have its own workroom, the reference department must have its, and the circulation processes must have theirs. Or, in larger buildings, every department wants separately located workrooms. Much can be saved, however, by providing a common work space which can be located where it adjoins two or more departments. This practice reduces the square footage that is needed, and it also saves on the equipment to be purchased. One typewriter, for example, may be all that is required in a shared workroom, whereas two would be needed if separate workrooms were established. In the same way, with this arrangement, one competent typist can be shared to the advantage of both departments, which otherwise might be required to use less skilled clerks.

5. The type of equipment to be used, and the manner in which it will be used, can also affect the space needed, particularly in workrooms. Practically every member of a library staff has some work assignments which should be carried out away from the public service areas. To attempt to provide desk space for each in a workroom would require far larger areas than necessary. On the other hand, simply constructed work stations, which are nothing more than deep counters with banks of drawers properly spaced below the counter, and book shelves above, provide all needed facilities. These can be constructed by the contractor for far less than separate desks can be purchased, and if placed along the walls the total area needed for an adequate workroom may be reduced in size sometimes as much as 40 per cent. This single device can reduce both the cost of the building and the cost of equipment with no loss in comfort or efficiency.

Flexibility of the Building

With library needs changing from decade to decade, either because of new professional developments or because of the growth of a city, no building, however wisely laid out today, will likely remain unchanged twenty-five years hence. For this reason buildings should be kept as free of fixed elements as possible. Those elements which are not subject to change of location, as elevators, stairways, toilets, etc., should be packaged in one area so the mass of the building will remain free for rearranging. Before installing any stacks, an over-all floor should be laid, with no feature borders marking what will become the stack or desk areas.

Avoid permanent partitions as far as possible. Free-standing book shelving, if imaginatively placed, may provide a desirable separation of service departments without giving the appearance or even providing the restraints of a temporary wall. Let me try to illustrate this point. Visualize if you can a medium-sized library with a large reference room on the north third of the building and a comparatively large home reading browsing room and lounge on the south third. Between the two is a bank of book stacks which houses the bulk of the library's open-shelf collection. With each range extending from the reference room to the home reading department, and with 6-foot aisles between the ranges, this collection provides a separation between the services while keeping the entire book stock as readily available to both as if duplicate book collections had been provided for each. Further, this total portion of the building is completely flexible and subject to change of use since there are no partitions. And what is also important, it has the simplicity, the openness, and the economy of warehouse-type construction.

Other items to be watched to keep a building flexible are:

1. Do not build-in listening rooms. They freeze the plan and create expensive ventilation and air-conditioning problems. Instead, grid some area of the floor with conduits so that electric power can easily be brought up to listening tables in various locations.

2. Avoid building closets for supplies or storage. It is cheaper to buy storage cabinets which can later be moved than it is to buy walls and doors for closets.

3. Built-in window seats or other similar built-in features also create problems when building changes must be made.

Over-all Plan

Two points which may have nothing to do with economy of construction or operation in any plan but have over-all importance are so frequently overlooked that they will be mentioned here even though not strictly a part of the assigned subject. To be successful a plan must be so simple and so direct that the patron visiting the library for the first time will quickly grasp the plan of the building and

its services. This is not always true, even in some of the important library buildings erected in recent years. Secondly, consideration must always be given to the normal flow of traffic to departments. Patrons should not be required to pass through the reference room, which is primarily a room for quiet study, to get to the circulation collection. Similarly, the movement of children through the building either to the children's room or to the story-hour room should not be through adult areas. Deliveries to the building should be directly to work areas so that the public services will not be disturbed. Freight elevators, catalog departments, extension services, public catalogs—all must be planned with a view to the traffic flow to those areas.

Conclusion

The wise use of building funds is less a matter of skimping on the needs of the service or even on the materials of construction than it is of exploiting to the fullest the areas and the equipment that can be made available from the funds provided, with attention being paid always to the effect the building plan will have on operating costs.

There is no clear-cut sure way to guarantee getting the most for your money, for each library presents a unique problem. Some compromises with ideals may become necessary in working out any plan, but it is important that you be able to appraise the effect of each choice made. In recapitulating, however, I would list as having major importance:

1. Select a competent library building consultant to guide you

2. Draw your building consultant into the project at the earliest possible time, even before selecting an architect

3. With the aid of your consultant, modernize all library procedures before plans are drawn

4. Instead of duplicating facilities, try to place each where it can serve two needs without inconvenience, as

One lending desk to control the entrances

Public toilets so located that they will serve both the reading rooms and the meeting rooms

A story-hour room that will double as a room for adult meetings

Joint workrooms instead of separate work facilities for each department

Work stations that may be used by several staff members

A book collection needed by two departments arranged where each will have direct, easy access to it

5. Keep the building flexible, so that it can be readily adapted to changed requirements by

Packaging in one area all fixed facilities, such as stairs, elevators, and toilets

Avoiding permanent walls between public service rooms

Equipping the library with movable furniture and stacks

Not using feature borders in the flooring

Avoiding built-in features, such as closets, listening rooms, and window seats

6. Strive for a plan that will not confuse patrons. Give serious attention to the flow of traffic in the building

Remember, too, that no program prepared in advance is ever complete. As a project develops, new problems and new needs will emerge, calling for new appraisals and new decisions. And, finally, let me say that if changes in a proposed plan seem desirable, make them without hesitation. It is easier to change a line on a print than it will be to move a wall later.

GETTING THE MOST FOR YOUR MONEY FROM THE POINT OF VIEW OF THE ARCHITECT

LEON CHATELAIN, JR.
Architect
Washington, D.C.

"How To Get the Most for Your Money" is a subject that is uppermost in everyone's mind in every endeavor we encounter. It is certainly one that confronts the architect with each commission he receives whether it is a residence, hospital, school, factory, or library. No one wants to waste his money these days on useless gadgets or unnecessary luxuries, and everyone wants to make sure that his dollar is buying the biggest dollar's worth possible. Architects are taught in school and during their many years of training and experience that economy in construction is of prime importance. It certainly is no surprise when I tell you that average building costs have risen over 200 per cent over the past twenty years. This is an average of 10 per cent per year, and it is continuing to rise every year.

Economy in building in its broad sense is the proper utilization of space—meaning the proper planning and designing of space for the function to be housed in the building—and it also includes the careful selection of materials and equipment with special emphasis on their life and their maintenance qualities. Of course, the architect must still design the building so that it satisfies the aesthetic senses. The building must look like a library; it must invite people to come in and browse or read or study. It must also be a pleasant place to work in and provide the proper atmosphere for the visitor.

Architect and Building Committee

How do we get the most for our money? Let us start at the very beginning—the site. The architect should be called into consultation in the selection of the site. With the selection of an unsuitable site you may actually lose money before you start. There may be all kinds of hidden expenses in the ground. It is surprising how often a site selection committee will actually purchase a lot only because it is the cheapest one being considered. A particular site may be over an old fill or dump yard, or an old marsh requiring expensive pilings, or it may be on solid bedrock requiring expensive rock excavation. The available utilities of sewer, water, gas, and electricity may be several thousand feet removed from the site, thus necessitating additional outlay of money to bring them to the site. Even some zoning or building restrictions can work hardships by forcing unnecessary plan arrangements and thus resulting in additional expenditures. We would all recognize that a lot with a rugged topography or a very odd shape can affect the ultimate cost of construction by handicapping the architect into necessitating a design with a complicated plan arrangement. So beware of a cheap or inexpensive lot—it may cost you many extra dollars in construction.

Somehow or other, building committees can often get the architect into all kinds of boxes. It would be well to consult an architect when you are about ready to write your program of requirements. Everybody wants the largest floor area built of the most expensive materials for the least amount of money. This is certainly utopia for the building committee but leaves the architect completely baffled. We must all be interested in the final cost of the building, or else we wouldn't be here discussing the subject. But what are we going to get the most of for our money? Efficient space, good material, good looks? The architect is no magician; he cannot plan a building of a given size with the most expensive materials and keep within some imaginary budget. Within reason, he could probably keep within the budget for a building of specified size if the materials were left to his selection. A carefully prepared program by a building committee will aid materially in producing an economical building.

Shape of the Building

Planning of a library involves many individual factors, such as, for instance, the general floor plan arrangement. We all know that a compact plan with a minimum amount of space lost in circulation is more economical than a plan with much space lost in circulation. Such a compact plan is also more economical in the use of employees' time in moving about the building. It is interesting to note that 10,000 square feet may be enclosed in a 100-foot square having a total perimeter of 400 feet. If this same area is enclosed in a simple "T"- or "L"-shaped plan with 50-foot-wide bays, the perimeter becomes 500 feet, a 25 per cent increase in length of exterior walls. "U"- or "E"-shaped plans are proportionately higher. This increase in perimeter will reflect a proportional increase in the cost of heating and of other services. Interior partitions are longer, piping is longer, wall footings are longer, roof flashings are longer, and you could go on with numerous other component parts of the building.

Windows, Materials, and Equipment

We could have an hour-long discussion on the subject of whether windows are necessary in a library. They take up wall space that could accommodate shelving. Windows do not save on the cost of electric wiring since we must design the building so that it can be used at night. They cost a great deal more than the blank wall into which they are installed. Windows must be washed, and they create a heat loss that means more fuel to buy. It may seem illogical, but in order to control the natural

daylight that they are put in to produce, we must purchase and maintain costly louvers, screens, blinds, or draperies.

You may ask what provision is made for ventilation. In this part of the country, at least, air conditioning is being used rather universally in buildings that are kept open all year. I am sure I need not explain to librarians that humidity-controlled atmosphere in a building helps preserve books and allows for the comfort and efficiency of people using the building. However, if you must use windows, I would recommend that you select those allowing the least amount of infiltration—the engineer's word for the leakage of air through window cracks.

This leads us into thinking about building materials and mechanical equipment. Experience dictates that many savings may be accomplished both in initial cost and in maintenance by careful and wise selection of these products. Today the heating and ventilation system of library buildings has become a rather complicated engineering system. We all demand more comfort. In order to get more comfort we often install very expensive control systems merely to take care of the extremely "hot-blooded" and the extremely "cold-blooded" librarians. Perhaps some lesser level of perfection would satisfy everyone just as well as the more complicated system. People didn't gripe nearly so much when they had only Franklin stoves.

We often spend many extra surplus dollars in our buildings by installing standby equipment that is rarely if ever used. Duplicating boilers, burners, pumps, valves, and controls is expensive. There was a time when we could not always depend on this equipment and, therefore, installed them in duplicate, including all the valves and gadgets. We have found that for the very rare and brief time such equipment may be out of commission, the building will usually keep warm enough to function. We often get over-zealous in the number of plumbing fixtures that we think we need in a building such as a library. Too often it seems we are trying to supply one fixture for each occupant in the building. Electrical service equipment, lighting fixtures, and overabundance of electrical outlets are factors that should receive close scrutiny. One of the biggest reasons why buildings are so costly today—outside of inflation— is that we demand so much more in heating, ventilating, plumbing, and electrical conveniences. The mechanical trades now account for about 45 per cent of the cost of the building. Twenty years ago they accounted for about 25 per cent of the total building dollar. Likewise, we now require better and more expensive flooring materials, acoustical treatment, and special wall finishes.

Today the architect is confronted with endless new materials and methods of construction, but woe be to the architect who blindly believes the salesman's silver tongue. Architects are tempted to specify to save money in installation and to save in later maintenance. Unfortunately many products have not been thoroughly tested against all elements and all climates. We do have many new materials being offered that drastically save in construction dollars and in construction time. Various panel walls are making their way into our buildings. They are much thinner than the usual masonry and plaster walls and often give much better insulation. It is interesting to note, in the 100 feet by 100 feet building we used as an example of perimeter of a building, that the saving in floor space using a panel wall would amount to about 400 square feet of floor area, or about 4 per cent of the total building area in the square building. Proportionately more would be saved in the other types of floor plans. Interior partitions are likewise subject to study and selection of the proper type. Here, again, we find vast improvements in design. I personally think we use too many interior partitions. Most areas in a library building can be easily separated by the casework. Think twice before you install ceiling-high partitions.

You have probably been struck, as is everyone who has either built, designed, or financed a building, with the great amount of waste that is hauled away from the building site—broken brick, end pieces of lumber, pieces of tile, pieces of glass, and endless bits of leftover building materials. In recent years the building industry has made great strides in many products by unifying dimensioning to eliminate this waste. We call it modular measurement. It uses 4 inches as a unit. There is very little waste when the materials manufactured and available in these sizes are used in modular-dimensioned plans. We in the building industry hope that some day all major building materials will be made to conform to this standardization. At present many units that are prefabricated of concrete, structural clay, steel, and aluminum are available. Modular measurement speeds construction and eliminates a great deal of the waste with consequent savings in dollars.

As part of the selection of a material we must always subject the material to a test to determine its maintenance cost. What good is it to save $5000 on an item of construction that will cost $750 a year ever after in heating bills, repairs, or painting? Or why save $5000 on a material or product that will have to be replaced in a few years? The building industry has made some substantial advances along these lines that will be explained later by Mr. Horowitz of the Building Research Institute.

Building Codes

Perhaps one of the problems of the architect over which he has little jurisdiction is building code requirements. Practically every building code in America is a specification code rather than a performance code. In other words the specification-type building code specifies exactly what and how to achieve the result, while the performance-type building code merely specifies the result to be obtained. For instance, the specification code will give the thickness of a stair enclosure wall and the kinds of material to be used in its construction; the performance code will only require the wall to withstand a two-hour fire test. Codes of each state or municipality differ widely. This, of course, adds to the cost of building because of lack of uniformity. Oftentimes local unions dictate the code to the authorities to make certain that their trade is not replaced by more efficient methods of building or by cheaper factory prefabricated units.

I ask you why in certain jurisdictions a library is classed along with a night club for egress requirements, while another code will require that a reading room of 5000 square feet shall have exit doors and egress requirements for 500 people, which in turn requires 154 inches or a 12-foot 10-inch door width? Our country would certainly be much more erudite if we could jam that many people into our library reading rooms at all times; perhaps we might introduce the night-club atmosphere to interest the young people.

Element of Time

Each new project creates a new problem for the architect, and the problem must be resolved jointly by the librarian and the architect. Don't press the architect into producing his drawings too fast. The over-all planning of the library from the preliminary concepts to its ultimate occupancy extends over a long period of time. Just as it is essential for the designer to have ample time for the preparation of plans, the contractor also needs sufficient time in which to prepare his estimates. Some savings can be achieved by taking bids in "off season" when the construction activities are curtailed because of weather or working conditions in the winter months, but this is not usually feasible.

It is probably not necessary for me to remind you that you will get a better and more economical library if you engage the services of a competent architect with a good reputation and pay him a just and equitable fee for his services. You will then get the most for your money.

GETTING THE MOST FOR YOUR MONEY FROM THE POINT OF VIEW OF THE RESEARCHER

HAROLD HOROWITZ
Assistant Director for Technical Programs
Building Research Institute
National Academy of Sciences
Washington, D.C.

Almost every discussion concerning use of the technical potential of our times to get maximum value out of new buildings gives a good deal of consideration to the trend toward industrial production of large building components and the reduction of operations at the building site to simple assembly. There is nothing new about these concepts any more, and everyone who has had any contact with buildings constructed in the past ten or fifteen years can see many examples of large components which were formerly fabricated at the site that have instead been prefabricated or preassembled before being sent to the construction job. My contribution to this session will concern the problem of the building owner and operator, in this case the library administrator, in making sure that he takes full advantage of the special opportunities offered by this trend toward industrial preassembly.

Not very many years ago, it was common practice for architects to detail a great many of the components and furnishings of library buildings that today are being selected from standard items in manufacturers' catalogs. I am concerned with one problem in this procedure, and that is the method by which you can be sure of having available to your architects at the proper time the kinds and qualities of preassembled components that you need. The average salesman will insist that his company's research and development department is always working in your behalf and can be relied upon to provide you with the best possible products for your particular needs. Up until recently, it was very unusual for a building owner or operator to question whether this was true or not. There is still little doubt that products manufacturers want to do the best possible job for you, but there is a very real question as to whether they have the best kinds of information with which they can plan their new product development programs.

Product Development Plan

The nature of this problem can be understood better if you review the processes by which new products are developed. My first figure shows the steps in a typical product development program in the form of a graph. The ordinate gives some idea of the relative cost of each step, and the abscissa shows the length of time involved. Of course, this graph is a generalization, and the estimates of rela-

tive cost and length of time vary from product to product. In the case of time, this chart shows a span of thirty-one months between the first specification of a new product and the completion of all of the development work prior to the beginning of production. Other estimates sometimes indicate a span of up to twenty years for this process where fundamentally new products are being developed.

To complete the abscissa, additional time would have to be added for the organization of the production facilities, production, and distribution. Here, again, we would have to guess to develop a generalization because every product is different in its time requirements. However, to give you some sense of scale about the production time required for a product whose development program has been completed, I will describe briefly a conversation I had about a year ago with a former college classmate who is employed in the new product development department of a large manufacturer of household appliances.

In my discussion of this problem with him, I asked about the experience within his own company on the time required to deliver a new line of products once the development work had been completed and the orders were given to go ahead. He said that normal experience was about twenty to twenty-four months. When a crash program is declared by top management, it has been possible to shorten this time to from fifteen to eighteen months, and under unusual circumstances on rare occasions the time has been reduced to twelve months. My friend was talking about residential appliances which normally have annual design changes and are in a highly competitive market.

You can see that it takes a manufacturer a very considerable period of time to bring a new product to the market. The generalization presented in Figure 1 of thirty-one months plus another twelve to twenty-four months for production and distribution give a total time span of at least three and one-half years and possibly four and one-half years. It is also evident that the investment in a new product increases rapidly as a manufacturer completes his product development program, and certainly when he is through with his investment in production facilities, he has such a great stake in his new product that he must attempt to secure very considerable sales before he can profitably consider modifications or new development work on the same item.

The lesson for the building owner and manager is that he must exercise any influence he believes that he should have on the development of new products many years before he begins the construction of a new building, if he is to have some assurance of finding the products he wants available to his architects. Studies of trends in his building requirements must be well established and of such quality that they permit reasonably good estimates of product characteristics three or four years before the time that products are being specified for a new building.

Manufacturers themselves attempt to study trends in building requirements to some extent through market research projects. However, since very poor records of the performance of building components have been kept by almost every party in the building field, the bases for these market studies are often generalized hastily from limited facts. If, someday, library administrators find that fins are the latest improvement to standard steel stack shelving, they may be able to claim a share of the responsibility because of a failure to provide a better statement of their needs to product manufacturers.

**Building Operation
and Maintenance Study Group**

A group of members of the Building Research Institute who are employed as managers of buildings by a wide variety of companies, such as the New York Life Insurance Company, American Telephone and Telegraph, Ford Motor Company, and John W. Galbreath and Company, together with a number of college and university plant administrators have formed themselves into a standing technical committee which we call the Building Operation and Maintenance Study Group. After their own consideration of the situation I have just described, they decided to experiment with techniques for feeding back information they acquire through the operation and maintenance of buildings, and then to attempt to state the problems they find as a means of clarifying their nature for the information of architects and to challenge manufacturers to develop solutions.

My next figure is a chart developed by the Study Group to express this idea graphically in terms of the chain of communication on building products. At about 1:30 o'clock on the chart we find a producer who designs, develops, manufactures, and distributes

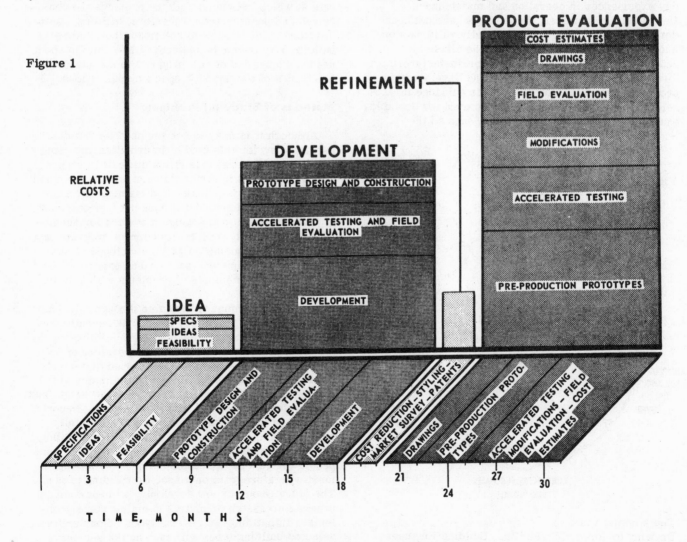

A Typical Product Development Program
Albert M. Rockwell, "Planning a Product-Development Program"
Battelle Technical Review, 78:211 (September, 1957)

building components. At about 4 o'clock we find the architect who selects and specifies components through his sources of information and reference files of current product data. At 6 o'clock we find the contractor who purchases and installs the products the architect has specified. Following the circle we find the completed building turned over to the owner who lives with it for years on end. The owner must adjust his program to any deficiencies in the building; he also profits by all successful aspects of the design. He must maintain all of the materials and equipment, modify or remodel them periodically, and eventually decide when his building is completely unsuitable and must be replaced.

Completed Buildings as Laboratories

Completed buildings can be considered as laboratories from which a great deal of valuable technical data can be developed as a result of the day-to-day experiences in operation and maintenance. Unfortunately, however, the methods have not been developed for collecting scientifically valid data on such experiences and completing the circle by reporting them back to the product manufacturers for use in planning their new product development programs, or to architects for their guidance in selection and specification. There are a few isolated examples of this kind of reporting, such as the

THE MISSING LINKS

Figure 2

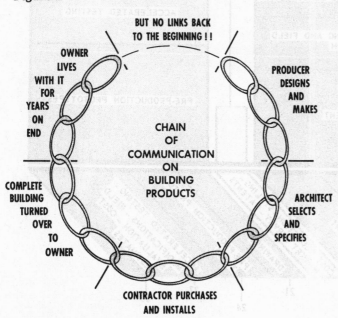

The Missing Links
Drawing by Howard E. Phillips, Building Engineer
American Telephone & Telegraph Co.
and Chairman, Building Research Institute's
Building Operation and Maintenance Study Group

annual survey of the National Association of Building Owners and Managers on operating costs for the office buildings administered by its members. A few large building owners also have engineering and architectural staffs which carefully study all of the factors that contribute to an accurate picture of the total annual cost of operating each building facility in such a way that helpful information is available to the designers and builders of subsequent projects.

The Building Research Institute's Building Operation and Maintenance Study Group is convinced that methods have to be found for more building users to communicate with the people who develop and produce products for their new buildings, so that the best possible use can be made in the future of the production capabilities of the industry. Although modern manufacturing processes offer a tremendous range of possibilities, the rate at which they can change and improve the building components they manufacture tends to be slower than the rate at which individual building projects are conceived and constructed. Therefore, building administrators must attempt to anticipate their future building requirements and convey information about needed properties of new products to manufacturers in advance of the need for specific applications.

Methods of Studying Problems

Although it is easy to see the need for building users to develop this kind of information and convey it to manufacturers, it is fairly difficult to suggest specific methods by which this can be accomplished. Our own Building Operation and Maintenance Study Group frankly admits that it does not feel confident, at present, that it can suggest a method for accomplishing this task. In fact, its current program is a series of experiments on various methods of summarizing operation and maintenance experience and of developing statements of problems with building components.

Using the techniques available through a technical society program, the Study Group has recently conducted a workshop on windows. In this workshop five subcommittees, composed of operators of a variety of types of buildings, developed statements of problems concerning window frame materials, glazing, glass area requirements, window height and width relationships, and window functions. Reports on these problems were presented to a carefully selected panel of architects, builders, and building products manufacturers' research and development people for general discussion. This was an experiment with a program on a specific building product. The Study Group is now developing an experimental program to assign priorities to maintenance problems with buildings of several types. Four or five selected building types will each be the subject of study by a small working group with the objective of reaching a consensus on the principal maintenance and operation problems.

There is a great deal of debate about methods which can be employed in these studies. Some people feel that maintaining accurate cost records for every building would provide valuable information, if done in a uniform way that would permit comparison with similar information for other buildings. They argue that the way to keep such data would be in the form of total annual cost of ownership and operation which would include initial cost, maintenance cost, repair, remodeling, and so on, prorated on an annual basis over the life of the building. Other people argue that such data would not really be helpful because of the tremendous differences in climate, building usage, and so on.

Another problem that is continually discussed concerns the propriety of engaging in studies which are likely to result in information that points a finger of criticism toward architects, building products manufacturers, or the building administrators themselves. In the case of managers of buildings where space is rented, there is great concern about identifying faults or other specific problems in their own buildings out of the fear that such information may have an effect on rentability. However, no one questions the ultimate value of reporting operation and maintenance experience which will provide a scientific basis for the engineering judgments made in the development of new building products.

At present, it seems that the methods of developing and reporting data and the selection of the significant facts for such documentation are research projects in themselves. There is no doubt, however, of the ultimate value of such programs in helping to realize the greatest possible value from our future buildings.

Questions from the Audience

QUESTION: If we wish to obtain information on a new product, would the Building Research Institute give us any information they have?

MR. HOROWITZ: Yes, if it has information on the product. The Institute also has publications containing such data to distribute. A list of these publications is available from the Institute, 2101 Constitution Avenue, Washington 25, D.C.

QUESTION FROM MR. DAVIS: We often hear or read that a building "looks like a library." What does looking like a library mean? Can you describe such a building?

MR. CHATELAIN: I cannot describe it, but we all know that buildings fall into such categories. We can recognize churches, school buildings, office buildings, and so on. I recommend that Mr. Davis take a look at the new New Orleans Public Library. This is an excellent example of a contemporary building which also looks like a library.

MR. ULVELING: I always quarrel with an architect when he uses the phrase and has in mind the old Carnegie-type library building. Now that he has mentioned the New Orleans Public Library

building, I know that I have no quarrel with Mr. Chatelain's concept of a library building.

QUESTION: Why has the use of glass block seemingly decreased?

MR. HOROWITZ: I do not know that it has decreased. It is a fairly expensive building material, however, and this may be the reason for a decrease in its use if there has been a decrease.

QUESTION: A few years ago we were told that balconies were wasteful of space, but now mezzanines seem to be in favor. What do mezzanines have that balconies do not?

MR. CHATELAIN: I cannot answer that question or describe the difference. I do not believe that either balconies or mezzanines give the most for your money.

MR. ULVELING: When it comes to deciding between a balcony or mezzanine and a second floor, I would prefer a second floor all the way.

QUESTION FROM MR. GIRARD: Generally speaking, what type of building gives the most wide-open space? What size module? What is the relation between cost and module size?

MR. CHATELAIN: There is not necessarily any one type of building which will give the most space. Space is determined by the distance between exterior walls and partitions. To gain space, one should keep partitions to a minimum. As to the module size, in America this is 4 inches. And this 4-inch standard saves money.

MR. ULVELING: Mr. Girard is probably thinking about the 20-foot module, pointed toward a larger bay probably.

MR. CHATELAIN: The size of the material is the determinant. Twenty-foot size is divisible by 4 inches or 4 feet.

MR. GIRARD: I was thinking of the module as used by MacDonald in his book, which is I believe a multiple of 3 feet or $3\frac{1}{2}$ feet.

MR. CHATELAIN: The Japanese were the ones who started modular dimension, and they used multiples of 3 feet. The size of their mats on the floor was 3 feet by 6 feet; the ceiling height of a room was 9 feet. Room size was gauged by the number of mats which would cover the floor.

MR. GIRARD: In terms of the library module, is there any optimum size that you know of?

MR. ULVELING: We use a 3-foot module in libraries, probably because the shelf size is 3 feet in length. There are differences in modular size in stack area because of the aisle space. Although I believe nothing has been accepted as a standard size, we usually look for 3-foot lengths plus aisle space.

UNITED STATES AIR FORCE ACADEMY LIBRARY

United States Air Force Academy
Colorado Springs, Colorado
Director: Lieutenant Colonel
  George V. Fagan

Statistical Data

Architect: Skidmore, Owings & Merrill, Architects-
              Engineers, 425 Park Ave., New York, N.Y.
Type of library: Educational
Population to be served: 2500 cadets and 1500
                            faculty members
Dimensions: 224' x 140'
Area: 78,500 sq. ft.
Book capacity: 300,000
Furniture and equipment: Designed by Walter
                            Dorwin Teague Associates
Bookstacks: W. R. Ames Co.
Seating capacity: 800
Size of module: 27'x 27'
Parking area capacity: 300 cars (lobby floor)

Presentation of Plans

LIEUTENANT COLONEL GEORGE V. FAGAN
Director

The Air Force Academy, which is located ten miles north of Colorado Springs, is not only one of the world's newest educational institutions but also a laboratory of military education. Like its sister institutions at West Point and Annapolis, the Air Force Academy has as its mission the undergraduate training of young career officers. Its curriculum is about equally divided between the sciences and technology fields and the social sciences and humanities. Each cadet is graduated with a B.S. degree and with a commission as second lieutenant in the Air Force. Like the other service academies, the classes (or, as they are called, *sections*) are small. We have only twelve to fifteen cadets in a section. In addition to having small classes, it is a practice in the service academies to use homogeneous grouping. In every subject, on the basis of the grade made previously or the results of College Board Entrance Examinations, the group is resectioned on a homogeneous basis.

United States Air Force Academy Library
Colorado Springs, Colorado

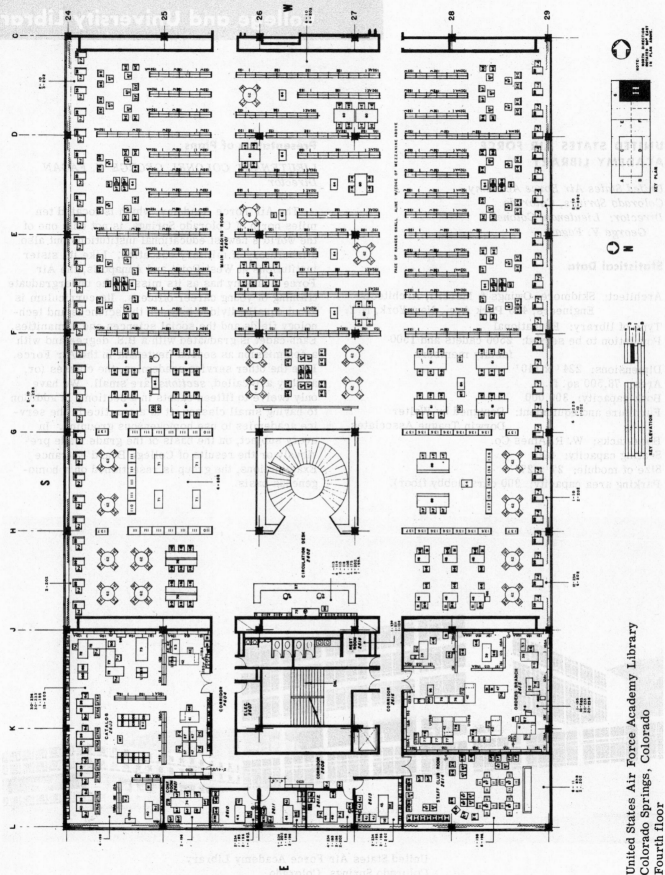

United States Air Force Academy Library
Colorado Springs, Colorado
Fourth floor

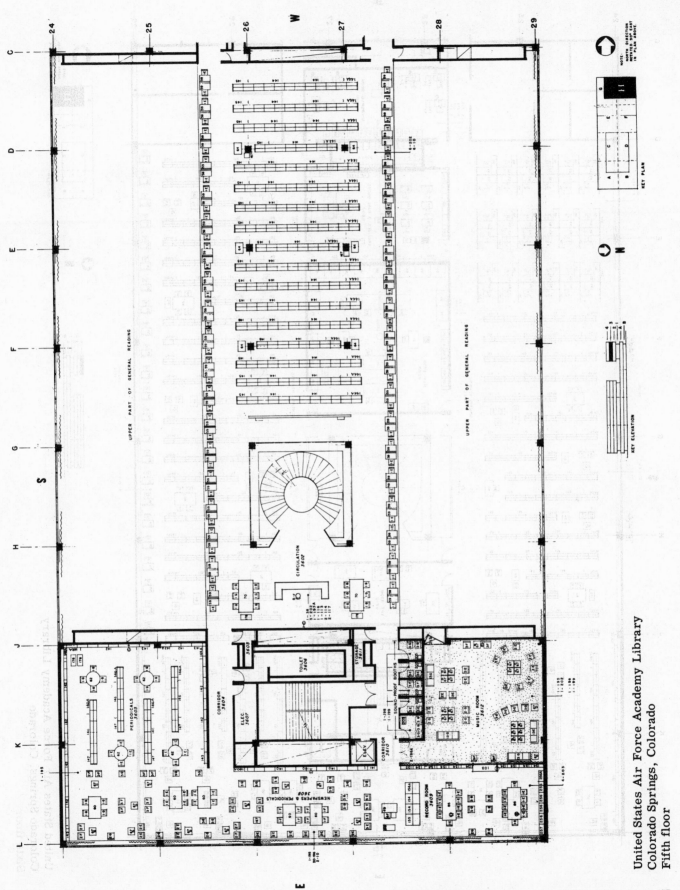

United States Air Force Academy Library
Colorado Springs, Colorado
Fifth floor

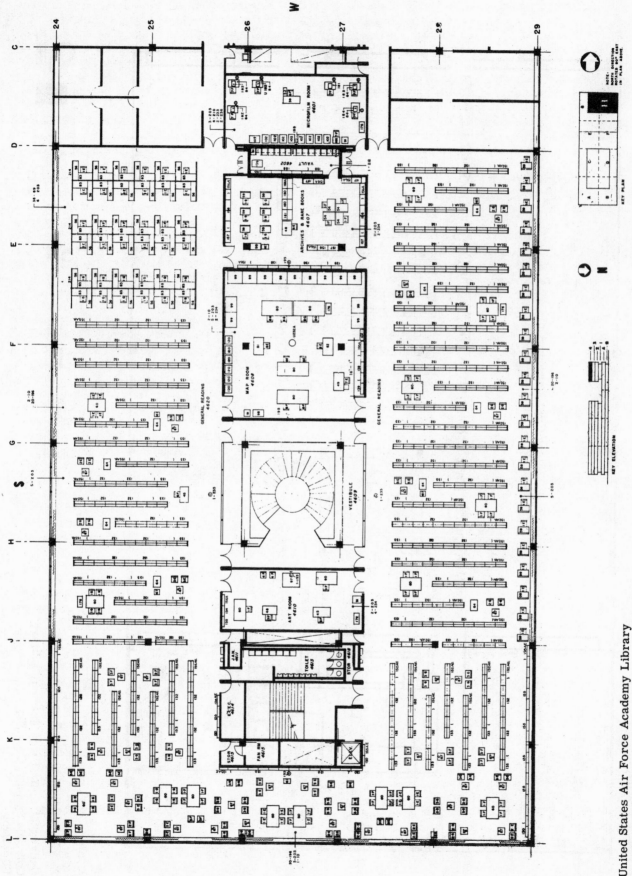

United States Air Force Academy Library
Colorado Springs, Colorado
Sixth floor

We use an elective system, called the *enrichment program*. The cadets may take validating examinations in any subject in which they have had previous instruction. If they pass the examination, they are then given credit for the prescribed course and allowed to take an enrichment course. This allows for a great ceal of flexibility and helps to individualize the instruction even further. The enrichment program has a big impact upon the library, and vice ·versa. We in the library are happy to be very prominent supporters of the enrichment program. By taking the enrichment courses, cadets are able to major in subject fields, of which five are offered at the present time. In addition to majoring, they receive additional academic credits and, as a result, accumulate about five years of academic credits in the space of the four years.

In order to understand the role of the library, one has to understand the academic complex of the Academy. By "academic complex" we mean the area of the Academy grounds which includes dormitories, dining hall, cadet social center, superintendent's headquarters, chapel site, classrooms, and library building. This corresponds roughly to the academic portion of a college campus. Whereas most university campuses were built piecemeal over decades, the Air Force Academy campus was built simultaneously over a two-year period. The whole Air Force Academy complex is a great tribute to the industrial and technological progress of the United States. It took twenty-six construction companies to build the complex. The buildings were designed to last for a minimum of two hundred years. They will last a lot longer. We planned that our equipment will last for one hundred years.

The library is one wing of the academic building and is situated right in the heart of the academic complex. It is open for service ninety-four hours per week. All of the professional librarians except myself are civilians. We have both civilian and military library assistants. At the present time, six of the twelve professional librarians are women; thirteen of the librarian assistants are women.

The library opened for service in August of 1955, at the Academy's temporary headquarters at Lowry Air Force Base in Denver. At that time, the holdings of the library numbered about 500 books. On January 5, 1959, the library moved into its new modular building; over 70,000 books were moved from Denver. By July 1, 1959, the holdings in the library had passed the 90,000 mark. The ultimate goal of the Academy is to have a library of 250,000, although the building is designed to hold 300,000.

Accessibility to all types of materials is a major objective of the Academy. As a result, the library is 100 per cent open stack. It is also the only major military library in this country which uses the Library of Congress classification system. During the 1957-58 academic year, over 38,000 books were circulated to about 1000 authorized users, consisting of three small classes and the faculty.

The library, along with all other phases of the Air Force Academy, reflects years of careful planning by military and civilian specialists. It represents many of the high ideas and ideals of librarianship; quality as well as quantity has been stressed.

The academic building is really one big building. The lobby floor is a parking lot for 300 cars. The third level from the street, called the terrazzo level, runs through the whole building. But above this floor, the library is a separate building, the same as the academic building is separate.

The huge windows in the main reading room are 24 feet high; there are 122 feet of glass across each side. It is heavily tinted glass, but the sun does stream in pretty brightly. The window drapes are operated by motors from the inside. The spiral stairway is a very distinctive feature of the library; it is a 93-step stairway, running right through the building. It is a cantilever, spiral stairway, concrete, with stone steps. In one part of the main reading room is the card catalog. We have a receded space for shelving on the back side of the card catalog. We place our reserve books on these shelves around the outside of the card catalog. This solves the problem of bringing the reserve books close to the desk.

All along the windows are individual study tables for the cadets, and there are also group tables. The seating capacity is 800, or one third of the Cadet Wing. One of the distinctive features of the furniture is that the tables and chairs are not library equipment; they were designed by Walter Dorwin Teague Associates for use throughout the Academy. They are aluminum-base forcatom. The small study tables are the same as used in the classrooms and in cadet quarters. The circular tables are used in various places throughout the Academy. Chairs are of one basic structure.

In another part of the main reading room is the reference collection in a "U" formation. I am aching to change that; but I cannot do it since changes in Air Force buildings cannot be made until quarters have been occupied at least a year.

On the second library floor, which is really the fifth floor from the ground, are the newspaper area, the magazine stacks, and current periodical area. All the current periodicals are laid out on the open shelves in alphabetical order.

Also on this floor is the music room. It is equipped with a stereo hi-fi system, and the room seats forty people. It is used not only for individual listening to records, classical and semiclassical, but for concerts presented on weekends. The music room is also used for language instruction by the foreign language department, as well as by the English and history departments, and for meetings of various types.

The top floor, the sixth, houses books in the L.C. classification N through Z, the microfilm room, special collection room and vault, map room, thirty-six faculty study carrels, U.S. government and UN documents, and the aerospace room.

The map room, a very attractive one, has map cabinets around three sides of the room. The special collection room houses the many fine and valuable gifts received from individuals.

The thirty-six faculty study carrels provide accommodations for many of our instructors, who are all on active duty. The large majority of the younger officers are graduates of West Point and Annapolis. Many of them are pursuing advanced degrees. It is necessary for the instructor to have at least a master's degree in the subject taught. About 25 per cent of the faculty members hold the Ph.D degree from leading universities throughout the country.

Besides the main library we have a community library, which is like a public library, for dependents, who are not allowed to use the main library.

Criticism

MR. DONALD C. DAVIDSON
Librarian, Santa Barbara Library
University of California
Santa Barbara, California

I did stop at the Air Force Academy on my way east because you really cannot understand the Academy without a visit. You can get some of the feeling of what it has to offer through pictures and words but not the full feeling.

Colonel Fagan used the word "modular" to describe the Air Force Library. Indeed, it is modular; it has a 27-foot module. But, unlike most of our libraries, I do not think there was much concern about the spans. The spans are tremendous; even the central mezzanine span, which is narrow, must be 35 feet. The reading room sides are 45 feet.

The foothills of the Rockies obviously challenged the architects to a great conception. Even though I think I have a rudimentary aesthetic sense, I think the Academy does come off. It is like the Jackson Lake Lodge at the foot of the Grand Tetons; the architect was really challenged.

I think the significant contribution of the Academy to the field of academic-library buildingmanship (if there is such a word) is visual; it is dramatic.

The architecture, I suppose, is a sort of mild brown plus black and gray and white. It is an effective use of matter. The very treatment of the library points it out, with its smaller pedestal of a terrazzo floor base, on which the three actual service floors sit upright at the corner. You can see that from every place.

I think there is excessive glass used throughout the Academy. The doors have to be closed carefully. Some of the panels on some of the buildings, which I thought were board, I was surprised to find (because one or two had been blown out) were also

glass. Color coating and the use of colors were very effective.

One of the things I had wondered about before I got there was if the over-all master planning, which went down even to the chairs, might create tedium; that is, would you get tired of the repetition all through the whole base? This did not seem to be true at all. The chairs, by their color, were different; they were comfortable. The chairs did have one defect; they are angular, like everything in the architecture. Rubber caps had to be put over the corners of the arms because they were damaging the underneath part of some desks. But this is about the only structural deficiency I think I noted about the equipment.

The library, then, is in a dramatic focal point within the scale of this quite overwhelming military installation. This is as I think most of us would have it. This, too, has an importance as a sort of international symbol of the importance of librarianship, as the Academy has become an international show place.

I do not think the Academy library is featured by detailed planning of interest to librarians. Some libraries have that character. The detail is good, but it is the over-all things on which I would like to comment.

I think the most dramatic part of the library is in realizing the full potential of the mezzanine as a dramatic, visual feature. I think I would go so far as to say it is probably the most effective treatment of the mezzanine which I know in academic libraries.

There is a luxury of space; there is a luxury of vertical space which cannot be changed; there is a luxury of space in the stack spacing with 5-foot 6-inch centers between ranges and stacks; 7-foot aisles between the stacks. This does not concern me because, when the library goes beyond the 250,000-volume mark, the stacks can be compressed. It is potentially fillable space.

The stairway is easy to climb. There are more than sufficient views. There are sufficient books although, again, the Academy is fortunate in having shelf space perhaps for its full-sized collection. The circulation space is sufficient. The tables are sufficient; there are sufficient officer carrels. There is certainly sufficient space. There is sufficient designation of smoking areas. There may be insufficient lighting in certain areas, but this may easily be remedied by the nature of the construction. There may be insufficient lighting in the work areas, maybe in the stack areas.

But it is very hard to find something really to criticize. There is not the flexibility or liberality of space in the staff work areas. I did not like the lack of a window for the personnel in acquisitions.

The building does have a nice interior symmetry created by the circular stairway; the utility core, which you remember was right behind the circulation desk, carries a conventional stairway and elevator. The symmetry is created by the mezzanine or central strip which goes through the reading areas on each floor. The reading spaces are primarily out toward the windows at the side, in an attractive effect.

The east end of the fourth level contains the staff or administrative areas. Westward of this space is the central circulation desk and a band 3 modules wide which contains the reference service area. The remainder of this floor is devoted to open shelving and reading space.

The fifth, or mezzanine level, is in the form of a "T," with music and current newspapers and periodicals occupying the horizontal section and back files of periodicals occupying the vertical section. This vertical section forms a bridge running the length of the general reading room.

On the sixth floor, the central third of the room, running east and west, contains four special purpose rooms, the stair well, and service core. On either side of this strip are stacks and tables intermingled.

I did like the Walter Dorwin Teague designs, which reflect that sort of Newbaugh House exterior. It is not of that school of the slab-layer pine laying, a phrase I picked up several years ago from the magazine *Interiors*. It has good, substantial appearance; it looks suitable to a military academy.

There is one question on the possibly minus side which I skipped over: there is not direct access from the academic building to the cadet quarters. This lack of direct access includes the relationship between the dormitories and the library.

Surely, we could find other things to criticize, but the things are small. We should regard the Air Force Academy, I think, with pride. It is (in Van Buren's words) a completed model of cultural beauty.

Discussion

MR. DAVIDSON: Before the questions we want to explain two things. First of all, the 27-foot module is not immediately apparent, but there are 22 modules around the outer walls of the building. Then, in the two reading areas, the central posts are eliminated; here the span is 54 feet. But the actual distance is not that because, I believe, the mezzanine represented here in the center, between these two bays, is sort of cantilevered up.

Secondly, I would like to mention some questions about the 93 steps of the circular stairway that goes from the terrazzo or main floor to the two upper floors. The climb of 12 feet from the terrazzo level to the first floor above is very easy.

MR. ESTERQUEST: I am curious about the circular staircase. It is dramatic; it is aesthetically wonderful; and you do not puff when you go up it.

But what about the problem of traffic? From the one picture we saw, it looked to me as if it were possible for just one person going up to pass one coming down. Is there enough space so

that you do not have a traffic problem?

COLONEL FAGAN: At least four people, if not five, can go up abreast. The largest group we have checked on in this limited space of time was on the 16th of May, which was Armed Forces Day. We had the Academy open; within the space of three hours, 900 people came up. We experienced no congestion. We found that during June Week with 10,000 people we had no more congestion than during the time we had the 900 people.

MR. HEINTZ: The furniture struck me as being very good; I am particularly interested in the rugged look of it, because I am in a men's college, where students are very hard on furniture. I wonder if the design is being made available to any manufacturer, or if a manufacturer has expressed interest in it.

COLONEL FAGAN: Several people have asked that same question. I am sure, if you inquired through Walter Dorwin Teague Associates, you would find there are manufacturers who are making similar material, if not the same.

MR. DeKOSTER: I wanted to ask about the mezzanine in your library. How wide is it in relation to the area underneath?

MR. DAVIDSON: 35 feet, approximately; isn't it? It overlaps at least 4 feet.

COLONEL FAGAN: It overlaps about 4 feet on each side. The stacks go down underneath the mezzanine; there are some reading spaces. The light is not too good. The light under the mezzanine is not fluorescent.

MR. METCALF: I wanted to raise a question in connection with the circular stairs. How wide are the treads at the outside, and how wide at the inside?

COLONEL FAGAN: I do not have the figures.

MR. METCALF: Then I would like to ask another question. When you go upstairs, do you go up on the broad side of the tread and come down on the narrow side; or do you go up on the narrow side and down on the broad side, which is the safe way to do it? There are two objections to circular steps. One is that they take space; the second is that they are dangerous to life and limb. I wondered if that has any effect here.

COLONEL FAGAN: Well, that is true. I do not know how the cadets go up and down those steps; but while taking groups through the building I go up and down the narrow side because I find it takes fewer steps.

MR. DAVIDSON: If you come down the natural way on the right side, you are on the narrow side of the steps. While I did not take the measurements, somebody did a very fine job, I believe, on the risers and width. You do not have any feeling of fear of falling. You go up this particular stairway in an entirely different manner than you do any other; I mean it is psychological.

Mr. Metcalf, you remember, undoubtedly, there is a conventional stairway not very far away, 40 or 50 feet to the rear, which the staff would normally use to get back and forth.

COLONEL FAGAN: I can assure you the staff never uses it, because it is easier to go up the spiral.

ST. VINCENT COLLEGE LIBRARY

Latrobe, Pennsylvania
Librarian: Rev. Fintan R. Shoniker, O.S.B.

Statistical Data

Architect: Nathan Cantor, R. A., Associates
            Pittsburgh, Pa.
Dimensions: 230' x 120'
    Square footage 44,000; cubage 490,000
Type of construction: reinforced concrete, steel skeleton, brick facing, stone façade and trim
Book capacity: 220,000 volumes (future 420,000)
Seating capacity: 318
    3 Reading rooms: 207
    3 Meeting rooms: 24
    Listening room: 15
    Microreading room: 6 (presently)
    Browsing area: 27
    Lounge: 15
    Carrels: 12 (presently)
    Index table and catalog tables: 12
Ceiling height:
    College and seminary reading rooms, lobby exhibit area, listening area: 15 ft.
    Preparatory school reading room, offices, meeting rooms, etc.: 8-10 ft.
Cost:
    Building: $500,760
    Lighting—fluorescent (except librarians' offices, etc.): $77,783
    Floors—vinyl, asphalt, marble: $12,369
    Heating and ventilating: $60,000
    Furniture and equipment: $116,482
    Site: no cost
Cost per square foot: $11.38
Cost per cubic foot: $1.02
Parking area capacity: 50 cars
Firm supplying major equipment: Remington-Rand

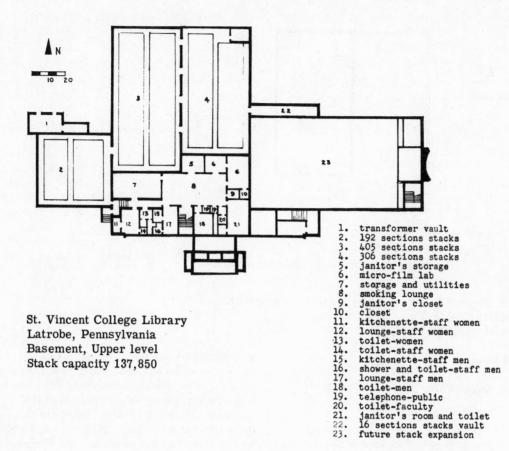

St. Vincent College Library
Latrobe, Pennsylvania
Basement, Upper level
Stack capacity 137,850

1. transformer vault
2. 192 sections stacks
3. 405 sections stacks
4. 306 sections stacks
5. janitor's storage
6. micro-film lab
7. storage and utilities
8. smoking lounge
9. janitor's closet
10. closet
11. kitchenette-staff women
12. lounge-staff women
13. toilet-women
14. toilet-staff women
15. kitchenette-staff men
16. shower and toilet-staff men
17. lounge-staff men
18. toilet-men
19. telephone-public
20. toilet-faculty
21. janitor's room and toilet
22. 16 sections stacks vault
23. future stack expansion

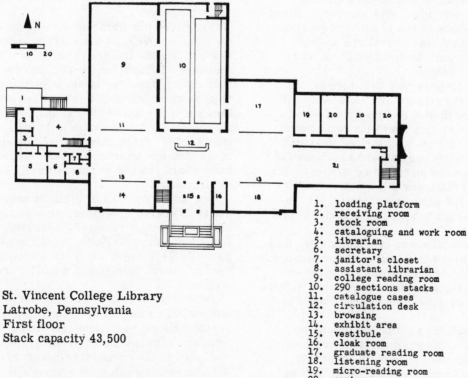

St. Vincent College Library
Latrobe, Pennsylvania
First floor
Stack capacity 43,500

1. loading platform
2. receiving room
3. stock room
4. cataloguing and work room
5. librarian
6. secretary
7. janitor's closet
8. assistant librarian
9. college reading room
10. 290 sections stacks
11. catalogue cases
12. circulation desk
13. browsing
14. exhibit area
15. vestibule
16. cloak room
17. graduate reading room
18. listening room
19. micro-reading room
20. seminar
21. prep library

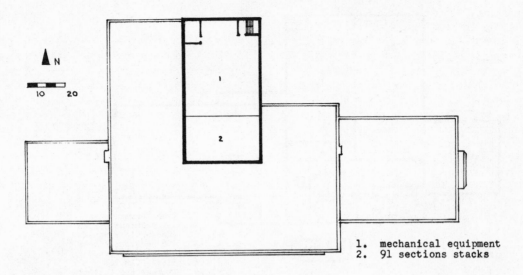

1. mechanical equipment
2. 91 sections stacks

St. Vincent College Library, Latrobe, Pennsylvania
Mezzanine
Stack capacity 13,650

Presentation of Plans

REV. FINTAN R. SHONIKER
Librarian

St. Vincent College is located in the foothills of the Allegheny Mountains forty miles east of Pittsburgh. Conducted by the Benedictine monks since its establishment in 1846, the institution comprises sixteen major buildings on a 1300-acre site, 90 acres of which are used for school purposes. Three academic units are maintained in adjacent quarters on the campus: a four-year liberal arts college, a six-year major seminary or divinity school, and a college preparatory school.

Currently the college enrolls 770 students, the seminary 207, and the preparatory school 240. All of these schools are limited to a maximum enrollment, the latter two already operating at maximum capacity, while the college is authorized to expand its enrollment gradually to an absolute maximum of 900 students. These are all full-time students. The Evening School and the Latrobe Hospital School of Nursing comprise 100 part-time students. At the present time the faculty in all schools numbers 113 priests and laymen.

The library has a collection of slightly more than 100,000 volumes served by a staff of six professionals (two half-time), five clerical workers, and the equivalent of two and one-quarter full-time student assistants. Accessions for 1958-59 numbered 5200 volumes.

A new library building for the institution was authorized in 1955. This was to replace one constructed for the seminary in 1892, to absorb the libraries maintained separately for the college and its departments, and to house the preparatory school library. A $500,000 building budget was established,

with $100,000 additional for furnishings. An escalator figure of 10 per cent was allowed for the total project. The closely adhered-to $500,000 building budget resulted in the elimination of five items suggested in the librarians' plans for the building: the audio-visual room, typing rooms, faculty studies, an elevator, and air conditioning. However, an unanticipated assembly room to seat 600 was incorporated in the building and constructed to bear two levels of stacks when this space is needed for library purposes.

Until 1958 our libraries were scattered all over the campus. We have been able to absorb in this new building the Biology Department library, the Chemistry Department library, and the record and book library from the Music Department. In planning we are thinking of a centralized library—first, because of our limited funds, and, second, because such a library would enable us to staff it more easily. The central library would be open longer hours than the department libraries, and we would know where most of our books were when they were in circulation.

Our divinity school or graduate school offers a master's degree; therefore, these students do a certain amount of research. Likewise, being a Benedictine monastery, the monks are interested particularly in research in ecclesiastical fields, such as church history and monastic and medieval studies.

In 1950 we were able to begin the reclassification and the full cataloging of the monastic collection. At that time we were somewhat daring in changing from an old Swiss classification system, which had been used in the monastery library, to the Library of Congress classification system with adaptation for Catholic literature. At the same time our college collection, a relatively small collection of about

30,000 volumes, was also fully reclassified. The preparatory school library was classified in the Dewey, and remains so classified; it continues to be a separate collection in the new library building.

The site of our new library was selected on the basis of units which are used by all departments of the institution. For example, the activities building, housing the auditorium on one side and the gymnasium on the other, as well as music rooms and art studios, is centrally located so that all departments have easy access to it. For the same reason the library is located close by. We suggested in our aims, objectives, and outline for the library building that the entrance be made at the ground floor. We were surprised when we saw all of the steps up to the main entrance.

As the building faces south, we have window drapes that extend from floor to ceiling, about 15 feet. There are certain disadvantages in the offices of the assistant librarian, reference librarian, the secretary, and the librarian, because the sun shines a great deal there in the afternoon. If we had secured our air conditioning, the orientation would have presented no problem.

The basement upper level includes the upper half of a temporary chapel, which we hope to use for two levels of stack expansion in the future. The footers are in to hold the weight of the stacks. This level also includes bookstacks, microfilm laboratory, staff lounges and kitchenettes, janitor's closet, toilet facilities, transformer vault, and telephone booths.

You will notice from the drawings of the first floor that the building is not modular construction. I believe Mr. Angus MacDonald mentioned that there is no need for modular construction in a one-story building. On this main floor much of the area is open. Three-foot shelving is used to separate the prep library from the browsing area. This is double-face shelving; thus we have the more common periodicals on the side facing the browsing area, and the high school or prep school periodicals facing into the prep library itself. The corridor goes down to an exit into the vestibule of the temporary chapel. The microreading room houses three microfilm readers, one microcard reader, and files for microfilms and microcards. We have three small seminar rooms with movable walls and the seminary or graduate reading room.

The circulation desk is centrally located with 3-foot shelving behind it for reserve books. We have open stacks everywhere except in the high school area. This level of stacks holds 290 sections. The assistant librarian and reference librarian has his office here close to the catalog and to the index table. He also at times serves at the circulation desk, and has a small area there where he is able to keep materials for answering reference questions. The cataloging and processing room is also close to the card catalog.

The upper, or mezzanine, level houses mechanical equipment and 91 sections of stacks.

Criticism

MR. JAMES D. MACK
Librarian, Lehigh University Library
Bethlehem, Pennsylvania

I want to make several general points and follow with only one or two details. Father Shoniker has already indicated that the building includes a chapel. I was struck by this immediately and wondered how temporary this location for the chapel was to be. According to my calculations from the stack capacity, the annual acquisition rate and expected rate, and the number of volumes they now have, I expect they will be wanting for space in about thirteen years.

Elements which have been omitted in the construction of the building are the audio-visual aids room, typing rooms, and private studies. I understand there is some discontentment about these omissions. The browsing room was in the program but also omitted. Father Shoniker and I worked over the addition of elevators in the building and thought tentatively of putting them exactly where the booklifts are located. Someone else may have other ideas on this.

The traffic pattern, as you can imagine, is simple—over to the catalog and the reading room, and circulation desk. I believe Father Shoniker would make only one change: that is, placing the circulation desk where it will allow for more control. The relationship between the principal functions of receiving, acquisitions, and cataloging seems to be sound.

The booklift does not accommodate book trucks; it is for books only and is hand operated. This is a disadvantage. The control of emergency exits is a problem that I do not think can be solved short of a system such as I noticed this morning in the McKeldin Library, a mechanically locking system for emergencies. I do not know if this type of lock on emergency doors is legal in Pennsylvania.

CASE INSTITUTE
OF TECHNOLOGY LIBRARY

Cleveland, Ohio
Director: Frederick L. Taft
Associate Librarian: Mary Frances Pinches

Statistical Data

Architect: Small, Smith, Reeb, & Draz
        1010 Euclid Ave., Cleveland, Ohio
Type of library: Central building, to be shared with
    Humanities and Mathematics departments
Population to be served: Faculty, undergraduate and
    graduate students
Dimensions: 42' x 86' plus additional space on
    second and third levels
Area: 34,078 sq. ft. devoted to library purposes
Book capacity: 172,300
Seating capacity: 494
    3 Reading rooms
    2 Meeting rooms
Size of module: 25' 10" x 27'
Ceiling height: 8' 4"; lobby and reading areas
    10' 10"
Cost per square foot: $25 (est.)
Cost per cubic foot: $2 (est.)
Parking area capacity: 26 cars under building

Presentation of Plans

MR. FREDERICK L. TAFT, Director
and MISS MARY FRANCES PINCHES
Associate Librarian

MR. TAFT: The Case Institute of Technology is
located in what is known as the University Circle
area of Cleveland. In the area is a rather re-
markable collection of cultural institutions, including within a few blocks the Cleveland Art
Museum (which recently received a bequest of
twenty million dollars), Western Reserve University, Severance Hall (the home of the Cleveland Orchestra), University Hospitals, and the
Natural History Museum.

The building in which we currently have our
main library was built in 1885. The physics
building was built in 1906. We have a chemistry
building which was just completed and an auditorium; the mechanical engineering building,
which will be enlarged, was built in the twenties.
The metallurgy building was built early in the
nineteenth century. The Student Union and two
dormitories were built since World War II, as
well as the Electrical Engineering Building.

The first level of our library building will be
on what I call stilts (I know this is the wrong

Case Institute of Technology, Cleveland, Ohio

Case Institute of Technology Library
Cleveland, Ohio
Third level

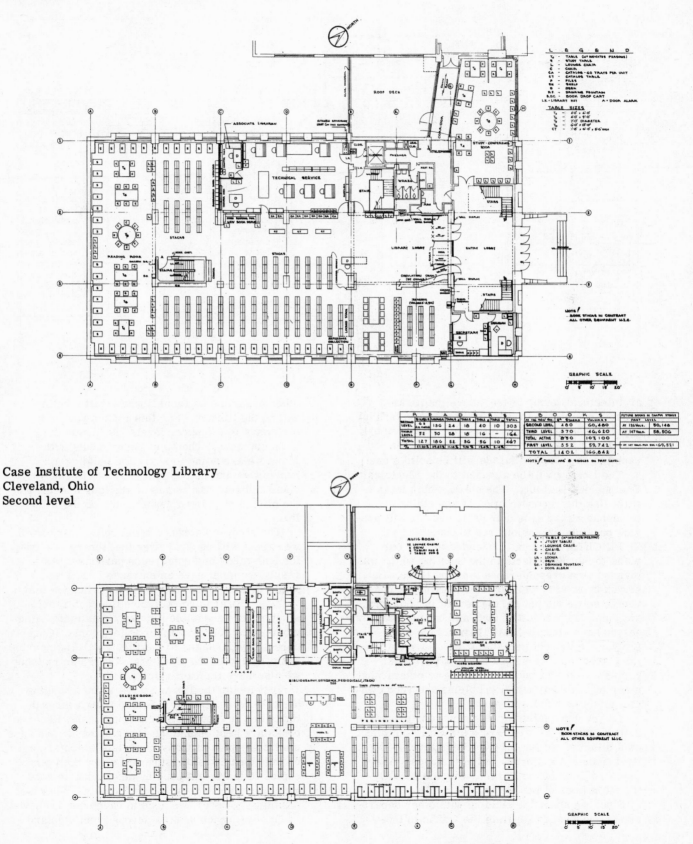

Case Institute of Technology Library
Cleveland, Ohio
Second level

Case Institute of Technology Library
Cleveland, Ohio
First level—first and second tiers

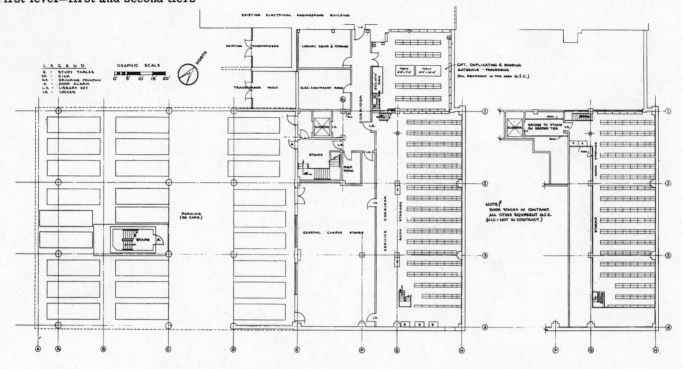

architectural term) 14 feet above the parking area. I would like to refer you to the western façade. The architect's birds (see photograph) have flown away since this was drawn, I am happy to say, and the façade will be solid stone.

The library will be attached to the Electrical Engineering Building. The plaza, which looks a little like the reconstruction of something of Nebuchadnezzar's, is only projected. It will provide possible expansion area for us.

MISS PINCHES: We really intended to take our plans to San Francisco, to the meeting which was planned as a preconference meeting there. But, as you know very well, that meeting never convened; so we did not get the benefit of your counsel then. As a result of that, and because we now, as you have already heard, have a hole in the ground, we thought perhaps, if we told you something about how we solved our own particular problems—and I find, from talking to others, that many of these particular problems are your own—this might be helpful to you.

As you can realize by this time, our plans are rather static. We will have a six-story building on a hillside. At the lower hillside level is the first floor of the library and at the upper level the third floor of the library, which is actually the main floor of the library.

Since we share the building with other departments, we want to separate the traffic to those other departments from library traffic before it enters the library. For this reason you find stairways to the upper levels just inside the main entrance. The other departments with whom we are going to share the building are humanities and mathematics. You will find their class and seminar rooms on the fourth level, and the offices of the two departments on the fifth level.

The study-conference room on the third level we expect will be used after the library is closed, for both study and conference purposes. As a result, we must have an entrance to it which would be away from the library, so that we may lock our library and still have the conference-study room accessible for use. This factor also dictated the location of our toilet rooms. Corridors allow passages to the Electrical Engineering Building and to the elevators. Off the entry lobby we also have the librarian's offices.

Just inside the library itself is the charging desk. Anyone leaving is forced to exit through turnstiles in front of the charging desk. Reserve books are kept behind the charging desk. We have multiple copies of many materials which are used by the humanities division, and a few multiple copies of materials used by other departments, which we plan to keep in this location. Wherever possible, however, we hope to have open reserves.

Our reference desk is across from the card

catalog and directly across from technical service. In technical service are located an apartment-house refrigerator, sink, and a small stove, and a desk and table for wrapping, mending, etc. Our order and accessions work is also done here. The associate librarian's office is in this area.

You will notice we have study tables around the periphery of the building; our study area is at the back, away from the traffic. On this level is kept the active book collection. One stairway goes to the level below, where periodicals are housed. The other stairway is dictated by housing codes, and is not ordinarily used.

We arrived at the division of materials by talking with a number of our faculty and asking how they used library materials. We were told that, as a rule, when they come into the library, they will select one or two books, then go to the periodicals and spend their time, usually, in the area where the periodicals are shelved. This is the reason we have decided upon this shelving arrangement—books on one level and periodicals on the other.

Again on the second floor we have study tables around the periphery; other study areas are located away from the traffic noises. On this floor, in addition to periodicals, there are rooms for Casiana and recordings.

We already have a very large record collection and expect, within the next year and a half to two years, to have about 7000 albums. The music room is to be used as a multipurpose room. The music department expects to have classes and to give lectures in music appreciation. I believe we are the only engineering college in the country which has an endowed chair of music. The room also is to be used for study. The plan is to have music played at intervals throughout the day. A conference-study room is also on this level.

On the first level the library has space for book storage, and for gifts, binding, and exchange. Also on this level are the general campus store, mechanical equipment, and parking.

The size of the module used in the building is 25 feet 10 inches by 27 feet. It will accommodate stack ranges on 54-inch centers. We are planning to use cork flooring on the upper levels and concrete on the first. Our walls will be plastered on the first level; the study areas on the second and third levels will be paneled. The music room will be paneled. We will have painted plaster above the dado on the second and third levels, wherever we do not have paneling. The ceiling height is 8 feet 10 inches in the stack areas. It is about 10 feet at the entrance, 13 feet in the music room, and 10 feet in the study areas.

MR. TAFT: I am now going to run through some of the more or less technical problems we faced and, we think, solved. I have tried to classify them.

First of all, on the matter of acoustics and noise control, we are going to have rubber or cork treads on the stairway to cut down the noise from traffic. For the same reason, we are having acoustical ceilings in the stair wells. All mechanical equipment which is possible, we feel, should be put in a penthouse, rather than in the valuable lower-level space. This is perhaps not quite an acoustic problem, but it has its relevance.

According to Dr. Shankland of our physics department, who is himself an acoustical expert and who has just worked on the acoustics of Severance Hall, the way to eliminate noise is to eliminate it at its source. If you do this, you really do not need acoustical ceilings. He recommended that we by all means have cork floors; we have used these extensively throughout. I must add that we have also put in metal-pan, acoustical ceilings in most of the areas, but this also is governed by certain other considerations.

Now, as to certain structural details—some of these are fairly elementary, I thought; but my experts said I should mention them. All underground walls below grade have waterproofing. This is done with a membrane. We have no painted concrete floors—only a sealer is used. One other thing, which is a structural problem, is minimization of the number of interior rooms, which is apparent in the floor plans.

One thing which the first floor particularly shows is that you can get space sometimes if you will pay for the cost of excavating. If you are tempted not to excavate, reconsider, because we have here, on one level, 7600 square feet of library floor at a cost to us of only $2 a square foot.

Recently we had a flood. We would have had probably 6 feet of water, which would have gone almost to the top of the stack ranges on the first level. Since then we have still further modified our plans. We are eliminating doors, making the wall waterproof. Also a little float device will ring an alarm if the water begins to rise. But adequate flood control is something all of you ought to take into consideration, to the extent of having floor drains for seepage. In our case— this is an interesting technical problem—there are no sanitary sewers at this level. We have here a pumproom which pumps our drainage up to the second-floor level, into the sewers which run at that level.

Another thing—the wall that appeared to be solid on the southwest exposure is not really a solid wall. It is a hollow-cavity wall, which is really two walls with an air space between, so that we minimize the sun's heat which might come through there. These walls, we hope, will also take out some of the noise of the thousands of automobiles which are hurtling along the high-speed boulevard just below us.

In regard to windows, those on the sides are to have Borg-Warner Kool shades to cut air-conditioning costs about 30 per cent.

The decision to use limestone on the large wall was made on the basis of the differential in the initial cost and in the maintenance cost. In our climate a wall must be pointed up within twenty years. Pointing up a brick wall is a real operation. In pointing up a limestone wall of large slabs you have far fewer crevices.

There are no separate switches on our stack areas because our lighting expert, Dr. Putnam of the electrical engineering department, says that with fluorescent lighting, unless you are going to be gone for three hours or longer, you need not bother about turning the lights off and on because you will only have to pay for replacing the switches more often and the practice saves no significant amount of current.

If you are considering air conditioning, be careful about using ordinary incandescent lights, because you must dissipate the heat which incandescent lamps produce, in addition to the other heat you are trying to dissipate. We have figured that perhaps the additional cost of fluorescent lighting is balanced by the cutting down of the amount of air-conditioning equipment required.

Mr. Metcalf, who consulted with us, told us to be careful about fluorescent lighting. He said quality of light was more important than quantity; 200-foot candles, which you can find some places, could be most uncomfortable compared with 50-foot candles of low glare and uniform intensity. In the microfilm area we have fluorescent lights on dimmers so that they may be dimmed from zero to full. In our building the air conditioning comes through the fluorescent fixtures. This, we are told by our experts, will add to the life of the fluorescent tubes.

This brings me to the subject of air conditioning. The air is prefiltered through an ordinary metal filter. Because we live in an industrial community, it then goes through an electrostatic filter. We are not located in downtown Cleveland, but we are in an area where the fume problem is a serious one. Then it is passed through what is called a *cathobar system* for both humidity control and air purification. This operates on a regenerative anhydrous solution of lithium chloride and removes odors, sulphur fumes, and bacteria from the air.

The air-circulating system is a high-pressure Weathermaster system with perimeter outlets maintained at a maximum noise of 30 decibels. We are trying to cut down the noise of the high-pressure system. The main duct sizes can be minimized with the high-pressure system. In our building the ducts are in the pillars, which are only slightly larger than usual.

All controls for the air-conditioning system are in the penthouse, which is actually the sixth floor.

Criticism

MR. H. DEAN STALLINGS
Librarian, North Dakota Agricultural
  College Library
Fargo, North Dakota

MR. STALLINGS: After Mr. Taft's opening remarks, my first thought was of the signs we used to have on the cars during the war: "Is this trip necessary?"

I think, in general, we have seen a fairly workable plan here. Not only have the experts from Case devised a workable plan, but they have also devised some fancy reasons for what they have done. Everything I was going to say has already been mentioned.

I might make this comment: Case plans to have a limited enrollment; consequently, the building is not planned for a greatly increased number of students.

I think the architects, the planners, did an excellent job on the main entrance lobby. They have designed it so that students have access to classrooms and offices without coming into the library. The Electrical Engineering Building can easily be reached. The library can be locked without interfering with other activities.

One comment I was going to make about most of the offices and the building in general is that I fail to find any clothes closets or very many janitor's closets.

The next comment I would make is that I would have been inclined to change the area on the third floor where the stacks are located for the reading area, because the students must walk the full length of the building to get into a reading room.

My next comment concerns the kitchen. The kitchenette is in the corner of the Technical Service room. My own library staff said they preferred a small staffroom where they could make their coffee.

MISS PINCHES: We included the staffroom in our plans, but each time it has been taken out by our administration.

CHAIRMAN COMAN: Can the staff go to the Union? I expect that you will lose more man-hours by having your staff leave the building than if you had a facility in the building.

Discussion

MISS HANBY: I wonder why the associate librarian's office is so far away from the director's.

MR. STALLINGS: I had that down as a question, too, when I first looked at the plan. My first reaction was that she, and perhaps every associate librarian, will be in charge of technical processing. Is that true?

MISS PINCHES: Yes.

MR. STALLINGS: It may not continue to be true—the next one may be a circulation librarian.

MR. YENAWINE: I was going to ask you if the cork tile was not contrary to the statement we had yesterday afternoon from the Armstrong people that this was not a desirable floor covering for heavy use areas.

MR. PIGOTT: I heard him make that statement, but I have been in a lot of libraries which have cork tile. I am not sure I agree with him 100 per cent.

MR. STALLINGS: From our investigation of this, I think the best example I can cite is Kent State Library in Ohio. Cork has been used in this building for thirty years and has a very low maintenance factor. The floors look as if they have several years' more wear in them. I think the product has been improved considerably since those floors were put down. For acoustical value, cork is superior to vinyl.

MR. YENAWINE: One of the reasons I asked the question is that about seven years ago cork tile was laid on the reading room floor in our building. It has been an impossible maintenance problem ever since.

MR. STALLINGS: Is it on a ground floor?

MR. YENAWINE: No, this is on the second floor. The dirt absorption presents an impossible situation. It has been sealed with every product recommended innumerable times, but is still impossible to maintain.

MR. WOODS: I think Mr. Taft mentioned the difference in ceiling height in different parts of the building—10 feet in the lobby and a different height for the reading areas and for the stacks. Yet, it was not double the height of the stacks. I was wondering how that was done without affecting the floor levels of the floors above.

MR. DRAZ: The general ceiling height in this library is 8 feet 2 inches. Above the ceiling are the ducts, conduits, lighting, and so forth.

MRS. ROBINSON: Even if the associate librarian is going to supervise technical services, that office bothers me. Why can't there be an outside door for the associate librarian? If she is going to bring anybody to her office, they have to wade through the catalog. Also, she does not have any escape door.

MR. STALLINGS: This is a glass wall, too, to complicate her privacy further.

MISS PINCHES: I have not even had a door in the past.

MR. PIGOTT: I think the answer there is that it is a choice of an inside door and an outside window. In this arrangement you can get the outside window.

MR. HEINTZ: Did Miss Pinches say the music room is a multipurpose room?

MISS PINCHES: I said it would be used for concerts, classrooms for music appreciation, and, when not in use in that way, for a study area where music would be played.

MR. HEINTZ: What kind of concerts? I am thinking about having some kind of kitchen unit adjoining that room, for Friends of the Library or concerts or that kind of thing, and make the kitchen unit serve more purposes than just for the staff. My president ruled out a staff lounge. I pointed out that we did have a Friends of the Library organization; we did entertain, particularly at commencement time, when we have a library open house. His only comment was that he had forgotten all about that. That ended the argument.

MISS HANBY: Is the cataloging department locked at the end of a work day?

MISS PINCHES: We can lock it.

MISS HANBY: You said you were keeping some of your catalog tools in there. Won't that prevent people from using those tools during the evening hours—some of your bibliographic tools?

MISS PINCHES: It would, but we can always provide keys if we find this is necessary.

CHAIRMAN COMAN: It would be better to duplicate the material.

MISS HANBY: Or you can put it out in another area.

MISS PINCHES: I am sure there are many possibilities.

MR. HUDSON: I believe Miss Pinches' reason for separating the periodicals from the books is that she asked the faculty members how they used them. I presume their arrangement was tempered by the current arrangements which, I gather, are separated.

MISS PINCHES: This is true.

MR. STALLINGS: I asked her about that, too. The magazines are not classified at present.

MR. HUDSON: One other thing. You mentioned the possibility of moving the reading area on the second level to the front of the periodicals collection, rather than behind it, to save walking through it. Did you think of intermingling the reading tables with the stacks?

MISS PINCHES: Yes, we have considered that, too. We have tried quite a number of arrangements. We have had reading areas more to the front of the building, and finally settled on this.

MR. DRAZ: Speaking to that point, I may say there are around the perimeter of both these floors individual study tables at the windows.

MR. GIRARD: I have two questions. In this construction which factors determine the size of the modules? The second question: Theoretically, what would be the ideal size of the modules?

MR. DRAZ: The module is 25 feet 10 inches by 27 feet. That was determined by book ranges at 54-inch centers.

MR. HUDSON: I wanted to ask another on this question of modules. Is there not a 27 by 27-foot module, or some such figure, which is divisible both by 54 and by the length of the section, so that you could turn your section in either direction?

MR. DRAZ: That is true. The reason we could not use it here is that we had an over-all dimension to meet on the east and west axis.

CHAIRMAN COMAN: I would like to ask one question. I did not see your microfilm study. Did I miss that? I did not have a chance to read your material.

MISS PINCHES: We have microfilm facilities on the second level. We have no typing facilities. You can bring your own typewriter in and we have some carrels where you could type if necessary.

CHAIRMAN COMAN: Where is smoking allowed?

MISS PINCHES: In certain areas throughout the library we will permit smoking.

TRINITY COLLEGE LIBRARY

Washington, D. C.
Librarian: Sister Helen

Statistical Data

Architect: Thomas H. Locraft & Associates
        1518 P St., N.W., Washington, D.C.
Type of library: College library
Population to be served: 700
Dimensions: 250' on longest side; 160' greatest width
Area: 45,417 sq. ft.
Book capacity: 150,000
Seating capacity:
    Reading rooms: 350
    Meeting rooms: 2 classrooms seating 75 each
Size of module: Not yet determined
Ceiling height: 9' 6" - 10'
Cost:
    Building: $1,235,520
    Furniture and equipment: $211,400
    Site: Part of present college campus; landscaping and roads: $32,500
Cost per square foot: $26
Cost per cubic foot: $2.03
Parking area capacity: Several areas on campus; nearest, 12 cars
Firms supplying major equipment: Not yet determined

Trinity College Library, Washington, D.C.

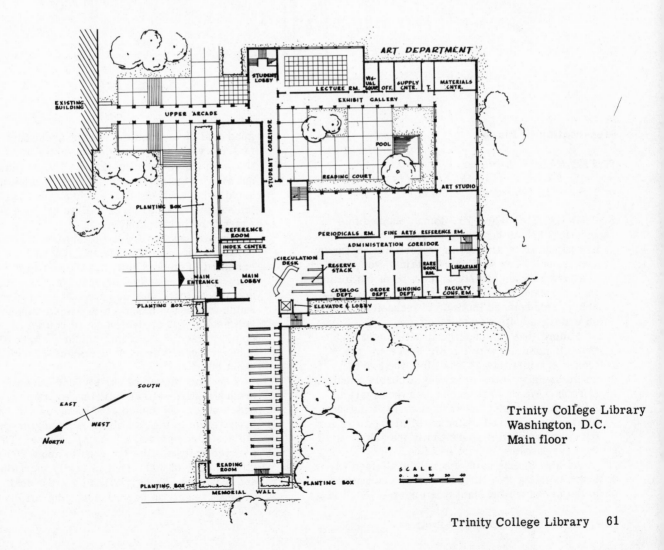

Trinity College Library
Washington, D.C.
Main floor

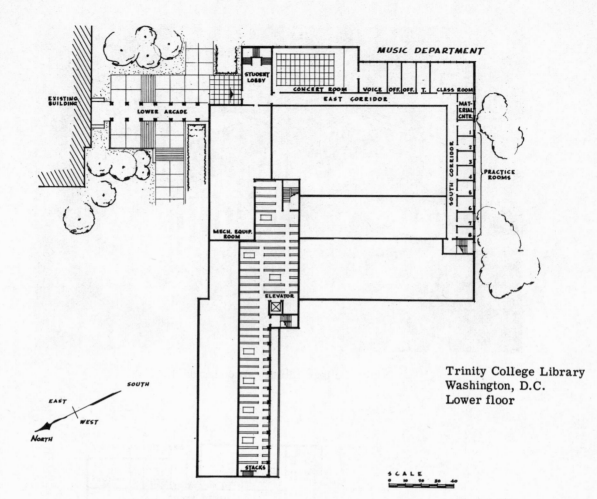

Trinity College Library
Washington, D.C.
Lower floor

Presentation of Plans

SISTER HELEN, Librarian
and MR. ERNEST FELLINGER, Representative
of Thomas H. Locraft and Associates

SISTER HELEN: When Mr. Coman planned this meeting, I think he really achieved what people are supposed to aim for in any artistic endeavor; that is, unity and variety. Certainly, you could not have greater variety in the type of institution than you have with the Air Force, a Benedictine abbey, an advanced institute of technology, and an undergraduate woman's college.

I admit that our undergraduates might find much in common with the Air Force and the technology institute at least, but whether they would begin with the library is probably a matter of doubt. We do have in common, however, an interest in bringing books to readers; today our interest is centered on the physical facilities for bringing books to readers and in the achieving of the best possible library building.

As Mr. Coman said, the Trinity College Library building is a little bit more than a gleam in the eye of a librarian; it is also the result of a

good deal of work on the part of architects, and of some very helpful criticism on the part of those who have seen the plans. But the plans are not even in the preliminary stage. I think the architects call them in the schematic stage. So the suggestions you make will be very welcome and will be particularly useful.

We are saying very definitely now that we will never go beyond 700 students. Whether we change our minds I do not know, but at least in planning a library you have to take some tangible objective and aim at that. Our objective is for a library which will accommodate a maximum student enrollment of 700 students and, of course, the concomitant faculty. At the moment we have 616 undergraduate women students and a faculty of about 60.

About one fourth of our students go on for graduate work—either full time or part time—which means we should give them a good, basic preparation in the use of research materials. We are very much of a reading college. The average daily circulation runs to about 200 in a student body of 600. That is really incredible, and it is true. The girls read a great deal.

One reason has been, I think, the very acces-

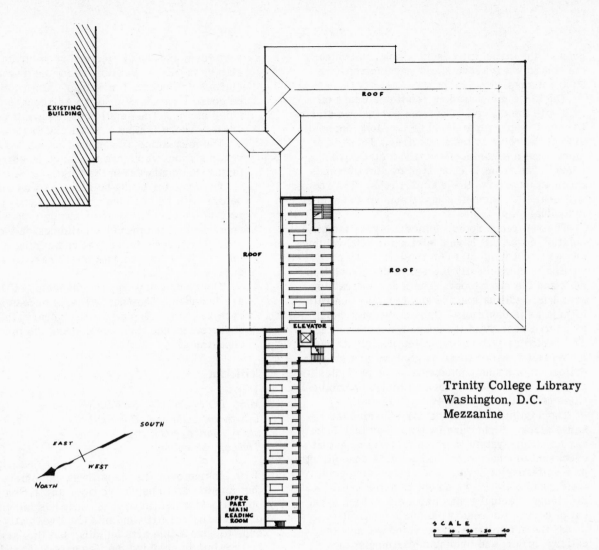

EXISTING BUILDING

ROOF

ROOF

ROOF

ELEVATOR

UPPER PART MAIN READING ROOM

SOUTH

EAST

WEST

NORTH

Trinity College Library
Washington, D.C.
Mezzanine

SCALE
0 10 20 30 40

sibility of our present library. We occupy two floors of one wing of the main administration building; it was with some reluctance that we faced the fact some years ago that we were outgrowing our quarters and would have to get a separate library.

We gave our architects our ideas of what the library should contain. They have worked out plans which we like and think you will like, but on which we want a critical and not just an admiring opinion from you.

We are asking for limestone, partly to harmonize with our present buildings, and probably because we feel that the upkeep on limestone through the years is going to be so low in relation to what it would be with brick or cinderblock that the initial expense can be justified, provided you can get the funds to do it. But that is what we hope for.

We asked for seating space for a relatively large part of our enrollment, a minimum of 40 per cent and a possible maximum of 50 per cent, as our student use is heavy, and of course we want it to continue so. We asked for great simplicity of interior planning so as to give an effect of openness which would be not only an effect but

an actuality. We want our students near as many books as possible.

We asked for ease and economy of supervision, which of course will go with that very openness. We do not have a disciplinary problem of any magnitude. We are not coeducational. We are dealing with older girls only, not with younger ones, so that the idea of supervision need not be extended to every last corner. But it should cover all exits and entrances of the library.

We asked for avoidance of any sort of monumentality in the building. In doing that we are aware that we are not a new campus—our buildings are not of the modern, streamlined, functional type. But we think the architects have planned very well indeed to tie in a building, which will be primarily functional, with the existing buildings on campus.

MR. FELLINGER: I quite concur with Sister Helen that we are in a "prepreliminary" stage on these plans. These are really earlier studies not detailed in regard to equipment layout. The module has not been determined for the building. We will very much appreciate comment.

Coming in by either entrance on the main floor we approach the control point for the library proper, the circulation desk, which has behind it the controlled reserve stacks, accommodating 3600 volumes.

The large main reading room is a cross on axis with the chapel. The front part is two stories in height, approximately 20 feet. Along the south side of the room is the stack area. There is a stack area mezzanine above and a stack area below. The room is connected by elevator and three staircases to these stack areas. The room will seat 100 readers—a large number of them at individual study tables.

The reference room, immediately off the circulation desk, will have shelving for 7000 volumes and will seat from 50 to 60 readers. The card catalog is conveniently located to the circulation desk and the main lobby. The index and catalog area has inadequate space and is not as centrally located as is desirable. Consideration is being given to a restudy of the space for these functions. The periodicals room is located just off the main lobby, and the stairs nearby go down to a large collection of bound periodicals. The periodicals room will have sloping shelves for 600 periodical titles and will seat from 40 to 50 readers.

The administration corridor is behind the reserve stack. Right here I wish to say that Trinity has an honor system in which there is no actual check-out or check-in of books. It is done strictly on a self-service level. The students sign out their own books; so we do not have the usual problems of actual control at a circulation desk, but of course the reserve stack is controlled.

Off the administration corridor we have the catalog, order, and binding departments; the faculty conference room, which will be a staff-room; the librarian's office; and a rare book room. The administration area will require considerably more study. One of the disadvantages, as we apparently have it, is the remoteness of the librarian from the heart or core of the building. I think this can be changed by having the librarian brought further toward the control desk. The binding room is now planned to be moved downstairs to give more space in the workrooms. There will be partitions within this area to separate the various functions. There will be shelving for 1600 books in this catalog-work area.

The fine arts and music reference room is also located on the main floor. It is adjacent to the art department, which is composed of an area separated from the main library by a reading court. It is possible to close off the library entirely and still utilize the music wing or the art wing.

The lower level is at the terrain level. The lower stack area is connected to the main floor by two staircases and an elevator.

The music area on this lower level has its own entrance and a concert room—both this con-

cert room and the art lecture room upstairs will also be usable by the library for instruction classes or for small meetings. The room will be sound treated, naturally. Adjacent to it is the voice studio. The small cubicles are practice areas. There is also a small classroom.

The mezzanine area is halfway up the large reading room which has the large fenestration facing the northwest in the front.

The exterior of the building, as was mentioned before, will be of limestone. The Ludowic tile roof is the clay tile of overlapping type which has been used on the previous buildings on the campus. The large administration building is on the left and is connected with the library by a closed arcade.

The landscaping and the diversion of the road are included. The road will give access to the receiving and shipping for the library, the art department, and, to some degree, the music department.

Criticism

MISS DOROTHY W. REEDER
Librarian, Albert S. Cook Library
State Teachers College
Towson, Maryland

In looking over the plans I was extremely startled that music was to be on one floor and art on the other floor of the library. Trinity has felt the need of a building for arts and music. Eventually they hope to have a fine arts building, but this seemed to be the time to combine the fine arts and the library. After Sister Helen explained that she felt it was quite certain that the sound in the music area would be absorbed and would not be noticeable in the library, and that there was nothing more to do about it, I was somewhat satisfied.

I think the general plan is a very expensive plan. When one departs from the square or the rectangle, one does get into higher building costs.

I wish to criticize first of all the connection from the main building to the new library building. It seems to me it is not at all necessary. The library has been in the administration building for years, and it may now be difficult to disassociate the two. The connection is going to make for more administrative problems, as there will be two entrances to supervise. The connecting arcade also cuts off the roadway.

Another suggestion is that because the campus is small, the science collection (now in the science building library) should be brought into the new building. This collection of 12,000 volumes could be more easily serviced in the main library. I rather expect also that the catalog area is small.

The next suggestion I have concerns the general traffic flow. I would reverse the locations of periodicals and reference. Then with the card catalog moved over near reference, you would have your reference person close to the card catalog, and the cataloger would be close to all this. It seems to me it would be a better arrangement. Also, the art and music materials might be moved to the main stack area if additional space were needed for reference.

The lower floor would take over the receiving room, the room for binding and extra workroom one would need, and storage. The lower level, which showed much space as being unexcavated, would be much better if it could be excavated.

On the lower level or on the upper level I did not notice any lavatory facilities. Also, there is no provision, either down on the lower level or on the mezzanine, for microcards, microfilm, and readers which would be needed or for any typing alcoves which could be placed on the lower or upper level.

Discussion

MR. ESTERQUEST: I should like to have the librarian's explanation as to why this main, central building is thought of as being library, though it contains art and music. By putting the art and music part in the wing which comes down to the north, the whole square could be all library. There is a mixture there which bothers me. I am sure there is a good explanation for it.

MR. HEINTZ: I would like to know why these functions are integrated rather than separated in two buildings.

SISTER HELEN: It is partly the cost. It is partly that on a campus where the curriculum is as largely in the humanities as ours is, there is a very great deal closer connection between arts and music and the library than you might at first think. For instance, we have for many years had co-operative supervision of audio-visual materials between the library and the art and music departments. Slides and records are used in many courses.

The reason for combining them is that both are so badly needed, and it is cheaper to put up one building than two. The plans for the art and music sections are definitely integrated for future expansion plans of the library in that all size dimensions as planned will take care of either book stacks or readers' tables.

The question which Mr. Esterquest asked first, I think, was: Why not use that—I think of the general shape of the building as the letter "P"—tail of the "P" for arts and music?

One reason is that music practice, located where it now is planned, will not interfere with library usage because of the unpleasant sounds of practice. Another reason is that the art and music rooms have the unfavorable orientation of the southeast and the east. Of course, the west is even more unfavorable, but we are planning on a blank wall at the west end of the main reading room. This gives us the long expanse of the northern light for main reading purposes, whereas, if we put the art and music there, we would be facing south and east for our reading light.

MR. MACK: I would like to know more about the reading court.

MISS REEDER: The reading court was planned as a pleasant spot for people to go out and sit in to read, because Washington has a long summer—it goes on into the fall and begins early in the spring.

MR. FELLINGER: There is the added fact that with the court we build up a level to isolate, in sound, the music department. The court was felt as being an auxiliary reading area.

MRS. ROBINSON: I would like to speak about the cost of this building and the fact that the music and arts are combined with the library so that it would cost less. It seems to me a great many things are being done here which will be costly to construct. Perhaps if the costly features were omitted, art and music would not have to be part of the library. The inside court certainly is a very costly item when there is an area right outside the building where people could go and sit with books.

Also, long, narrow corridors and a lot of long, narrow passages are very costly features and inconvenient. It seems to me a number of the rooms are closed in with walls which could be opened. All these things are going to add to the cost of the building.

MR. BERNBROCK: I would like to have the architect explain why the importance is given to the entrance on the northeast side of the building.

MR. FELLINGER: This is something, I admit, which is not in accordance with the center of full campus development of Trinity. We felt it was essential because it is the public entrance off the main way into the whole campus. Admittedly, a large percentage of the campus is to the rear; students will be using other doorways. This essentially, though, is an entrance not only for the students but also for the public, and a front door, so to speak, to your library.

MR. GIRARD: If the reading court is to be such a feature, I do not see why the entrance should be so restricted. It would seem to me that a maximum-sized entrance should be used because of the pleasant qualities.

MR. FELLINGER: This is a true point. I think it deals in relative control.

MISS CRAWFORD: I have lived with a long, narrow reading room for many years. I question why the stem of the "P" needs to be a long narrow room. Could it not be made chunkier? Putting stacks on one side removes all need for windows on that side. If more reading area were placed along the windows, that part of the building could be chunkier; there would be fewer jogs. You would have less cutting-up by corridors; then a double row of tables could be placed along the windows. The stack area could be put along the windowless wall. There is no particular reason to extend the wing unless you want to have windows on both sides.

MR. METCALF: It was on that point which has just been spoken of that I want to comment. The main part of the library, both for readers and for books, is on the stem of the "P" on three levels which are so narrow. How wide is the book stack on that? That is, how long are the book ranges on that floor?

MR. FELLINGER: I think they are 18, becoming 27 when you get past the elevators.

MR. METCALF: All right, you come into this most used part of the building at the center of the short side and have to walk the full length. Any reader, to come to the end of the "P," has to walk the full length of the reading room past everything else in it, which violates one of the first principles of keeping a quiet reading room. You should always, if possible, plan a library so that you enter near the center of the long side of the reading room, so as to walk just as little as possible past people.

The same holds with the bookstacks. To get books you have to go the full length to get the books at the end. You have as much distance to cover in getting them as you have in many libraries with several times as many books. That does not make very much difference most of the time, but if you count up the time spent to get your books and put them away in the course of the next generation, it is going to add up a good deal.

I have no suggestion to make with the building in this shape, but I would try always to arrange the building so as to make less tracking back and forth in the reading area and in the stack area.

SISTER HELEN: I think perhaps one thing is that, as the plans evolved, the reference room seems rather more cut off from the main reading room than we had considered in our initial thinking. We had thought of a "T"-shaped building, which is the shape used successfully in other buildings, and that the reader use would be at both the left and the right of the entrance. However, I certainly see the desirability of avoiding unnecessary steps by having an entrance halfway along.

MR. FRAZIER: I would like to ask why it is necessary to have two entrances in such a small building. I would like to ask the question in the context of the student use of this building. With the students approaching the building mostly from the administration building, isn't it satisfactory to consider that one entrance along that arcade is enough for such an arrangement as this?

MISS REEDER: You are counting on the arcade's being there as the second entrance.

MR. FRAZIER: I am counting on the arcade's being the entrance, doing away with the main entrance

which, it seems to me, is unnecessary.

MR. FELLINGER: It is possible that this main entrance could be closed entirely, but then anyone on the outer campus would have to make a detour and use the far entrance. This is possible, but it would mean that this group of people would have to retrace their steps, particularly to get to the main reading room.

MOLINE PUBLIC LIBRARY

Moline, Illinois
Librarian: Mrs. Kathryn A. Devereaux

Statistical Data

Architect: William F. Bernbrock, A.I.A.
           1630 Fifth Ave., Moline, Ill.
Type of library: Central
Population to be served: 45,000
Dimensions: 141' x 130'
Area: 33,000 sq. ft. first and second floor
      2000 sq. ft. basement
      Remainder unfinished for expansion
Book capacity: 160,000
Seating capacity:
   Reading rooms: 200
   Auditorium: 200
   In each of two meeting rooms: 20-30
Size of module: 25' x 27'
Ceiling height: 12' on first floor and basement
              11' on second floor
Cost:
   Building: $675,000
   Equipment: $75,000
   Site: none
Cost per square foot: $19.30
Cost per cubic foot: $1.39
Parking area capacity: None
Firms supplying major equipment:
              To be determined

Moline Public Library
Moline, Illinois
First floor

Moline Public Library
Moline, Illinois
Second floor

Presentation of Plans

MRS. KATHRYN A. DEVEREAUX, Librarian
and MR. WILLIAM F. BERNBROCK, Architect

MRS. DEVEREAUX: The "quad" cities on the western edge of Illinois and the eastern edge of Iowa,
separated by the Mississippi River, include
Davenport, with a population of 85,000; Rock
Island, with a population of 50,000; Moline, with
a population of 45,000; and East Moline with a
population of 16,000. The total metropolitan
population is approximately 300,000. The community is industrial and primarily manufactures
farm machinery.

The Moline Public Library was built by a
grant in 1933. The present square footage is
17,000 square feet. Only about 11,000 square
feet—basement and first floor—are being used.
The second floor is not used because of the number of steps up there. The site is two blocks
from the business center on the main street and
adjacent to the post office on the side street.
The outlying area is served by a bookmobile.

The Library Board is in the preliminary
stages of discussing the inadequacy of the present
building and the need for better facilities. It
secured the services of an architect and asked
him to go into the various possibilities of remodeling the present building as compared with
the cost of a new building of adequate size. The
estimated cost of remodeling came to $500,000,
which would provide a face lifting but leave us
with the same inadequate size. It is a case of too
much cubic footage and too little square footage.

Mr. Hoyt R. Galvin was hired as a consultant
to work with us on planning a new building to cost
$750,000. Of this amount, it was planned to spend
$675,000 for the building and $75,000 for the
equipment.

MR. BERNBROCK: We are planning to build on the
site of the present library. The site is on a one-
way street—the most important street in the
town. In addition, it's on a corner with the secondary street being rather heavily trafficked.

There are two municipal parking areas of a
full block each, one to the north and one to the
south. There is a private parking area immediately across from the post office which is next
to the library.

We have a piece of property that is 160 feet
along Fifth Avenue and 140 feet along the secondary street. Thirty feet of the 160 is going to be
sold off to our neighbor to the east who will also
be building. It's a newspaper publishing house.
They are going to build on that 30 feet to enlarge
their plant and they will precede our construction.
We have been told that we may use their building
for the period of time during which ours is under
construction, which is an advantage because we
can keep the library in the immediate vicinity of

where it is now.

Our proposed building is 35,000 square feet.
It is two stories above the ground. We will
develop 2000 square feet below ground for heating
and air conditioning. We also hope to develop an
unfinished complete area underneath these two
floors. We went to two stories above ground for
the reason that most of the business buildings in
Moline are two and three stories high.

The first story on the secondary street will
have a rock face comprised of native granite
boulder. Its warm gray and brown tones will
give a warmth and informality to the design
which will be inviting for people to enter. We
have opened up the north, or Fifth Avenue, side
to glass. The reading area is along that side of
the building and can be viewed by passers-by.
The second story of the building has no windows.
It is of ceramic tile in an abstract design planned to give color, dignity, and richness.

The building is on a corner and features an
air door. The latter is a rather new development and is simply a blanket of air to keep the
hot air out, the cool air in, and the leaves and
dirt outside. The idea is that if you are handling
books and packages, you don't have to push or
walk on the treadle or anything.

Both the book drop and the circulation desk
are near the air door. The circulation desk is
about 20 feet long and provides for complete
control of those entering and leaving. Also, there
is a glass-enclosed area and a court which sur-
rounds a handsome elm tree. It would be very
dramatic as you enter the building to see this
glass-enclosed area of two stories with a tree
growing in a court.

The library will provide open stacks for
30,000 volumes. The reading area will seat 100
people, and there is a lounge around the glass-
enclosed court.

Criticism

MR. HARRY N. PETERSON
Librarian, District of Columbia
Public Library

MR. PETERSON: The planning of a new library
building requires a considerable amount of thought,
work, and close co-operation on the part of many
people. A great many factors have to be taken
into account including the population—present and
projected—the educational level of the people, the
staff available and its qualifications, the budget,
and other community facilities.

The final result should be a building that will
make it possible to carry out the objectives of
the service in the most efficient manner possible.
The library is, or should be, the physical ex-
pression of the service planned and the thinking
behind it.

Louis H. Sullivan put it more succinctly when he said, "Form follows function," but Frank Lloyd Wright probably came closer to the truth when he proclaimed that form and function are one. I suggest that these ideas be kept in mind as we review the plans for the Moline Public Library.

The new library is to be situated at the intersection of Fifth Avenue and Seventeenth Street, only two blocks from the heart of the downtown shopping center. I think this comes as close to being an ideal site for a library as anyone could hope to get, and certainly great credit is due the trustees who acquired this land way back in 1903. It is quite evident that they had foresight.

The new building contains approximately 35,000 square feet of space including the 2000 square feet in the basement. The basement will accommodate the heating and air-conditioning units, incinerator, custodian quarters, and so on. The rest of it will be unfinished for future expansion.

The present population is about 45,000; it is anticipated to be somewhere between 80,000 and 90,000 in twenty years. While the building is more than adequate for present needs, it will not provide enough space for the population anticipated by 1979 as it now stands. If we apply the Wheeler and Githens formula of .55 square foot per capita, we find that the Moline Public Library should contain between 44,000 and 49,500 square feet instead of 35,000. However, if a full basement is provided, the total square footage will run around 54,000, or more than enough to take care of the needs for twenty years.

If the whole basement area is not to be excavated, I think it would be a good idea to provide footings strong enough for another floor to be added at some future date. As a matter of fact, it would be a good idea to do so even with a full basement excavation because libraries never seem to be built to a plan large enough.

The estimated cost of construction, as you have been told, is $675,000, and there will be an additional $75,000 for equipment. Omitting the equipment cost, we find we have a construction cost of approximately $19.30 per square foot, and that seems to me to be a very reasonable price.

The new building is very modern. No doubt it will attract the attention and interest of many potential users visiting the downtown shopping area. The building is virtually square—130 feet on Fifth Avenue and 140 feet on Seventeenth Street. However, the plan is not developed as a conventional square.

As a part of the unusual treatment, the main entrance is at an angle of the intersection of Fifth Avenue and Seventeenth Street. This in itself does not offer any particular difficulty, but the interior treatment, of which the entrance is a part, imposes very serious problems because of the angles and odd-shaped rooms that result from the design.

The entrance to the building is on grade and this is good. The library as you saw has an air door. This is the first one I have seen in a library. Its chief attractions are that it imposes no barriers to those entering, it stops a great deal of dirt from getting into the building, and according to the manufacturer's catalog it is economical to operate. Presumably a conventional door will be installed so that the building can be locked at night.

I note with misgivings the court at the rear of the building diagonally opposite the main entrance. I was interested in seeing that one of the reasons for having the court was to preserve the tree. Obviously this is intended as an architectural feature. It is emphasized by the fact that all the furniture on the first floor has been carefully placed out of the line of vision from the entrance to the court.

Although this may be interesting from an architectural point of view, it seems to me that it is more appropriate to a gallery than to a library. It should be remembered that people come to the library to study and read. I regret that such a feature is built in as a fixed and permanent part of the building because the space is lost for library purposes. You can rest assured the day will come when the area occupied by the court will be needed for library functions.

It is apparent that the advantage of a conventional square design is lost as a result of the diagonal angles from the entrance to the court. Library administrators have learned by bitter experience to avoid triangular and other odd-shaped buildings because of the peculiar angles and lost space that they generally impose. Here we have a square building which, so far as design is concerned, actually consists of a pair of artificially created triangles.

The preoccupation with an architectural gimmick results in an unsatisfactory service arrangement throughout the building. In other words, in order to achieve an effect the library function has been sacrificed. In this design form and function are obviously not one; nor does form follow function. A library is not just a building. It is a building specifically designed to house books and related services. It should be planned so that these functions can be performed with maximum efficiency at the lowest possible cost.

The circulation desk is not entirely satisfactory for a building of this size. There is no clearly defined space for charge and return or registration, which may cause some confusion during rush periods, and mind you, we are looking ahead to an ever increasing use because the population will almost double in the course of twenty years.

The desk permits satisfactory supervision of the stair well to the second floor, but from a practical point of view, I should have preferred a "U"-shaped circulation desk with the entrance on one side and the exit on the other, even at the expense of losing the air door. This would make it possible to have separate stations for the major functions and afford a far better control over the entire lobby area. The elevator is close to both the circulation desk and the stairway.

The public services on the main floor are poorly arranged. For one thing, the business and technical books should not be so far removed from the rest of the adult collection. I should also prefer to see the young adult service brought into closer relationship with the other public services. The same thing applies to the local history and genealogy unit on the second floor. The bringing-together of the presently dispersed adult services is particularly necessary because of the small staff. The total staff now is twelve, which includes the two janitors.

Incidentally, if the young adult service is to stay where it is, it will need larger quarters as the room designated contains only a little over 700 square feet. As the partitions are fixed, it cannot be readily enlarged.

The reference desk or counter looks like a fixed installation. There is little to recommend such an arrangement. Furthermore, in my opinion, a counter creates a psychological barrier between reader and reference assistants. A desk would be better. A major criticism concerns the location of the reference desk. Good administration requires that the reference assistant be near the readers serviced and near the reference and other books used in this connection.

It is also desirable that the reference assistants be fairly close to the catalog. In the Moline plan the reference desk is close to the catalog but is far removed from both the readers and the open stacks. The reference desk does not have to be next to the circulation desk. As a matter of fact, if it were moved from its present location to the reading room where it should be, it would give the staff better supervision of the entire service area. Furthermore, people seeking reference assistance would not then be disturbed by the confusion and noise usually associated with the circulation desk.

The arrangement of tables and chairs leaves much to be desired. It is obvious that they have been placed in this rather peculiar and arbitrary pattern in order to maintain the passage from the entrance to the court. I repeat that this arrangement will interfere with the function of the library. The seating capacity for readers will be 100 in the main reading room, 12 in the business and technical department, 15 to 20 in the young adult department, about 25 in the lounge area, and 35 to 40 in the children's room. If we take the maximum figures given and include the lounge area as reader space, which in a strict sense we

should not, there will be a total of about 200 seats available. The formula calls for 3 seats per 1000 of population. At the present time, 135 seats are needed. However, in twenty years with a population of 80,000 to 90,000, the library should have seats for 240 to 270 people instead of the 200 as now indicated. If the basement is finished at a later date, perhaps arrangements can be made for the additional seats for readers.

Book capacity of the new building is approximately 160,000 volumes. The accepted formula calls for 2 books per capita for a city of this size. With an estimated population of 80,000 in twenty years this capacity is adequate. If the population goes to 90,000 or more, additional shelving space will be needed.

There should, of course, be a workroom close to the circulation desk. The size of the circulation workroom will be determined by the charging system used and the volume of business. However, not all of the book work has to be done at this point. In any case I do not think that workrooms as large as those indicated for circulation and reference should occupy space in the front of the new building. It would be better to utilize this area for displays of books and other materials or some other public service.

It seems to me that there are too many small rooms and too many fixed partitions throughout the building. This results in a rather rigid design. It would be better to have larger areas and use double-faced bookcases or movable partitions to create small offices and workrooms as needed. That would afford greater flexibility.

I deplore the fact not only that there are a great many small rooms, but that they are of such peculiar shapes. This, of course, is the by-product of the double triangle design. There are many examples, but the microfilm and film storage rooms on the first floor are cases in point. Films and microfilms could be stored more effectively in cabinets or on shelves.

The second floor as designed not only repeats but compounds the errors of the first floor. Again we are faced with a double triangle design, and so far as I am concerned that is double trouble. Obviously from the library point of view it would have been far better to eliminate the diagonal hall going from the stair landing to the court at the opposite corner of the building. While this would have destroyed the effect the architect sought to obtain, it would have avoided the wasted space and multiplicity of odd-shaped rooms.

I think it would have been an improvement to put the stacks over the adult reading room, with stairs that the staff members could use for ready access to books and shelves in that area. This would be particularly desirable if the reference desk were moved to the reading room area on the first floor as previously suggested.

A booklift would also be useful in this connection because of the triangular-shaped space wasted in the stack area. A conventional square or oblong stackroom would permit much more shelving. I fail to see that the ledges provided will be of any real benefit, particularly since they seem to be fixed and take up a considerable amount of floor space.

The children's room is convenient to the stair well. However, it measures only 30 feet by 40 feet and therefore contains only 1200 square feet. In my opinion this is much too small. I think it should be at least 2000 square feet at the present time. Usually 25 per cent of the reading room seats should be for children. The Moline Public Library plan calls for 30 to 40 seats for them. This is less than 25 per cent of the 200 total, and is too small for the anticipated growth in the next twenty years.

The doors to the auditorium and conference rooms open in instead of out. The auditorium is apparently built in.

MRS. DEVEREAUX: It is not.

MR. PETERSON: I am glad to hear that. It would be better to have a square or oblong room for the auditorium in any event so that the space could be more readily converted to additional service space at a later date, if that should be necessary. The auditorium has seats for 200 people, and these are not included in the count of seats for readers. There is a narrow hall in back of the stair well leading from the children's room to the auditorium, presumably for the use of the children when they attend story hours.

The area beyond the auditorium contains a jumble of odd-shaped nooks and corners and peculiar-looking rooms. These include the kitchen, staff lounge, quiet room, the conference rooms, the chair room, and the exhibit room. They are all a product of the double triangle design, of course.

The exhibits preparation room connects with the staff lounge, though I don't know why. I can see no particular reason why it should be adjacent to the auditorium, either. As a matter of fact, there seems to be no logic in the design of the rooms and arrangement of the facilities on the second floor. The wide hall from the stair landing to the court contains exhibits. While this is apparently attractive, it is not the best use of space, and, of course, its existence is what caused the triangular areas which flank it.

The elevator door obviously should not open into the catalog and ordering room but into the shipping and receiving room. There should also be a door connecting shipping and receiving with cataloging and ordering.

I think it is apparent from this resume that the plan for the new Moline Public Library leaves much to be desired. Should the design be carried out, the city will have a smaller library than the outside walls would permit if a more conventional design had been developed.

MR. BERNBROCK: Some of the criticisms have come about as a result of our trying to solve some of the points that Mr. Peterson made. For instance, having the door on the corner, which created the two triangle design, was an effort on our part to try to open up the north side of the building to do just what he was talking about—merchandising!

Discussion

QUESTION: Why the tree? What if the Dutch elm disease hits the tree?

MR. BERNBROCK: It can be taken down if the disease hits it.

QUESTION: What happens to the court if you remove the tree?

MR. BERNBROCK: You can put in another tree.

I don't remember how the statement was made about the room being a place just for reading, and that these sorts of things are embellishments that are not necessary, but I can't agree with that sort of thinking. I think in order for a person to be attracted to a building first of all and then to enjoy being in that building, it has to have something besides four walls and a lot of books packed in the space. There has to be something about it that makes it more like home for them really to appreciate and enjoy.

QUESTION: I would like to know why the catalog department had to be put on the second floor.

MRS. DEVEREAUX: I don't see any argument about it. We tried to put all of our public service areas and those used most on the first floor, and we put our audio-visual department on the alley so that materials could be picked up and returned easily. I know of other libraries that have catalog departments on another floor and don't suffer from it.

QUESTION: If Moline is going to grow as fast as they say, it is going to be a busy place. I don't see that the children's room is going to take care of this. How large is that children's room?

MRS. DEVEREAUX: It is 1200 square feet. Our children's room is used very little. We have no school libraries and we loan books to the schools. Most of the children use the bookmobile. Our main children's room is used very little.

QUESTION: Will the new children's room pull in more children?

MRS. DEVEREAUX: I doubt it.

QUESTION: Why is the auditorium upstairs where all the traffic has to go through the main door?

MR. BERNBROCK: There wasn't enough room to put it on the first floor.

QUESTION: How about the basement?

MR. BERNBROCK: I think many people get a feeling when going down to a basement that it is like going down to the bargain basement or some of them get claustrophobia. Also, there are light and ventilation problems that you don't have when you go up.

QUESTION: I should think you would want to have a separate entrance and exit to the auditorium so it could be used after the library is closed.

MRS. DEVEREAUX: It will be used after hours. There are other libraries that have their auditorium on the second floor and you go in through the building, and it doesn't seem to be a problem.

MR. PETERSON: It is a problem in that point just made. You should be able to cut off the other public service areas so you don't have to light, heat, and staff them when the meetings in the auditorium go beyond normal service hours. This plan does not permit that.

VOICE: I would like to help out a fellow architect. On this business of the auditorium, I think it is a good idea to have it upstairs because it will have a greater span to support it. It is easier to support the roof load than a floor load. Therefore, we can eliminate one column in the middle of the auditorium without decreasing the effectiveness.

MR. BERNBROCK: Somebody asked about light in that area. If we wanted light, it would be a simple matter of skylights as well as ventilation. I am not saying we would advocate that, but it could be done.

QUESTION: Do you think that the Wheeler formulas for square footage and number of seats are realistic in the present-day use of libraries in view of the fact that he prepared those formulas based on libraries built from 1910 to 1930 or thereabouts?

MR. PETERSON: My own experience has been that the formulas are very good. The book was published in 1941, so it is a little later than suggested. I do agree that sometimes it may be a job to sell the extensive space for a twenty-year development to the local purseholders and the voters. If there is such a problem, I would say, first, to go along on the Wheeler formula and get as much money and as much building as you can, but in the event that it is not possible to get all you are going to need for twenty years, by all means plan a building for the twenty-year interval but do not build all of it at once. In other words, you can have footings as I suggested earlier for upward extensions and place your building on the site if the site is not large enough to have lateral extensions.

QUESTION: On your first floor plan you had the small corner area in the rear for the bookmobile, and I take it the alley is at the right of the drawing.

MR. BERNBROCK: That is right.

QUESTION: Then you have the docks for the bookmobile from the opposite side of the loading platform. Otherwise they would have to back in.

MRS. DEVEREAUX: They back in now.

MR. BERNBROCK: The post office parking area is right opposite that, and there is plenty of area to turn around.

QUESTION: Why do you have public toilets on both the first and the second floors? That is rather luxurious.

MR. BERNBROCK: Because of the auditorium and children's room on the second floor. Definitely you need toilets there, and you wouldn't want to ignore the first floor.

MR. BERNBROCK: I would like to say something about Mr. Peterson's remarks about putting the stacks over on the north side. The elevator, freight elevator, and books and all are coming up on the south side. I presume you would then be contemplating another lift of some kind over in that area.

MR. PETERSON: I suggested that a booklift be placed close to the reference desk because that is your main point of need for a kind of facility to get ready delivery of books in the stacks. Magazines, newspapers, and books not on the open shelves would be sent down by a dumb-waiter which would be near the ready assistance desk.

NORTHWOOD BRANCH
ENOCH PRATT FREE LIBRARY

Baltimore, Maryland
Chief, Extension Division: Mrs. Lee B. Gorsuch

Statistical Data

Architect: Smith & Veale
              Baltimore, Md.
Type of library: Major branch library
Population to be served: 54,000
Area: 14,441 sq. ft.
Book capacity: 40,472
Seating capacity:
    Adult and young people: 68
    Children: 52
    Meeting room: 145
Ceiling height: Varies
Cost:
    Building: $285,689
    Equipment: $30,000
    Site: None
Cost per square foot: $18.62
Cost per cubic foot: $1.26
Parking area capacity: 34
Firms supplying major equipment: To be determined

Presentation of Plans

MRS. LEE B. GORSUCH, Chief, Extension Division
and MR. WILLIAM B. FLACK of Smith and Veale

MRS. GORSUCH: The Enoch Pratt Library services a population of 982,000 by means of a central library, 25 branches, and two tractor trailer bookmobiles. The central library is ideally located in the center of the city so its resources are easily available to all of the branch libraries by daily truck service. This, plus the fact that Baltimore's population is actually very small in comparison with cities like Philadelphia, New York, Detroit, and Los Angeles, eliminates the need for regional libraries in the sense we usually speak of them—that is, libraries administratively responsible for smaller units within the service area. In order to avoid confusion in terms, we classify our branches as major, medium, and small. And, of course, the size of the building, the book collection, and the staff and type of service offered varies in each category.

    The Northwood Branch is classified as a major branch with a staff of at least six professional librarians, six desk assistants, an opening book collection of 31,000 volumes, and a capacity

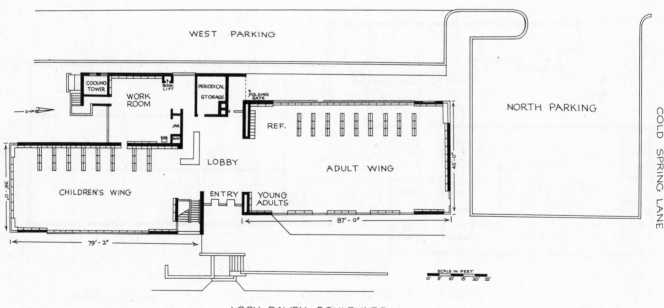

Northwood Branch, Enoch Pratt Free Library
Baltimore, Maryland
Main floor

growth to a collection of a little over 60,000 volumes. The staff will carry on an active community program—story hours, school visits, film and discussion meetings, and book reviews—as well as the usual informational services given within the library.

The neighborhood is a middle-class residential area. There are some individual houses, but the majority of them are built in groups or as row houses, and there are many large apartment units. Most of the homes are owned or occupied by young or middle-aged married couples who are on the way up the professional or white-collar ladder. The adults are unusually civic-minded and actively participate in many community organizations. In an area of this sort, of course, there are a great many children. Schools, public and parochial, and churches abound in the neighborhood. A large state college is less than half a mile away.

There are three shopping centers in addition to one that is in the rear of the site of the branch, and these shopping centers are all within a mile radius. The largest of these is six blocks away, and we have had a very successful bookmobile stop there for many years. We have also had a

very successful bookmobile stop about eight blocks to the north of the present location, so that our present site is actually between two bookmobile stops that have proved the need for branch service in this area.

The site is a block long, and while the adjacent shopping center is not as large as the one to the south, the site is at a very important intersection of two main traffic arteries, Cold Spring Lane and Loch Raven Boulevard. The first, Cold Spring Lane, is one of the main east-west arteries across the city, and the latter, Loch Raven Boulevard, is a six-lane parkway which serves as one of the main arteries, not only for the city but also from the county to downtown Baltimore. Bus routes along this thoroughfare increase the library's accessibility.

There are two more shopping centers north of this radius of our present site. A stipulation of the gift site was that parking must be provided in the adjacent shopping center, and this we have done with a parking lot at the north end of the building and off the public alley to the rear.

As frontage on Loch Raven Boulevard is residential, it is necessary for an ordinance to be passed to permit the erection of the building, and,

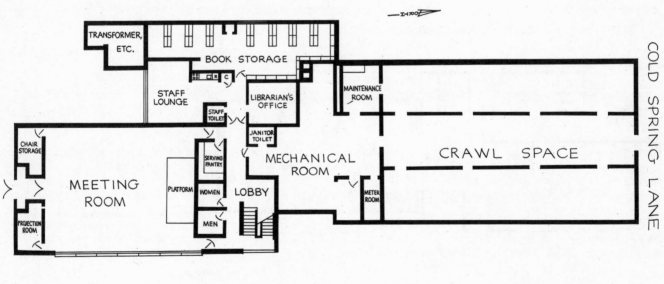

Northwood Branch, Enoch Pratt Free Library
Baltimore, Maryland
Ground floor

of course, we had to abide by rather strict zoning regulations. These, plus the parking requirement mentioned before and the sloping lot, present many problems which had to be resolved by the architects.

The main entrance to the building is in the center of the building and in the center of the block. The secondary entrance is to the rear, and this entrance is put in to accommodate the people who would be using the shopping center and also the people who would be using the parking area. The circulation desk is halfway between the two entrances. It is immediately visible through either entrance and is flanked by the adult wing and the children's wing.

MR. FLACK: The building is located on a sloping site, and it is restricted by law to a 25-foot set-back, so that it was not possible to have people strolling past and looking into the library. Feeling that the major foot traffic would be coming from the north, we developed a plaza in front of the library so that you can enter the grounds and walk down past the building to the main entrance.

The children's area and the adult wing, while perfectly open on the plan, are separated by the scale of the ceiling heights.

Criticism

MR. J. ARCHER EGGEN
Director, St. Paul Public Library
St. Paul, Minnesota

I would like first of all to call attention to some of the things I deem critical in branch library planning. One of these is ease of accessibility; another, identification as a library; and, finally, some provision for display, be it artificial or integral as a part of the building.

This building makes particularly good use, in my opinion, of a very difficult site. In fact, it takes advantage of that site to provide certain features which would otherwise be difficult of attainment. It has street level access from two points. It also has access from two or even three parking lots to the building.

I was interested in the way Mrs. Gorsuch and others presented the capacity of the building. So many of us think in terms of only the actual number of books a library holds. We forget that a reasonable percentage of our books are out in circulation. Mrs. Gorsuch assumes one third out in circulation, giving an effective inventory capacity of this building of 60,000 volumes. I certainly agree with that figure.

The potential population served by this branch is 54,000. Assuming a normal or an average, I had better say, two-week loan period, the building then is designed for an ultimate circulation capacity of about half a million volumes a year. I haven't

discussed this with Mrs. Gorsuch. It is just a conclusion I reached.

The separate entrance for the meeting room is certainly good. However, I can see no provision on the plan for closing the room off from the main library, but it probably could be easily accomplished by a door or pair of doors. As it is now, if the rest rooms are used by people in the meeting room or made available to them, and if the serving pantry is made available to the people who use the meeting room, it is impossible to block off the meeting room from the rest of the library.

Down in the book storage area, the stack sections are shown on 6-foot centers. For mere dead storage of material, 4-foot 6-inch centers would be adequate. This would allow at least two additional 6-foot ranges. This is a detail, and I am not sure whether the metal shelving is a part of the contract or not. I believe it is, but two could easily be added.

When I discussed this plan with Mr. Flack, he made a rather interesting comparison with a residence. He likened one wing to the bedroom wing of a house, and the other to the living and service wing with the central entrance. I think this is a wonderful plan. There are two equally accessible entrances. I suspect, and I think both Mr. Flack and Mrs. Gorsuch would be inclined to agree, that probably the bulk of the traffic will come from the parking area at the north end of the building or on the west side of the building.

It is interesting to note that there is a folding gate which can close off the west entrance when the library is not open. Probably any vandalism that might occur would come from this direction because it is not as well lighted as Loch Raven Boulevard. The folding gate should eliminate that.

When people enter the library, they are not faced with an imposing loan desk or control center. However, excellent visual control of the adult wing, the children's wing, and the entrance is provided at this focal point.

Your attention was called to the fact that the only public toilet facilities are in the basement. I would like to see public rest rooms on the main floor as well as in the basement. Someone questioned having two sets of toilet facilities in the Moline building. I couldn't help but be reminded that most houses now of six or seven rooms have two bathrooms. A big public building like this certainly ought to have two sets of rest room facilities.

I don't know what processes are taken care of in the workroom. It seems larger than necessary, which led me to believe that a corner could be taken from the workroom for the librarian's office; or periodical storage could be made available in the workroom, and the room now assigned to periodical storage could be the librarian's office.

I like the way the stacks are located on the west side of the building. The only glass on that side, I believe, is opaque glass. Very little heat from the west sun will enter the building.

Discussion

QUESTION: Why the enormous mechanical room?

MR. FLACK: I can say that while it looks enormous to you, you would have to go into that room sideways, practically, to get by all the equipment that is in the room. The library is air conditioned and requires a considerable amount of equipment.

QUESTION: How about the cost? What is the construction cost on this building and how much in furniture and equipment?

MRS. GORSUCH: The contract bid is around $254,000 and the equipment $30,000. That is an allocation. We actually expect not to spend the $30,000.

QUESTION: I was wondering about the roof overhang. It seems to me that is just a step probably in the right direction, and with a larger roof overhang maybe you could control the glare on the windows and perhaps make some savings on the 75-ton air conditioning.

MR. FLACK: The second floor overhangs the first floor by 4 feet, and then the roof overhangs that by another 4 feet. As far as the east façade is concerned, which is the other possible area, a roof overhang would have to be excessively bulky from an aesthetic standpoint to do the shading job.

QUESTION: Why have any roof overhang at all, then?

MR. FLACK: The 4-foot overhang on the south is effective but not on the east, and anything greater than that would be aesthetically undesirable.

QUESTION: Is any glare-reducing glass used?

MR. FLACK: Yes, on the west elevation and on the staffroom in the basement on the south elevation. We are using gray glass as an experiment.

QUESTION: In what areas?

MR. FLACK: That is the west elevation. What was referred to as opaque glass in most cases is gray glass, which takes the glare off looking from inside out and cuts down somewhat on the heat load, but normal high efficiency heat-reducing glass is quite undesirable from a color standpoint.

QUESTION: If Mr. Eggen's estimate is correct that circulation is expected to approach half a million, the size of the circulation desk appears rather small.

MRS. GORSUCH: Before we reach that circulation I am sure we would have another branch to the north of this particular branch library because we are thinking in terms of a service area at this point of at least a mile or a mile and a half, and I am sure that a branch library would go to the east, which would take some of the circulation off this branch that we are planning. There is another major branch that is just a mile and a half to the east of this and still another major branch that is about a mile and a half between the two branches on the west, so that we had not anticipated a circulation of more than 315,000 or 350,000 at any time.

QUESTION: In that connection were you planning to discontinue the bookmobile stops?

MRS. GORSUCH: We will discontinue both of these stops and possibly put one farther north where we said we might eventually build another branch.

QUESTION: What about the toilets in the basement area? Are those for adults and juvenile combined?

MRS. GORSUCH: Yes.

QUESTION: It would be less of a problem if you had them up on the main floor where you could supervise them.

MRS. GORSUCH: We have had toilets on the main floor, and they have not worked out either. In fact, sometimes they are harder to control because they put notions in children, whereas if the children don't see them, they don't desire to go to the toilet.

QUESTION: With the traffic coming in from the back of the building away from the front door, which way does your circulation desk face?

MRS. GORSUCH: The circulation desk is actually an "L." We have part of the circulation running parallel to Loch Raven Boulevard, and the other runs parallel to Cold Spring Lane.

QUESTION: On the west entrance do you have any facilities for displays in that area?

MRS. GORSUCH: Yes. They are very shallow so we would use them mostly for posters, but there is a display on the west as well as on the east of the main entrance.

I do feel that I should point out, when we are talking about control at the circulation desk, that in none of our branch libraries is control actually the responsibility of our desk assistants. In a branch of this size we would always have a professional librarian on duty in the children's wing as well as a professional or two on duty in the adult wing at our least busy time.

QUESTION: What were the considerations in putting the librarian's office in the basement?

MRS. GORSUCH: That has created a great deal of discussion at home as well as here. All librarians' offices are actually on the main floor in all of our buildings at present. We have felt this is a very valuable area, and we tried to review actually how the librarian's office is used.

Our librarians are not supervisors in the sense that they sit in their office and watch what is going on on the outside of the building. They actually work at the information desk at times, and when they are not working at the information desk, what do they do? In many cases they are writing their reports. They are consulting with staff. They are meeting with community leaders, and often they want to be where it is quiet. The librarian's office is also used by other staff members who have the same kind of reports to prepare.

So we called in the librarians of four of our major branches, when we thought we would experiment with the librarian's office in the basement, and asked them what they thought about it, and they said that they thought it would be an excellent idea. Now, we haven't actually tried it, but we are going to see whether it does work out. We might be all wrong.

QUESTION: Are circulation routines such as overdues taken care of at the branch or centrally?

MRS. GORSUCH: They are taken care of at the branch now, but we hope in the very near future they will be taken care of at the central library.

QUESTION: With two entrances where do you have your charge-out desk?

MRS. GORSUCH: At this point we actually haven't designed the circulation desk. However, we do feel that the return will be facing the main entrance and that the charge-out desk will be on the long end as will the registration.

QUESTION: At the same desk?

MRS. GORSUCH: Yes.

QUESTION: Is your mechanical room large enough to take care of your custodian quarters as well?

MRS. GORSUCH: Yes; if you notice, there is a room that is called the janitor's workroom and we provide a toilet and locker and sink for the janitor in the basement.

QUESTION: In the building we just saw [Moline], it was my impression that the children were more or less discouraged to come to the library, their room being so small. I would like to know what the Enoch Pratt standpoint is on that.

MRS. GORSUCH: There is a difference in the location of the Moline Library. It is downtown and would not have the use by the children as in a branch.

FAIRFAX COUNTY PUBLIC LIBRARY

Fairfax, Virginia
Director: Mrs. Mary K. McCulloch

Statistical Data

Architect: J. Russell Bailey
      Orange, Va.
Type of library: County headquarters
Population to be served: 225,000 (estimated
    population)
Dimensions: 105' x 160'
Area: 30,708 sq. ft.
Book capacity: 111,850
Seating capacity:
    Reading rooms: 155
    Meeting and conference rooms: 135
Cost:
    Building: $522,036
    Furniture and equipment: $50,000
Cost per square foot: $17
Parking area capacity: 35
Firms supplying major equipment: To be determined

Presentation of Plans

MRS. MARY K. McCULLOCH, Director
and MR. J. RUSSELL BAILEY, Architect

MRS. McCULLOCH: Fairfax County, Virginia, consists of 403 square miles of rolling terrain. Our site has a 30-foot slope from the street level to the rear property line, so that will account for some of the problems and possibly the appearance of our building.

It is located on the Virginia side of the Potomac River and is considered a part of metropolitan Washington, D.C. Arlington County and the city of Alexandria are surrounded by Fairfax County. The town of Falls Church, population approximately 10,000, although located within the county, maintains its own municipal services including library service.

Since the 1950 census, the population of Fairfax County has grown from 98,557 to an estimated 225,000 including the towns. We are growing at the rate of one and three-eighths persons per hour! According to the County Planning Commission, growth of Fairfax County has just begun

Fairfax County Public Library, Fairfax, Virginia

and the influx of population will continue at a rapid rate for several years. The present rate of growth is one thousand per month.

As a result of this rapid growth and development, the demand for all public services is pressing the county government. However, with progressive county government it is felt some services should be given an immediate start, with additions and expansions to come later. This theory applies to the new central library plans of the county.

At the present time development is chiefly residential, which means real estate taxes are the chief support of the county. Large industry is gradually being attracted and encouraged to settle in the county. An eight-lane highway is in process of construction through the approximate center of the county. It will bypass Fairfax, however.

The Central Intelligence Agency is in process of constructing its headquarters in the northwest section of the county near McLean. Near the west end of the county, referred to as Chantilly, construction is proceeding on the International Airport for Washington, D.C.

In six years the County Library has grown from one bookmobile serving the entire county to a headquarters circulation library; administrative and technical processes offices, which are housed in a building located about one-third block from the circulation library; five branches with another proposed for the next fiscal year; two bookmobiles covering 122 stops; and two sub-stations and deposit service to schools. There is a total of 59 full-time employees on the entire library staff. The circulation library at our headquarters location in Fairfax town circulated 116,290 books in 1958 and has a total net registration of 6231.

As the "bedroom of the Nation's capital," the county's population has a high intelligence level and is well acquainted with the uses of a public library. Circulation for 1958 was 707,674 for the entire system. Total number of registered borrowers was 44,021, and our new registrations are averaging a thousand or more a month. Circulation is increasing at the rate of 33.1 per cent this fiscal year over last year. Total book collection is 111,997. Juvenile circulation at the end of the fiscal year was slightly more than one half

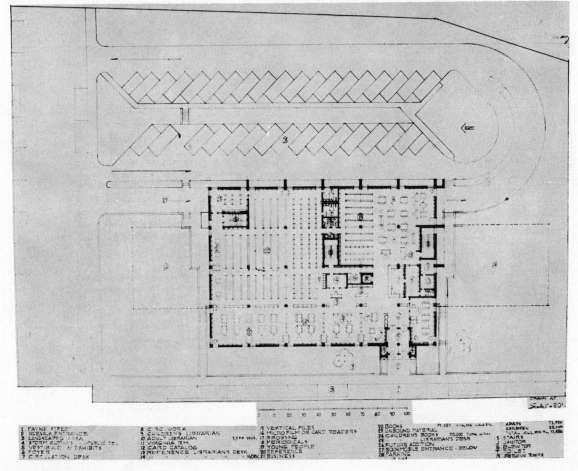

Fairfax County Public Library
Fairfax, Virginia
Main floor

the total circulation of the system. Adult non-fiction circulation has recently been exceeding fiction.

The central library is the core from which the whole county system will operate. It will house the largest book collection, and it will supplement branches and bookmobile collections via intraloan service. The administrative offices, bookmobile services, school deposit service, and any additional services added to the extension department will all emanate from the central library.

Our site is two acres and is very hilly. It is difficult to obtain level land in Fairfax County in the proper location. The library will be located beside the new post office building which was recently constructed in the town of Fairfax. So we are very much in the heart of the town. We are anticipating that it will cost approximately $17 per square foot, which will bring the total to around $522,036. We have estimated $50,000 for furniture and equipment and $50,000 for outside work. We will have a total of 30,708 square feet.

MR. BAILEY: The 30-foot drop from the street side to the back poses a real problem because we had to build parallel to the slope of the ground, and parallel to the street. The plans show the first

installment of the library. It is designed to have three additions which will double the size of the building as it is now projected. Two lateral additions, plus an addition on the roof, are planned.

The two divisions of the library plan are those of adult-young people's reading toward the front of the building, and children's reading toward the upper right-hand corner of the plan. The collections, of course, for these two groups of readers are adjacent to their reading areas.

There are three stairways. The staff would use the stair at the right; the children the one at the left, which means that the children do have to walk across through the book stack area to go to story hour. This is a criticism we make of our own plan. We don't like this, but we don't see a better way to do it.

The toilet facilities are rather hidden away in this case. We have even considered using a series of mirrors to make sure people were directed properly. However, our feeling is that having the facilities somewhat remote from the entrance and somewhat supervised by persons going through to stack, probably the situation can be handled. We do have children's facilities adjacent to the children's room.

Fairfax County Public Library
Fairfax, Virginia
Second floor and north elevation, south elevation,
     and front elevation with future additions on ends

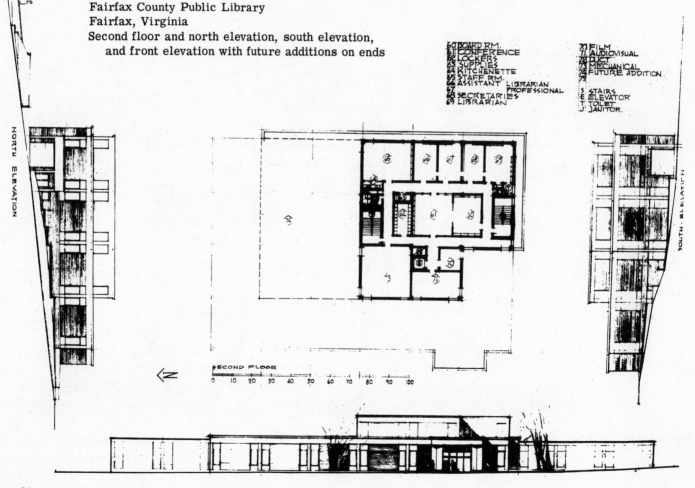

About one third of the ground floor plan is given over largely to bookmobile and bookmobile entrance and library receiving entrance. As a result, the enclosed area of the ground floor plan is quite small, yet it is all we could afford to buy. We were not able to afford the cutting-away of that portion of the site which is parallel with the front of the building. This will be a step in the steep bank and will not have to be excavated and means we will have a part of the main floor poured on grade.

There are three main elements on this floor, or four perhaps. We will start with the one at the left which is the meeting room. This room can be reached rather easily from the parking lot. It can be reached also from the second floor by the stairway which is in back of the meeting room entrance. In back of the stair, and to the right of the meeting room, you will notice the public toilets for use in the evenings when the rest of the library is closed.

The next unit is the extension work office with its extension book shelving. There is a loading dock with two bookmobiles housed within the building.

A panel truck is shown in the garage backed up to the entrance of the receiving room, where materials come in and are worked on in the processing room and where acquisitions, cataloging, and processing are handles for the whole system. This is a large area which we think will be sufficient to do the job even though at a later date the building will have to be enlarged. The elevator on the main floor is a very important piece of equipment which comes down close to the processing and cataloging area.

In summary, there are three departments on the ground floor. They are the meeting room, the department which has to do with mechanical and janitorial and supply services, and the department which has to do with extension work including the bookmobile and its entrances.

The top floor has a series of offices reached by two stairways. One might have been enough, but when we add on, we will need the other one; so we have the two stairs, the staff lounge and kitchenette and toilets directly over the stairway to the left, and those offices which have to do with the operation of the whole system. The board room is a combination space where I understand the library staff have their big powwows. They bring people in and lay out their work and have their staff branch conferences and so on.

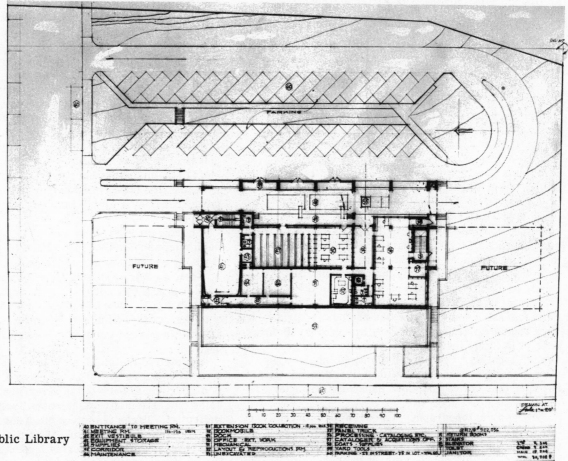

Fairfax County Public Library
Fairfax, Virginia
Ground floor

Criticism

MR. WALTER H. KAISER
Librarian, Wayne County Public Library
Detroit, Michigan

I think my first ammunition concerns the site. The site for the County Library headquarters in Fairfax County should be selected primarily because of advantages which relate to the County Library service as a whole and not just to that of the town of Fairfax. The town has 6900 persons living within its boundaries. The county has 225,000. The town of Fairfax is approximately 3 square miles. The county of Fairfax is 403 square miles. From my analysis, the site selected is so poor from the county standpoint as to justify delaying construction until a more suitable site can be obtained.

The County Library headquarters should be near arterial highways and not be in the heart of the town. I have a feeling this headquarters is selected because it is next to the post office. This has nothing to do with the proper functions of a true county library headquarters. It is possibly a very good location for the town of Fairfax as may be inferred from data already presented. I feel that this site is town-locked. It is three quarters of a mile from a major arterial highway. I believe this building will be flooded with University of Virginia students whose needs should be satisfied by the state and not by the county. I think they are just a bit south. I think the University of Virginia is located on 150 acres just below this present site, and I have seen what university students can do to a public library branch. I feel that this headquarters will be taken over by the University of Virginia students.

This is perhaps a rather radical proposal, but I would suggest that you consider a site perhaps up as far as Fairfax Circle or some point which may be on the periphery of the town. If you put the library at Fairfax Circle, you would be only $2\frac{1}{2}$ miles from the center of Vienna and some miles from the center of Fairfax. I think there is a possibility of considering a new site between these two, but if that is not possible, consider the town of Fairfax as a separate entity because I think you have a real problem here in thinking too much about the town of Fairfax. The registration figures indicate the possibility that two thirds of the present usage of a library in the town of Fairfax is by nonresidents of the town. Fairfax Circle is about 2 miles from the center of Fairfax town and $2\frac{1}{2}$ miles from the center of Vienna. Before long, it is likely that the proposed site would be a central location. Consideration should be given to the separation of the Fairfax town library from the headquarters building, if such expansion endangers the selection of a good site.

Now, on the topography. The architect correctly classified the terrain as rugged, there being a 30-foot drop which gives in 240 feet an average drop of 1 foot for each 8 feet. The disadvantages stemming from this fact will result in many burdensome steps and excessive site development cost, loss of flexibility in using available land area, and possibly other disadvantages not easily ascertainable at this time by this critic. I assume that the present site was free; possibly the unusually large cost for site development, estimated at $50,000, would permit the purchase of a more suitable site.

Now, on the size. The proposed site provides 74,000 square feet or one and three-quarters acres. I am assuming that you are giving away 30 feet of this land to the county. This is much too small. I would recommend a minimum of five acres and up to eight or ten if funds and a suitable parcel are available. It is comforting to remember that the library is a permanent institution, or so it has appeared. If the future indicates that the land is not needed, it can be disposed of more likely with gain than loss. From the foregoing considerations, as you can see, I am most unhappy and disturbed by the site of this building.

Now, to the building. Making the assumption that this site has been selected, unwise as it may prove to be, let's move to the consideration of the building itself. While the character of the site obviously prevents the consideration of a one-floor building, I still desire to note that if at all possible the building should be on one floor with facilities being located in a basement area and with, possibly, the use of mezzanine areas rather than full-story levels for offices, staff, stack, and meeting room purposes.

Let's look at the ground floor for a moment. First, the garage occupies too much space in the present building.

Second, the space allotted for technical processing, 1204 square feet, is much too small. It should be two or three times the size, and within ten years this increased area will likely be too small. A staff of 13 (some figure 100 square feet per staff member) and 4000 volumes constitute too much material and staff to be placed in that particular location.

Third, the office of cataloger and acquisition personnel (100 feet) will not comfortably hold two persons.

Fourth, the corridor which is just back of the auditorium should be consolidated in some way with the supplies and maintenance rooms.

Now, insofar as expansion is concerned, my first look at this area indicates that it might be rather difficult to expand this auditorium and integrate it with the library. The rest room facilities on the ground floor area I consider too small for a staff of 23.

Let's go to the main floor now. There is waste space around the elevator. If you will notice, there is a corridor in back of the reference workroom. I raise a question of why the room itself should be walled off. There is quite a bit of interior wall in the building, and I think that the building seems a bit unnecessarily complicated because of that. Should the microfilm readers have such privacy as planned? Is there danger of mutilation? I am asking a question there. I really don't know, but I wonder about it.

The children's area of 3250 square feet is about twice the size it needs to be—that is, too large for a population of 6900. If the children are coming from outside the town, let's locate the library out there. The total proposed, 1500 to 2000 square feet, I think would be adequate for the children's room. I think the public toilets are improperly located. They should be relocated to a space near the elevator, near the center stairs if stairs are retained. I have a suggestion for eliminating those center stairs. They go only to the third floor, and later on I am recommending elimination of the third floor.

Now the business collection. The location may be a matter of just placing it somewhere. It was noted the final areas were not set up, but the business area as it shows on the plan is quite hidden, isn't it? For better control, I would have the adult stacks running north and south. That would be just opposite from where they are now.

Back to the ground floor for a moment—the garage runs completely the full width of the building. What I am suggesting is that it be cut off so that the cataloging area can be extended.

My recommendation is to do away with the third floor. I would bring part of those facilities down to the ground floor and part to the main floor, and excavate where the unexcavated area now shows. You will gain 3750 square feet and the topography of this land would seem to suggest such a change.

And then, on the main floor, there are islands in with several stairways. I would take all this out and try to package my things and try to open up the area.

I would relocate the unbound materials in stacks near reference. The stacks could be sealed off in some way by a gate or some device if put near the reference department. They should be there, not back in the corner. I would also consider relocating the Virginia Room in an area near the reference desk. Use the present Virginia Room for more active materials. Children's activities may be located here. The Virginia Room can still be given sufficient prominence and better service if located near the reference desk, and better supervision of its valuable material.

Now, to the third floor. My main criticism of the third floor (it's called your second floor) is that there is too little "pay area" left. It is mostly corridors and stairways. I calculate that there are 2559 square feet of a total of 5304 that are of no public or staff use, and I think that is a rather high percentage.

One more criticism that I have is the movement of staff from way down in this basement ground floor all the way up. There are three floors to go up, and the staffroom and facilities are on the top floor.

The audio-visual service area, I think, should be on the main floor. I imagine the audio-visual would be a busier place than the Virginia Room. The staffroom should be on the ground floor, not two floors away from where most of the staff are employed. There are only six people on the second floor, and I think the supervisory staff are too far removed from the working areas in a library of this size. They shouldn't be on the ground floor, however. I wonder whether the lockers might not be decentralized if the second floor is retained. There is much time lost in moving staff. I would recommend the elimination of the whole top floor and excavate the west portion of the ground floor to line up with the main floor, as I pointed out. In this area there are 3750 square feet. The executive offices could be located on the main floor.

One other problem with this library, to get back to size again, is that this area is a tremendously growing one and this building as it is now set up can be expanded 50 per cent, or some 16,000 square feet. I just don't feel it is looking far enough into the future to get a building of this size in this location and plan it this way for this county.

I have watched a similar situation in Wayne County. It is difficult to grasp how fast these mettopolitan areas are growing. I know one and three-quarters acres is simply too small. The Detroit Public Library is one of the few main libraries in the United States that could expand on its own grounds. It has nine acres. The purchase of this site was one of the most foresighted actions in library planning in that city.

This facility in Fairfax County will be serving maybe as many as a million people within twenty or twenty-five years, and you have one and three-quarters acres on a very poor site. I want you not to take my comments too personally. As I say, this is just the first go-around, and it would be a lot of fun to work with you later on as your plans develop.

Discussion

QUESTION: Were any other sites considered?

MRS. McCULLOCH: No, we didn't actually consider any other site. I will tell you one reason for selecting the site we did. We are located very close to the Court House, which serves the whole county. We have a great deal of business in connection with the Court House. Our purchasing agent is located there. Our legal advice is located there. The finance department is located there. Therefore, we felt that it would be wise to locate our central library building near the Court House where we have so much business to transact—plus the fact that it was located in the geographical center of the county. Mr. Kaiser suggested we go out to Fairfax Circle, but Fairfax Circle is still Fairfax town. So we still would be within the town and farther away from the Court House. The University of Virginia site was just recently settled. We had no idea when we purchased our site several years ago that the University would be located nearby. It is presenting a kind of problem for us.

QUESTION: What is the road network? Does the road go where you are now?

MRS. McCULLOCH: The library location will be almost at an intersection of two major highways going through the county. They will not be near the big interstate limited-access highways, but we are on major routes going into the District. We will also be on a major highway running from the south to the north end of the county.

QUESTION: Do you use your central collection on the main floor both for services within the building and for extension agencies?

MRS. McCULLOCH: Yes, it will be drawn upon for service to our branches and to the bookmobiles. Even though we will have an extension collection, there will be certain materials which will not be in that collection. Therefore, we will have to draw on the collection upstairs.

QUESTION: Following that up, since the town is relatively small in population but the county is very large, I would assume a great many of those books would be going in and out through your bookmobiles and trucks.

MRS. McCULLOCH: Yes, they will.

QUESTION: Wouldn't it be better to put a larger share of your collection where you won't have so much vertical transportation up and down?

MRS. McCULLOCH: I am a firm believer that library books should be available to anyone who walks in. I dislike seeing a lot of books stored in the basement where a librarian has to get them, so we thought we would put them on the main floor for our public to see. We do have a large circulation in our headquarters location now, and it is increasing tremendously. We feel that this collection would not be too large for that area. We are really serving the whole county.

QUESTION: As a matter of economy in plumbing, it is very expensive having toilet facilities in so many parts of the building, is it not?

MR. BAILEY: We would, of course, like to have all the plumbing lined up in a vertical fashion so there wouldn't have to be any pipes going through floors where we don't like to have them. However, you will notice if you look at the top floor that we have tried to run the pipes down along stairways, elevators, and places where they can easily be concealed. The plan just didn't seem to work for lining them up one above the other.

QUESTION: You indicated that the first addition would be to the south. What facilities do you plan which would be incorporated in that addition?

MRS. McCULLOCH: At the present time we really aren't too sure because our plans have changed. They change overnight because we are going so fast. A little thing like the University's being located next to us suddenly pops up, and here we have this problem we are faced with; and, with all the new highways coming through the county,

the belt highway or the interstate highways that are going to bisect the county to get into the District quicker also present problems to us; so right now we really aren't sure because of the possibility of change.

QUESTION: What is the longest-term population projection now available for Fairfax County?

MRS. McCULLOCH: I believe the Planning Commission have taken us up to about 1975, and they keep raising that each year that they project because they find their projections are always too low. By that year we are anticipating a good 500,000 to 800,000

QUESTION: Is the building air conditioned?

MRS. McCULLOCH: I am pushing for that with all my might.

QUESTION: Mr. Bailey, you mentioned the site problem you have. This has to do with your addition. Wouldn't it be easier or cheaper to plan your future addition just out in one direction rather than two?

MR. BAILEY: I think it is a perfectly good suggestion, and it may be that we could have a more economical addition if we were to do it that way. However, it seems that you have to please the public somewhat in the first appearance of the building, so we had that in mind—to try to get it on the site in a way which would be pleasing, for a while at least—and sometimes you have to wait ten years or fifteen years, even though these towns grow very fast, to get the money. Yet I think that is a very good criticism.

QUESTION: In connection with the ground floor mechanical and maintenance spaces, it has been my experience that the tendency is to give them too much space or overemphasize their needs, whereas any library function is tended to be squeezed down. Are you sure you need that much space for those three rooms there?

MR. BAILEY: The library staff kept after us to make it bigger and bigger, so we have it at this size at this moment.

MRS. McCULLOCH: Maybe I should answer that, and take Mr. Bailey off the hook. We hope that our maintenance will be centrally located. We will have a custodian who will supervise all the custodians of our branches and also maintain supplies. The maintenance area is also planned to be the central supply agency for our branches. At the present time our branches have actually no space for supply storage, so it is up to the headquarters or central library to supply the storage; and by being able to purchase our supplies in large quantities and keep them in storage, we can get them cheaper, too.

QUESTION: I wondered about the supervision of public areas from the circulation desk.

MRS. McCULLOCH: We felt that we had that pretty well under control, but perhaps we don't. We would appreciate any suggestions you might have. Attendants at the circulation desk will be able to

see into the children's room when that is necessary. They will also be able to see into the
Virginia Room, because there will be a glass
partition there and an entrance to the Virginia
Room is near the circulation desk. People will
have to walk past it to get in and to get out.

QUESTION: In your business section there is no
arrangement for professional coverage, is there?

MRS. McCULLOCH: We will have an assistant near
the business section.

QUESTION: I don't remember if you said the rear
property line is as far as your property goes or
not.

MR. BAILEY: There is a little distance between the
rear property line as shown on the drawing.
There is a creek which will have to be filled.
When the creek is filled, the property will adjoin
that of the city hall.

QUESTION: What happens to the creek?

MR. BAILEY: It will be underground.

QUESTION: Since we are talking about the possibility of increasing the ground floor or the main
floor area, couldn't it go back and even over
your parking area?

MR. BAILEY: There is enough variation in elevation to have a three-step arrangement, but it
would be difficult. We would have to build out in
a balcony fashion if we went back another step.

FREEPORT PUBLIC LIBRARY

Freeport, Illinois
Librarian: John F. McAvin, Jr.

Statistical Data

Architect: Lankton-Ziegele-Terry & Associates
    1100 Main St., Peoria, Ill.
Type of library: Central Public Library building
  remodeling
Population to be served: 25,600 in tax-supported
                             area
                          85,000 in immediate
                             trading area
Dimensions: 82' x 92'
Area: 14,140 sq. ft.
Book capacity: 55,500 (@6/lin. ft. shelf)
Seating capacity:
  Reading rooms: 100
  Meeting rooms: 100
Ceiling height varies: 8' 0" minimum
                       17' 6" maximum
                       9' 6" average
Cost:
  Building (including air conditioning): $146,750
  Furniture and equipment: 25,000
  Total: $171,750
Cost per square foot: $10.40 (building only)
Parking area capacity: 8 cars
Firms supplying major equipment: To be determined

Presentation of Plans

MR. JOHN F. McAVIN, JR., Librarian

Present planning is for interior remodeling and renovation of existing facilities. Plans are in a preliminary stage and are the result of deliberations among the librarian, architect, and consultant based upon a survey made in 1957 of library facilities and operations.

Freeport, incorporated in 1855, the county seat of Stephenson County in northern Illinois and the largest community within a 30-mile radius, has had a moderate and sporadic population growth. The population in 1902, when construction of the present library building was completed, was 17,514. The present figure is 25,601. Estimates of the population twenty years hence average out to a 10 per cent increase or 28,000. Freeport retail business serves approximately 65,000 residents in the area, and its industries, which are engaged in the manufacturing and processing of electronic equipment, metals, hardware and household aids, toys and looms, and patent medicines, have an international market as well as a national one. The residence of these specialized skilled and semiskilled workers in Freeport and the area is reflected in an active cultural and educational community program and, consequently, in a well-patronized public library service.

The library building, a two-story brick construction of the modified Carnegie style, is set back from the street on a sloping lot facing south and is located on one of the main east-west streets (one-way outbound traffic). It is within two blocks of the downtown area, centrally located for the schools, and close to public parking lots. The library parking area has an 8-car capacity which is used by visitors and library personnel.

Library resources consist of a 59,000-volume book collection, 700 recordings, and 150 periodicals to which the library subscribes. Eighty per cent of the book collection is located at the main library and the remainder at one branch library, two hospitals, and five rest homes. Circulation is approximately 10 volumes per capita. Main library service constitutes about 75 per cent of the total and is steadily increasing. The children's department is on the second floor, adult facilities on the first, and the rest rooms, meeting and storage rooms, as well as the heating plant are in the basement. The staff at present consists of 7 full-time or, in effect, 9 full-time equivalents. A program employing 12 staff members or equivalent has been recommended by the consultant and will be approved almost in its entirety by the library board after the remodeling project has been completed.

The children's department will be moved from the second floor to the basement area where the collections can be adequately shelved and displayed, and where entrance is possible from one of two places (northeast side or front entrance) and egress possible from one of three locations (the third being an emergency exit from the children's reading room) instead of as at present from only one (front stairway). Additional storage for the children's collection as well as for the adult book collection will be available in the far north end of the basement area. The degree of supervision intended here will be sufficient for this community.

Technical processing and other workroom activity will be located within the basement area and on the east side of the building. The advantages here will be more space and easier delivery of shipments. Whereas now deliveries must be made through the front door, as proposed they can be brought in at the northeast end at nearly basement level immediately from the adjacent parking lot. Also, processed material and books in storage can be sent to the adult department on the first floor and to the second-floor area (historical room, film previewing area, and smaller meeting room) via a booklift which will be located near the loan desks. During the evening hours, when the children's department is closed, the children's reading room will be available for public meetings. The basement area will include also the rest rooms, staffroom, and maintenance room, all or part of which can be closed off while the community meeting room is in use.

It is planned that adult service will remain on the first floor. Construction of a mezzanine in the

northern part of the room primarily for bookstacks, presently in use near the front of the room, will afford the department more reader space, effective display of books and recordings (the "marketplace"), and a more desirable location of the public service desk which at present is immediately in front of and facing the entrance way. The card catalog will be to the right in the foyer and easily accessible both to the public service desk and to the reference room.

The popular reading room will be the "quiet" room where current periodicals, some browsing material, and the stereo collection complete with the listening truck will be within easy reach. The librarian's office and secondary workroom will form a unit with the public service desk and will be accessible to the basement by way of the nearby stairway.

The second floor will remain structurally the same. The local history room will be enlarged to include the former children's room. Facilities for film previewing and a smaller meeting room are planned.

Total estimated cost of the project including renovation of the heating system and installation of air conditioning would be $146,750. Alternates were contemplated and would change the estimated cost to some extent. The over-all result of this project would be a service substantially equivalent to that obtainable from a new construction designed for a population of 28,000.

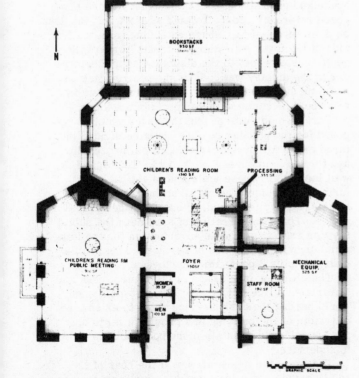

Freeport Public Library
Freeport, Illinois
Basement floor

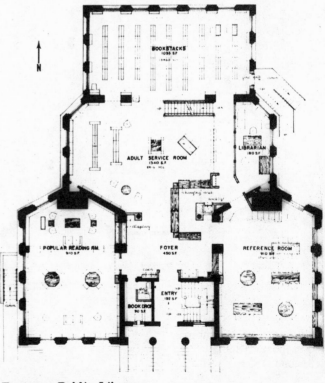

Freeport Public Library
Freeport, Illinois
First floor

Criticism

MR. CHARLES M. MOHRHARDT
Associate Librarian
Detroit Public Library

Here we have the unusual situation of a library building that is of approximately the recommended size for serving the community in which it is located but with space arrangements which make adequate and efficient library service nearly impossible. In addition to poor space arrangement the problem of remodeling is further complicated by (1) the existence of numerous bearing walls which divide the space into a number of small rooms and (2) the proposal to provide public service on four levels— the existing basement, first floor, second floor, and a new mezzanine. The operation of a multiple-story building for a library of this size is far from ideal in that it breaks up the book collection, limits the availability of the staff, and thus hampers service to the public. A larger staff is invariably required when service is given on more than one floor. Ideally,

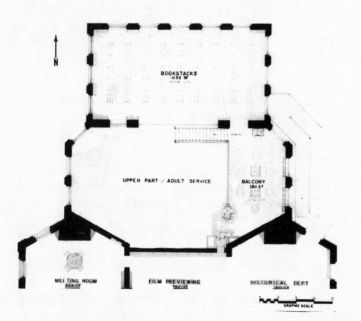

Freeport Public Library
Freeport, Illinois
Second floor

for a public library of this size, all public service should be on the ground floor.

Before I begin to discuss the proposed remodeling plans I would like to mention one essential which is often overlooked by librarians and that is a critical examination of their operating methods. Procedures and methods should be simplified and modernized as they inevitably affect the planning, staffing, and equipment requirements of the library. As an example of this let's take a look at the book charging system of the Freeport Public Library.

At present this library uses the Newark charging system with its cumbersome files of book cards and book slipping operations which are performed at the control desk. I would plead with them to adopt one of the simpler and equally effective charging systems. For example, the adoption of the Wayne County transaction charging system would enable this library to make a substantial saving in staff and equipment costs. The use of the Wayne County system would enable the Freeport library to eliminate the purchase and typing of book cards, the filing of book cards, and the slipping of returned books. The control desk could thus be smaller in size as space would not be required for the book card files and for the shelving of returned books which are being held for slipping.

Let's begin to discuss the proposed remodeling plan with a look at the layout of the first floor. Upon entering the building one sees the large control desk which extends from the foyer into the adult service room. This desk takes up an unnecessarily large space and partially blocks the entrance to the proposed reference room. I would suggest that the desk be of an inverted "L" shape extending from the left side of the foyer wall marked "coats" toward the adult service room to the display area and return left to the display wall. Thus the control desk would be on the borrower's left as he enters the building and would be contained totally within the foyer.

Next I would suggest that the space which is proposed for the popular reading room be divided into three areas for the librarian's office, processing, and for the loan bureau workroom. This space is well located for these units and might have the further advantage of permitting the staff to share typists, typewriters, and, in case of illness, staff duties. This concentration of staff near the public service area would be an advantage in this building which provides 68 hours of service a week with a staff of 8 plus 2 part-time employees.

The changing of location of the control desk and librarian's office to the positions just mentioned would permit the adult service room to extend the full width of the building and provide a large open area which would contain more books and be easier to supervise.

The proposed new stairway at the rear of the adult service room is planned to rise from the basement stack level, adjoining the new children's reading room, to the first and second stack levels, the adjoining new mezzanine (over the librarian's office), and the new third bookstack level directly over stack two. It seems to me that this stairway is poorly placed as it reduces the size of the children's reading room (basement) and the adult service room (first floor). It would be more efficient to place this stairway in a small addition at the east end of the bookstacks. This small addition would also provide space for the booklift and would place the booklift near the concentration of books in the bookstacks rather than in the center of the building.

The adoption of the building changes which I have just discussed would make a more desirable and attractive first-floor layout and would have the added advantage of staffing two public service rooms instead of three.

Now let's take a look at the proposed basement plan. One enters the basement directly from the entry way on the first floor. Under the present arrangement a separate control desk is required for the children's reading room. If it were possible to relocate the stairways to the basement and the second floor so that they would be entered from the foyer instead of the entry, a single control desk would suffice for the entire library. As the building is presently planned, the library patrons who use the services in the basement and the second floor could leave with uncharged books unless additional control desks were established at both the basement and the second floor. The savings to be made by manning one control desk instead of three are quite evident.

The basement area contains a maze of walls which break up the available space into a number of rooms and result in a considerable amount of waste space. The proposed remodeling calls for the removal (shown by dotted lines) of the angle wall at the lower left-hand corner of the children's reading room. The economy of this change is questioned as it would add a very small area to the children's room at the expense of removing the wall and raising the floor level, which is now one step lower than the children's room. This wall could remain, and the children's room could be enlarged by moving processing to the first floor, removing the bookstack stairway, and eliminating the control desk. (The elimination of the control desk is dependent upon the feasibility of changing the main stairway as mentioned previously.) Concentrating the children's service in the one enlarged room would be much more efficient and less expensive than using the two basement rooms. Another new room in the basement is proposed for the staffroom which is now located on the second floor. The addition of a staff toilet in the area south of processing is suggested.

Now let us consider the remodeling plans for the second floor. The main change on this floor is the addition of a new balcony extending over the east end of the upper part of the adult service room. This balcony is on the same level as the new third bookstack but is a few steps below the existing second-floor level. Access by means of a short stairway should be provided between the historical department and the new balcony.

In area this building approaches the recommended total space requirements for a community of this size, but because of the mass of walls, fireplaces, and usable space it is far below the actual requirements. In fact, only 75 per cent of the space is usable and it is distributed over three floor levels. Compare this with a usable area of 95 per cent in the new Louisiana State University Library. Incidentally, the economy of space is only one of the significant differences between the old Carnegie libraries and the contemporary type of library buildings.

In concluding my remarks I would like to offer a practical suggestion to the librarian and the board of the Freeport Public Library. I would strongly recommend that they scrap their plans for remodeling and plan for a new building. This is not as radical as it sounds in view of the fact that more than half the funds needed for a new building are already available and the rest can be obtained in about four years. This four-year estimate is based on the librarian's statement that it may be possible to set aside about $40,000 per year for a new building.

The construction of a new building of the required size could be financed as follows:

Estimated amount required for a new
air-conditioned building

16,000 sq. ft. @ $20	$320,000	
Equipment	40,000	
Total		$360,000

Funds on hand for remodeling

Construction	$70,000	
Air conditioning	76,750	
Equipment	25,000	
Total		$171,750
Amount to be financed		$188,250

Funds for the building could be obtained by accumulating $40,000 per year over a four-year period, and funds for the new furniture and equipment could be accumulated during the year in which the building is under construction.

It seems to me that the librarian and the board of the Freeport Public Library are in an unusually favorable position in being able to give the people of their community a new library building which will enable them to provide more and better library service in the years to come. I hope they will make this choice.

Discussion

QUESTION: What would the value of the old site be?

MR. McAVIN: We have investigated pretty carefully the front-foot value of the property in this community and this property is on the fringe, but the community is developing westward. The value is approximately $700 a front foot, and it runs up to about a maximum of $1500 in a commercial area.

QUESTION: And what is the footage?

MR. McAVIN: It is about 150 feet in front, and 150 feet deep. We have been told that in terms of square feet the building can accommodate our present population. The population is not developing other than simply at a steady, moderate rate. In approximately twenty years only about a 2500 increase in population is expected. The real sleeper in the whole affair is the factor of service to the rural area. If we are to provide that service, then there would have to be a complete change in our thinking, but the city is not growing rapidly enough and at an alarming-enough rate to jar the community into any kind of fundamental rethinking of the whole situation.

QUESTION: Would it be possible to raze this building and build on the present lot?

MR. McAVIN: I think it would be possible because the public buildings nearby are such that we could use them temporarily. The church buildings could accommodate a considerable part of the service during construction.

QUESTION: If you rebuild in this spot, will the populace get left behind?

MR. McAVIN: No. As a matter of fact, the commercial area is centralized.

QUESTION: Was there a place in the remodeled building for a young people's section?

MR. McAVIN: They have access directly to the adult collection. The building is such and the size of the library is such, it simply won't accommodate a separate area.

CHAIRMAN WILLIAMS: Maybe one answer to your question is, what is the size of the professional staff you have.

MR. McAVIN: It is one. That is a very material factor.

QUESTION: Even more reason sometimes to have at least a section of book shelves with a collection for young people.

QUESTION: I just wondered if Mr. Mohrhardt would feel that in this case, or in a similar case where you have an old building, it would be worth while to move to a lot that was as far as five blocks from the present location in order to get a one-story building?

MR. MOHRHARDT: Unfortunately there is no pat answer as to the exact location of a main library. There is extensive literature on library site selection, most of it repetitious, which applies identical solutions to the village, the town, the medium-sized city, and the large city in selecting library sites, but does not provide constructive help for a community which seeks a thoughtful approach to its own problem. Without knowing your community I cannot give a complete answer. I feel that a move of five blocks to a site where there can be a one-story building might be an advantage, especially if the site was in a prominent location, easy to reach, and with adequate parking nearby.

QUESTION: How do the architects feel about remodeling versus a new building?

MR. McAVIN: They certainly would be in favor of a new building. However, they are willing to give the library board what they ask for.

INTRODUCTORY STATEMENT

AS REPORTED BY M. BERNICE WIESE
Supervisor, School Libraries
Public Schools, Baltimore, Maryland

The study and evaluation of school library blueprints and plans by institutes and workshops prior to the construction of the building are impossible, because school library facilities are only one part of the total school plant. The purpose, therefore, for viewing plans of new school libraries was not to provide a means for the individual school planners to obtain recommendations for improvements in proposed plans. The committee responsible for planning the school library group meetings of the Institute thought that school librarians could acquire background that would help them in their own present or future planning from seeing and discussing the advantages and disadvantages of plans and photographs of some new school libraries from various sections of the country.

Committee members contacted librarians and supervisors in all sections of the country to secure colored slides and pictures of new elementary, junior high, senior high, vocational, and college laboratory school libraries. In order to have slides which would show the whole library and all its facilities, each school agreeing to co-operate was sent a list of views desired to provide for complete coverage, and was asked to provide facts about the school and its library program according to the sample form for the fact sheet. Blueprints of the plan and black-and-white pictures were also requested. Twelve schools, as included below, supplied colored slides, blueprints, and fact sheets. Several other schools sent incomplete sets—the blueprints only or pictures.

The technique adopted for studying and evaluating the slides worked effectively for the group of twenty-five. Every person had copies of all fact sheets. The panel members—consisting of Jackson P. Ketcham, Tyler, Ketcham, and Myers, Architects, Baltimore, Maryland; James A. Sensenbaugh, Superintendent of Schools, Frederick County, Frederick, Maryland; Audrey Newman, State School Library Supervisor, State Department of Education, Tallahassee, Florida; and Carolyn I. Whitenack, Assistant Professor, Library and Audio-Visual Education, Purdue University, West Lafayette, Indiana—had previewed the slides and were ready with comments as they were shown. Since the group preferred to ask questions and discuss overall planning and individual features as the slides were shown, this pattern was adopted. Architectural principles, school administrative thinking, practical experiences of librarians, types of good lighting, floor coverings, location of exits, placement of equipment, and types of equipment were discussed as they related to school library planning in general and as they related to the pictures being shown. During the morning session the group examined together one elementary, one junior high, and three senior high schools. All of the other sets were seen by small groups during free time.

The fact sheets and comments on the slides follow, along with plans and pictures.

The school librarians attending the Institute recommended that the Committee on Planning School Library Quarters make these sets of slides available for borrowing through the American Library Association Headquarters Library. It was thought that school library workshops, library school classes, and meetings of school librarians, as well as school library supervisors and school administrators who were planning new libraries, might find it valuable to examine the slides. This recommendation has been followed, though it was not possible to duplicate all slides for several sets. The slides will be available on loan from the American Library Association.

MT. ROYAL ELEMENTARY SCHOOL
Baltimore, Maryland

Statistical Data

Architect: Taylor & Fisher
              Baltimore, Md.
Staff: 1 librarian
Enrollment: 700
Location of library quarters in school: Second floor; middle of wing facing playground, near intermediate classes
Book capacity: 5000
School library quarters:
    Total space: 2016 sq. ft.
        1 Reading room: 1568 sq. ft.
        1 Conference room: 192 sq. ft. (This is separated from work area by counter-height shelving.)
        Workroom: 256 sq. ft.
Type of school: Elementary, grades K-6
Type of community: Baltimore is a large metropolitan community of nearly 1,000,000 population with a large seaport and many industries such as Martin Aircraft, McCormick Spices, and Bethle-hem Steel. The school is located on the fringes of the downtown. Nearby a big redevelopment area has just been completed to house the state offices. Adjacent to this area is an old established community of the younger members of the best social families, who have good educational background and have middle or upper middle incomes. To the north of the school the neighborhood has been deteriorating and most of the families are transients from the South, in the lower economic and social brackets.

Type of student: Predominantly average with many below average and a few above; some students with good cultural family background, but the large transient and Negro group come from underprivileged homes. A few Chinese children.

Type of curriculum: Typical elementary curriculum with consideration for special groups of slow students.

School philosophy: To provide meaningful learning experiences to help the individual child grow and develop to his best potential.

Relation of library to school program: Five-day library service under the guidance of a superior elementary librarian to enrich the curriculum

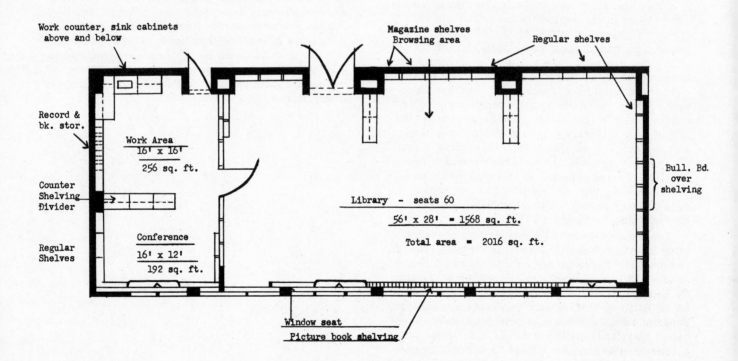

Mt. Royal Elementary School Library
Baltimore, Maryland

and provide books and library materials to meet educational needs and interests of children. Special attention given to developing a wide and varied literature background.

Community library resources: Nearest public library is the main library in the downtown section, which is not easily accessible to these children because of traffic.

Special services and comments: This school opened February, 1959, and has been designated as a pilot school to demonstrate the type of education that could be provided for all elementary children if money were made available to keep class sizes limited to 30 students and to provide all the resource services such as counselors; art, music, and physical education resource teachers; and librarians. The Department of Recreation has provided facilities in the building and administers a recreation program for the community.

Comments

Good features

1. Adequate space
   Reading room and conference area are large enough to work with class groups, work groups, and individuals.

   Work area is adequate, since all book processing and cataloging are taken care of by the central cataloging section of the school library department.

   Shelving will house 5000 to 6000 books or 8 books per pupil. Shelving for 500 more books could be added, if the need arises, by placing island counter-height shelving on other side of entrance and beneath glass partitions in front of conference room.

   There are 2 informal areas with lounge furniture near magazines and the window seat near charging desk.
2. Attractive colors in walls, floors, and a touch of color on chair legs.
3. Adequate bulletin board space.

Suggestions for improvement

1. Need more space to house recordings and maybe additional cabinets for housing filmstrips, since the school will be used as a pilot school. Since the school has been built, it has been decided to house, index, and circulate the school-owned audio-visual materials in the library.
2. Use Venetian blinds instead of window shades (budget prevented supplying these).
3. Either the window sills should be raised (this is an architectual feature, which it is difficult to change) or the "toe kick" of the shelving under the window should be reduced to 2 inches instead of the 4 inches of the standard plan. As the picture book shelves beneath the windows have only $11\frac{1}{2}$ inches between shelves, books larger than 11

inches must be shelved on their sides. Reducing the base would provide an extra inch and be more convenient for shelving picture books.

4. Reduce length of work counter on corridor wall to permit room for housing two vertical files. The original plan did not indicate that the back wall corner would not be flush with the wall, so the standard units were not adapted to the length. As a result one vertical file will have to be located in the reading room.

WATKINS ELEMENTARY SCHOOL
Hollywood, Florida

Statistical Data

Architect: Start & Moeller, Architects
            Hollywood, Fla.
Staff: 1 trained librarian
        1 half-time clerk
Enrollment: 502
Location: First floor, separate building in forefront
    of cluster type school
School library quarters:
    Total space: 1470 sq. ft.
        Reading room, seats 44: 1010 sq. ft.
        Conference room, seats 8: 150 sq. ft.
        Workroom
        Storage room   } 310 sq. ft.
        Librarian's office ⌡
Type of school: Elementary, grades 1-6
Type of community: A very small, newly developed
    incorporated suburban area, having some light
    industry but principally catering to tourist ac-
    tivities. The outline community fringes on a
    large metropolitan area. The population is pre-
    dominately middle to lower economic level.
Type of student: The majority are average students,
    with a few superior and many below average.
Type of curriculum: General fundamentals in ele-
    mentary work with special emphasis for the
    lower and slower learning element.
School philosophy: The object of education in a
    democracy is the fullest development of the in-
    dividual. One of our first aims is to help each
    child make a good adjustment to his group and to
    develop a feeling of "belonging." We are trying
    to develop happy children who are secure, socially
    acceptable, self-confident, independent, and self-
    reliant.
Relation of library to school program: Every student
    is given an opportunity to use the library and is
    encouraged to do so. It is open for circulation
    and group or individual study throughout the
    school day.
Community library resources: The nearest com-
    munity library service is more than 5 miles
    away—the Hollywood Public Library

Comments

Good features

1. Size and location seem desirable for size of
   school.
2. Counter desk in workroom with lower height for
   typewriter should be functional.
3. Workroom well planned.
4. Informal area in library seems attractive.

Suggestions for improvement

1. Backs on all shelving would prove more serv-
   iceable in the long run.
2. Vision panel between workroom and conference
   room would help with supervising space.
3. Table tops seem to reflect too much light. Is
   this effect created in the picture only or are the
   table tops glossy?
4. Are vertical partitions in picture book shelving
   the standard distance apart? Six inches is functional, but new standards may approve 8-inch
   divisions. The slides give the impression that
   the dimensions are rather wide.
5. Table with plastic top and draperies create a
   "luncheon room" appearance in the conference
   room. More informal furniture and plain draperies might have avoided this look.

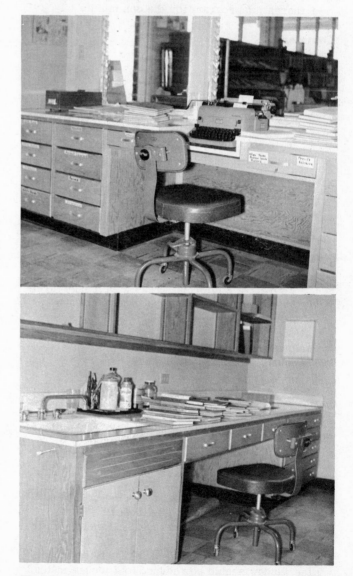

Watkins Elementary School Library, Hollywood, Florida
Desk counter with file drawers, lowered for typewriter
Work counter with poster drawers and supply cabinet

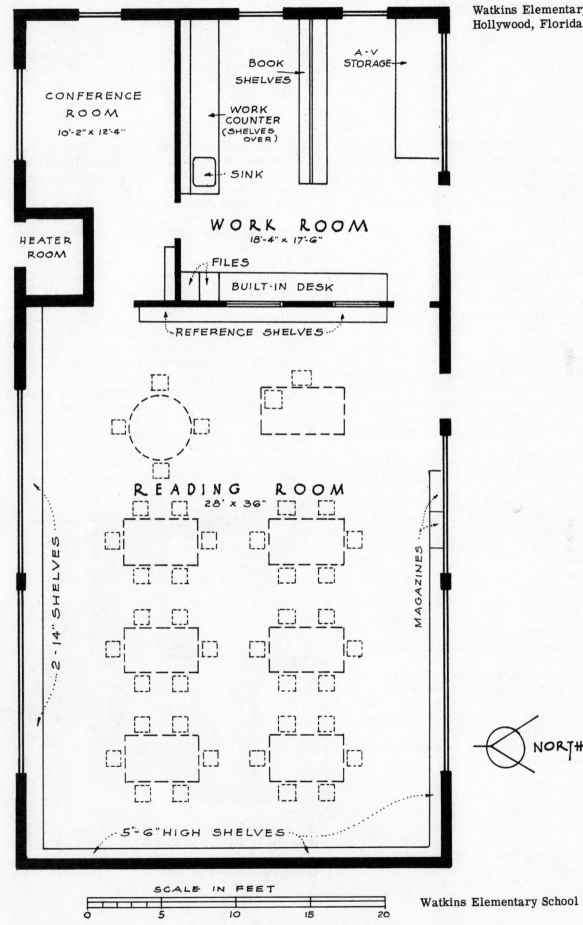

CONFERENCE ROOM
10'-2" x 12'-4"

BOOK SHELVES

A-V STORAGE

WORK COUNTER (SHELVES OVER)

SINK

HEATER ROOM

WORK ROOM
18'-4" x 17'-6"

FILES

BUILT-IN DESK

REFERENCE SHELVES

READING ROOM
28' x 36"

2-14" SHELVES

MAGAZINES

NORTH

5'-6" HIGH SHELVES

SCALE IN FEET

0   5   10   15   20

JUDSON JUNIOR HIGH SCHOOL
Salem, Oregon

Statistical Data

Architect: William I. Williams
             Salem, Ore.
Staff: 1 trained librarian
      3 hours paid student help daily
      Processing of orders and cataloging done at
        central library office
Enrollment: 860; next year 1000
Location: Front of one-story building, near student
    lobby and office area
School library quarters:
    Total space: 3996 sq. ft.
      Reading room: 2080 sq. ft.
      Conference and A-V preview room: 150 sq. ft.
      Workroom and storage: 786 sq. ft.⎫ Can expand in-
      Textbook library: 560 sq. ft.   ⎬ to each other
      Combination office and A-V room: 420 sq. ft.
Type of school: Junior high, grades 7-9
Type of community: Suburban area of middle-class
    residents on northern and southern extremes of
    state capital, located in an agricultural area of
    the state. The city population is 50,000 and school
    district population 75,000 as suburban and rural
    areas are part of the consolidated district.
Type of student: Predominantly average with many
    superior.
Type of curriculum: Typical junior high program of
    instruction with block classes for English and
    social studies.
School philosophy: In general to meet the needs of
    the early adolescent and to prepare him for his
    senior high school years. The guidance program
    provides the basis for individualization in this
    school program.
Relation of library to school program: The library
    is definitely the heart and the core of the in-
    structional program. This has become more
    evident in these new schools, where the librar-
    ians have also become responsible for audio-
    visual materials, which come from the central
    A-V library.
Community library resources: Within the city
    limits are the city library and the state library
    from which suburban patrons may borrow; how-
    ever, neither branch nor bookmobile service is
    near these schools. The school librarians sup-
    plement their collections by borrowing from the
    state library.

Comments

Good features

1. High ceiling gives a spacious look to room with
   no low windows.

2. Cork bulletin boards above shelving provide
   space for informative labeling and attractive
   bulletin displays.
3. Storage facilities for audio-visual equipment
   should encourage efficient housing and handling.
4. Slot for returning books into depressible book
   truck from outside corridor may have advantages.

Suggestions for improvement

1. No windows at eye level to effect a feeling of
   openness of room. A school superintendent believes that one wall should have had low windows to permit view of outside.
2. An architect recommended more light be thrown
   on the ceiling than is given by the type of lighting
   provided—slides may not show the effectiveness
   of lighting.
3. With bulletin space over high shelves is there
   need for much additional bulletin space? Librarians seeing the slides differed on total
   amount of bulletin board space needed in a
   library.
4. A school superintendent thought the stalls for
   A-V equipment unnecessary, but some librarians liked the arrangement (see pictures).
5. If the librarian is in charge of textbook library,
   the Institute participants were opposed to making
   this a librarian's responsibility. School superintendent was against it, too.
6. Total space is a bit cramped for serving 1000
   students. No library classroom provided. Since
   library serves as a materials center, possibly
   more space over-all would be desirable.

Judson Junior High School Library, Salem, Oregon
A-V storage—shelving, cabinet, space for projectors;
work counter; depressible book truck for return of books
through corridor slot

Judson Junior High School Library
Salem, Oregon

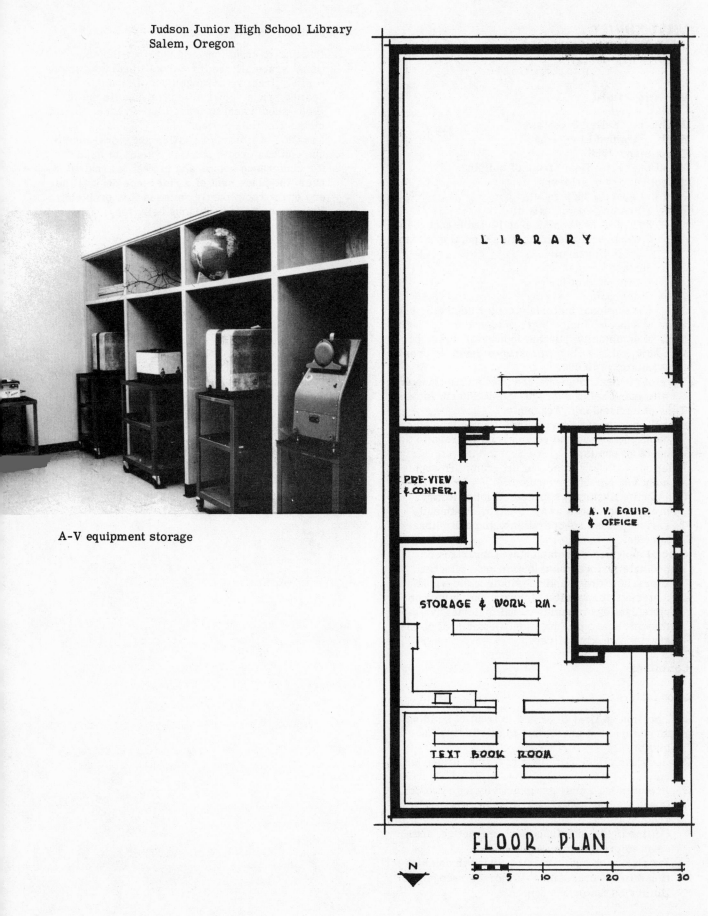

A-V equipment storage

L I B R A R Y

PRE-VIEW
& CONFER.

A. V. EQUIP.
& OFFICE

STORAGE & WORK RM.

TEXT BOOK ROOM

FLOOR PLAN

N

0   5   10   20   30

WEST KINNEY
JUNIOR HIGH SCHOOL
Newark, New Jersey

Statistical Data

Architect: Kelley & Gruzen
Staff: 2 trained librarians
Enrollment: 1388
Location: First floor, front of building
School library quarters:
    Total space: 3625 sq. ft.
      1 Reading room seats 48
      2 Conference rooms seat 12 and 6 each
      1 Workroom accommodates 6 pupil assistants
        plus librarian
      Storage room
      Librarian's office
      Classroom
      Instructional materials center seats 20
Type of school: Junior high, grades 7-9
Type of community: Urban, industrial, lower eco-
    nomic, middle class; housing-project children.
    Population 450,000.
Type of student: Students are predominantly average
    with many below average. Some Puerto Ricans.
Type of curriculum: Academic.
School philosophy: Curriculum, though labeled aca-
    demic, has shop and commercial courses to suit
    needs of pupils.
Relation of library to school program: To supple-
    ment and enrich curriculum.
Community library resources: Public library
    branch two blocks away. Nearby bookmobile
    service; close co-operation with public library
    service.
Special services or comments: Librarians co-
    ordinate textbook distribution and collection.
    Librarians order and distribute audio-visual
    materials for faculty. Library maintains com-
    plete catalogs of audio-visual material available
    through Board of Education, Department of Li-
    braries, weekly delivery.

Comments

Good features

1. Location on first floor and in front of building
    should make it accessible to all students (see
    plan).
2. Good use of color in floor covering, draperies,
    etc.
3. Provides for small group activity with two con-
    ference areas and also a browsing area in
    reading room.
4. Ceiling lights look functional, attractive, and
    seem to provide proper lighting.
5. Provision for audio-visual housing in combina-
    tion office-workroom-A-V storage recognizes
    library as materials center.

Suggestions for improvement

1. Reading room is long and narrow—the conven-
    tional space alloted for school libraries, which
    limits attractive arrangement of space.
2. Seating space very limited for enrollment of
    1388—should seat at least 100. Present seating
    means limited service.
3. Location of librarian's office and workroom at
    one end can create some problems of supervision
    for conference rooms and browsing area. How-
    ever, the placement of a reference desk at the
    end of the room partly relieves this problem.
    Having two librarians does help, too.

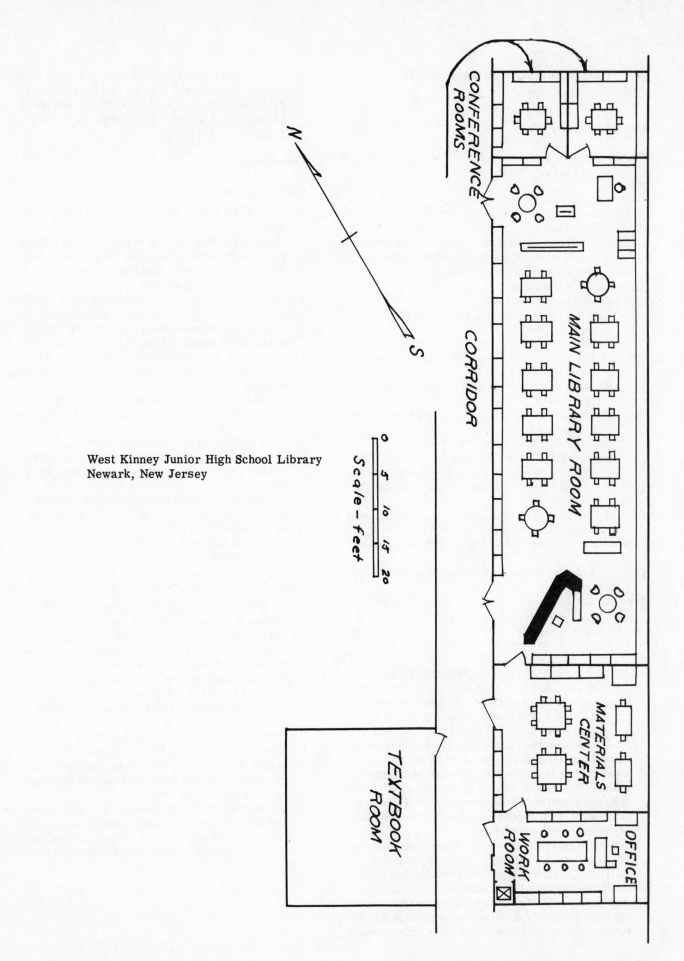

West Kinney Junior High School Library
Newark, New Jersey

Scale – feet

CONFERENCE ROOMS

CORRIDOR

MAIN LIBRARY ROOM

MATERIALS CENTER

TEXTBOOK ROOM

WORK ROOM

OFFICE

WOODROW WILSON HIGH SCHOOL
Tacoma, Washington

Statistical Data

Architect: Lea, Pearson & Richards
Tacoma, Wash.
Staff:
Number of trained librarians: 1
Number of clerks: $\frac{1}{2}$
Enrollment: 1400
Location of library quarters: Library is at center of two classroom wings and directly connected with the administration building
School library quarters:
Total space: 6000 sq. ft.
Reading room: 3500 sq. ft. (50' x 70'), plus alcove space
Conference rooms: 745 sq. ft. (one double 16' x 36' divided by folding door; one, faculty, 13' x 13')
Workroom, combined with office: 312 sq. ft. (13' x 24')
Storage room: 330 sq. ft. (11' x 30' magazine stackroom)
Classroom: 720 sq. ft. (24' x 30')
Audio-visual facilities: 169 sq. ft. (13' x 13' double conference room used for films)
Type of school: Senior high, grades 10-12, campus type building
Type of community: Urban, industrial; fishing, outdoor recreation, and beach areas are close by; middle and upper middle class; 160,000 population.
Type of student: Predominantly average with many superior.
Type of curriculum: Comprehensive high school, offering largely academic and general program with opportunity for commercial courses. Technical training is given for the most part at a separate vocational school.
School philosophy: To provide opportunity for students to develop their aptitudes in proportion to their capabilities and drive. To provide exploratory and high achievement environment for all.
Relation of library to school program: The school library serves the curriculum needs of the school and provides materials for enrichment and to meet the needs or special interests of the individual. The school library program is planned to help students learn how to use library facilities and materials independently and to develop skill in careful research work.
Community library resources: Fine public library service at central library. Co-operation is excellent. There will be a new branch a few blocks from the school within a year.
Special services or comments: The librarian does not have charge of A-V, but some classes are scheduled to view films in the double conference room. The librarian is building a record collection for English and foreign language classes. There is a district A-V department, but the librarian will buy some filmstrips for social studies.

Comments

Good features

1. Central location and attractive entrance (see plan).
2. Open, airy, and inviting appearance of reading room with outdoor view and patio at one end.
3. Facilities and space adequate for seating 140, or 10 per cent of enrollment.
4. Recognition that school library service provides books and audio-visual materials to enrich and supplement educational program. Provisions for space for student and faculty conference needs, classroom for instruction in library skills, listening room, previewing room, and magazine storage.
5. Folding doors in conference area provide space for small groups and for expansion to take care of larger groups.
6. Good ceiling lights—attractive and effective.
7. Placement of reference materials in counter-height shelving between columns makes columns functional and incorporates them in space arrangement. Treatment of columns provides contrast of materials and adds to attractive appearance of room.
8. Plain flooring without pattern adds to feeling of spaciousness.

Suggestions for improvement

1. No outside light in conference rooms. When folding doors are drawn to create two rooms, the space may feel closed in. The ceiling illumination may help to reduce this feeling. The use of this area for seeing films may require less light. Closed area may lead to some supervision problems. Vision panels into the library would facilitate supervision, and dark draperies could be used for film showing.
2. Only two shelving sections for magazines are shown. Is this adequate for magazine needs in a school this size? Is the magazine room supposed to provide current magazines for general use in addition to back issues?
3. Doors from magazine room to library classroom and conference room seem remote from circulation desk and supervision. Would placement of doors nearer to reading room have been possible?

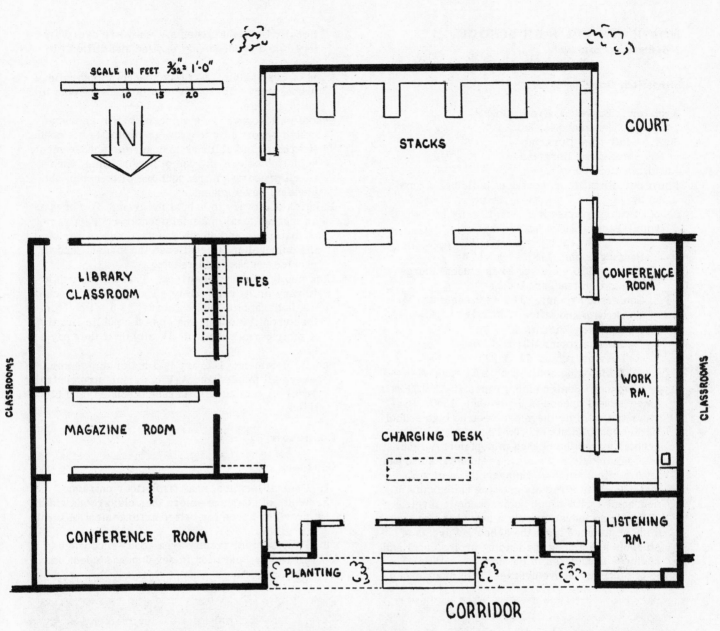

SCALE IN FEET $\frac{3}{32}$" = 1'-0"

5   10   15   20

N

COURT

STACKS

LIBRARY CLASSROOM

FILES

CONFERENCE ROOM

CLASSROOMS

MAGAZINE ROOM

WORK RM.

CHARGING DESK

CLASSROOMS

CONFERENCE ROOM

LISTENING RM.

PLANTING

CORRIDOR

Woodrow Wilson High School Library
Tacoma, Washington

NORTH CENTRAL HIGH SCHOOL
Indianapolis, Indiana

Statistical Data

Architect: Everett I. Brown Co.
      Indianapolis, Ind.
Staff: 1 full-time librarian
     1 half-time librarian
Enrollment: 1400
Location: First floor, center of building, off main lobby
School library quarters:
  Total space: 118' 6" x 46' 6"
              seating capacity: 146
    Reading room: 118' 6" x 32' 6"
      seats 120 including 24 in student lounge and 8 in teachers lounge
    Conference room: 13' x 15'; seats 8
    Workroom and office: 13' x 15'
    Audio-visual facilities:
      Storage room: 12' x 13'
      Preview room: 13' x 23'
      3 Listening booths: 4' x 7' each
Type of school: Senior high, grades 10-12. This is a new school opened in September, 1956. Previous to this time there had been no high school in this school district. Two new junior high schools were also opened in September, 1956.
Type of community: Wealthy, residential suburban area 5 miles north of Indianapolis, a city of 500,000. It is a rapidly growing community of new homes with a high socioeconomic level. There is no industry—only a new shopping center a short distance from the school. Parents of students are among the leading professional and business executives in the city.
Type of student: Above average, with many exceptionally brilliant students. Many are overprivileged, and consequently spoiled and difficult to discipline.
Type of curriculum: Largely academic and college preparatory. 75-90 per cent of students plan to go to college.
School philosophy: To give each student an unexcelled opportunity to grow according to his needs, interests, and abilities in academic achievement, social poise, worthy use of leisure time, vocational preparation, responsible citizenship, and physical development.
Relation of library to school program: To serve as an instructional materials center where a variety of materials and media are available to enrich the curriculum, to challenge the student, and to provide recreational reading.
Community library resources: There is no public library in the community. The nearest branch of the Indianapolis Public Library is 5 miles from the school. Students may use the public library if their parents work in the city or if they pay a fee.
Special comment: Library is a materials center, where all printed and A-V materials are centrally ordered, cataloged, processed, housed, and circulated.

Comments

Good features

1. Central location, near first-floor entrance.
2. Width of quarters—more than classroom width—provides space for better arrangement of furniture, etc.
3. Provision for faculty area good—encourages closer co-operation in developing student use of library.

North Central High School Library
Indianapolis, Indiana
Charging desk and stacks

North Central High School Library
Indianapolis, Indiana
Listening booths, workroom, conference room, and teachers' lounge in background

4. Placement of stack area behind charging desk and use of counter-height shelving make supervision and service more efficient and helps to prevent closed-in look.
5. Use of glass paneling between reading room, office, and conference rooms makes supervision easier.
6. Provision for audio-visual service good—3 listening booths, space for housing audio-visual machines on carts, previewing room, special catalogs for indexing filmstrips and slides, storage cabinets, and work counter with sink.
7. Multiuse of conference room for magazines in addition to books has some advantages.
8. Use of file boxes and open shelves for storage of magazines in stack area makes them accessible.
9. Provision of index table for reference use should be practical.
10. Pegboard for bulletins.

Suggestions for improvement

1. Long rows of tables monotonous and give crowded appearance.
2. Wall space for placement of card catalog and index file for filmstrips and slides might have prevented the crowded look. Slides give impression of clutter and obstruction of view for supervision by one librarian.

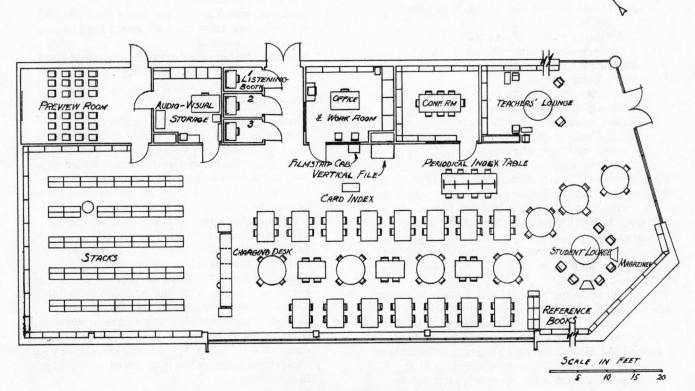

North Central High School Library
Indianapolis, Indiana

MYERS PARK HIGH SCHOOL
Charlotte, North Carolina

Statistical Data

Architect: J. N. Pease & Co.
Staff: 2 trained librarians
Enrollment: 1222
Location: First floor, Language Arts Building,
  center of campus
Book collection: 8032 vols.
School library quarters:
  Total space: approximately 9000 sq. ft. (incl.
    mezzanine)
    Reading room (total): 5207 sq. ft.
      Left wing: 2360 sq. ft.
      Right wing: 2847 sq. ft.
    Mezzanine (low stacks and reading area):
      1812 sq. ft.
    Downstairs stack: 288 sq. ft.
    3 Conference rooms: 120 sq. ft. each
    Librarian's office: 120 sq. ft.
    Workroom: 216 sq. ft.
    Storage room: 240 sq. ft.
    3 Listening booths: 32 sq. ft. each
    Audio-visual (total): 609 sq. ft.
      Machine storage: 180 sq. ft.
      Rec. and film storage: 45 sq. ft.
      Previewing room: 348 sq. ft.
Type of school: Senior high, grades 10-12
Type of community: Upper middle class, urban area,
  in a city of approximately 200,000 people. The
  school is located in a residential community on
  the southern edge of the city limits.
Type of student: Predominantly average with many
  superior; 90 per cent of the 1958 senior class
  entered college.
Type of curriculum: General and college academic.
School philosophy: To help each child develop to his
  fullest potential, taking into account his interests,
  abilities, and life goals.
Relation of library to school program: The library
  is the instructional center of the school. It
  serves as a source for research, curriculum
  enrichment, and recreational reading. The
  librarians guide the reading of pupils, give instruction in the use of the library, and work with
  class groups in the use of the library materials.
Community library resources: Public library is
  accessible to all students. A branch of the public
  library is centrally located in the school district.
Special services or comments: The library was
  planned for a 2000 pupil, campus type, senior high
  school. Until this school year it has served as a
  junior, senior high school. A junior high school
  has been built on adjacent campus, and we expect
  the senior high to grow to its 2000 pupil capacity.
  The mezzanine floor is over the office, workroom,
  periodical storage, and audio-visual rooms. It
  was provided to give room for growth of the
  library.

Comments

Good features

1. Central location for campus type school near
   language arts classrooms.
2. Attractive seating with view of outdoors. Use of
   glass walls around doors adds to outdoor setting
   and creates a pleasant atmosphere inside library.
3. Spacious quarters to provide ample opportunities
   to serve students and teachers with enrichment
   and supplementary materials including audio-
   visual materials. Ample space for books and
   magazines. Room for growth of collections
   within present quarters.
4. Placement of charging desk to serve both entrances and for good supervision of most areas
   including mezzanine.
5. Browsing space around fireplace most inviting.
6. High windows allow for wall space for high
   shelving on one wall.
7. Adequate storage facilities for periodicals and
   audio-visual equipment and service.

Suggestions for improvement

1. Floor pattern gives a "busy" look.
2. Mezzanine, no doubt, can serve dual role—as
   library classroom space for instruction and as
   reading area for large enrollment. Would separate classroom be more desirable?
3. Can two librarians supervise and serve all these
   separate areas? Some hidden spots not visible
   from charging desk—sections of bookstacks,
   parts of storage room, materials storage room,
   and A-V room. Should consideration have been
   given to vision panels for some of these?
4. Consideration might have been given to one large
   conference room, with folding doors to divide
   area when smaller conference rooms were
   needed. The mezzanine might have areas which
   could serve as conference areas and be under
   supervision. The A-V room might be used as a
   conference room, when it is not being used for
   film showings.

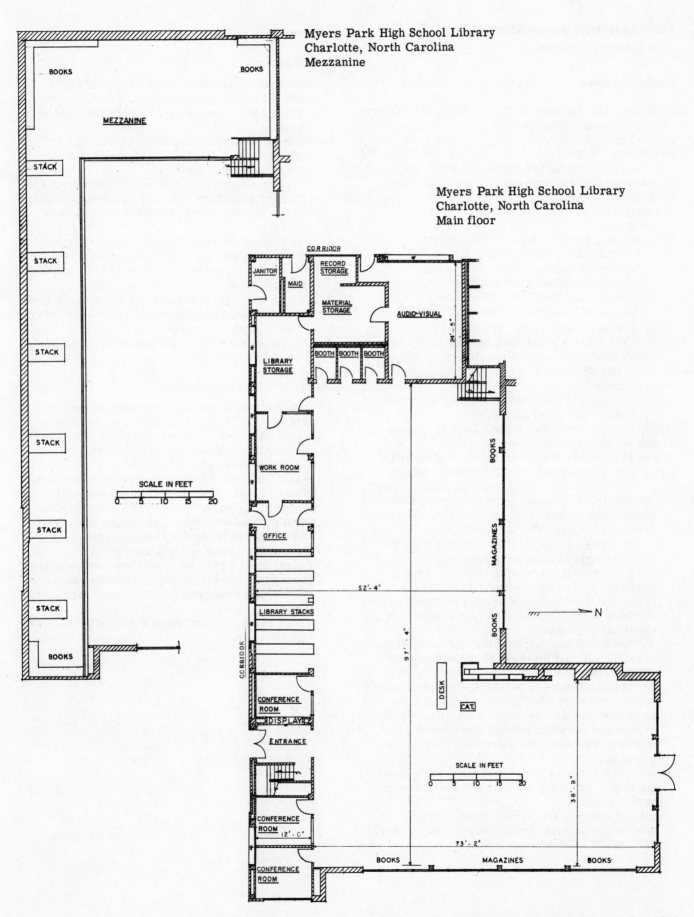

Myers Park High School Library
Charlotte, North Carolina
Mezzanine

Myers Park High School Library
Charlotte, North Carolina
Main floor

EAST LANSING HIGH SCHOOL
East Lansing, Michigan

Statistical Data

Architect: Warren Holmes Co., Malcolm M. Williams
Lansing, Mich.
Staff: 1 trained librarian
Enrollment: 823
Location: Central part of English language class-
room section with room for 1 wing expansion
Book capacity: 12,260
School library quarters:
Total space:
Reading room or rooms: 1937 sq. ft.
3 Conference rooms: 496 sq. ft.
Workroom-storage room: 413 sq. ft.
Librarian's office: 270 sq. ft.
Audio-visual facilities: 225 sq. ft.
Teachers' curriculum library: 300 sq. ft.
Type of school: Senior high, grades 9-12
Type of community: Suburban, upper middle class,
university town—home of Michigan State Univer-
sity. Population of city is 20,000 without M.S.U.
population.
Type of student: Predominantly average with many
superior; many able, not genius.
Type of curriculum: Academic. Library science
offered with academic credit.
School philosophy: Education begins at birth and
continues throughout life. It involves helping
people to grow physically, mentally, socially, and
spiritually. The school provides a framework
which seeks to make this growth continuous in its
duration and positive in its direction.
The school program offers opportunities for
boys and girls to understand themselves. One of
its main aims is the building of skills, such as
reading, writing, comprehending number concepts, and objective thinking. All phases of school
life seek to promote the constructive growth of
individual personality.
The school has responsibility for leadership
in the educational process. With the home and
other social institutions, it helps mold the basic
habits and attitudes of the child. The community
looks to the school for the impartial and non-
sectarian education of all its youth. Our society
expects the school to provide experiences which
will help boys and girls understand the American
way of life.
Relation of library to school program: Enrichment
materials center for students and staff. Integral
part of program.
Community library resources: Public library,
bookmobile service, county library, state library,
Michigan State University library.

Comments

Good features

1. Placement of teachers' curriculum library in
library quarters should help to develop teacher-
librarian teamwork in promoting student use of
library.
2. Location of library in relation to language arts
classrooms and provision for expansion of library space seem good.
3. Corridor display case and use of intervening wall
space for placement of poster file drawers under
library bulletin board show imaginative use of
space.
4. Use of glass paneling between office, curriculum
library, and reading room aids supervision.
5. Storage facilities for "pixmobiles" in A-V room
seem practical.
6. Folding doors provide for three small conference
rooms or one large conference space—flexibility
of space good.
7. Plain floor covering important when space is
limited to narrow width.

Suggestions for improvement

1. Use of conventional long narrow plan limits arrangement. The slight angle for office, workroom, etc., does little to relieve this (see plan).
2. No classroom space for library instruction.
3. Too much floor space is utilized by counter-
height shelving. Space is needed for tables and
chairs to seat 10 per cent of enrollment—90
students. Using some of the space in a narrow
room for shelving running the length of the room
and crosswise leads to a cluttered look.
4. No backs in counter-height shelving.
5. Access to A-V storage room from library reading
room a bit remote. Would there be any advantage
to reversing this room with teachers' curriculum
library?
6. Vision panel into workroom would help to supervise the area.

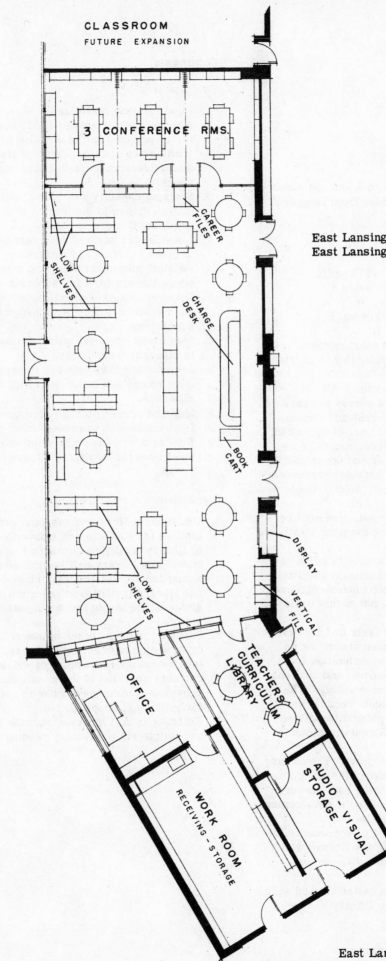

CLASSROOM
FUTURE EXPANSION

3 CONFERENCE RMS.

CAREER FILES

LOW SHELVES

CHARGE DESK

BOOK CART

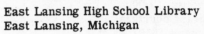

East Lansing High School Library
East Lansing, Michigan

DISPLAY

VERTICAL FILE

LOW SHELVES

OFFICE

TEACHERS CURRICULUM LIBRARY

WORK ROOM
RECEIVING - STORAGE

AUDIO - VISUAL STORAGE

ESCAMBIA HIGH SCHOOL
Pensacola, Florida

Statistical Data

Architect: Frank J. Sindelar
Pensacola, Fla.
Staff: 2 trained librarians
Enrollment: 1900
Location: First floor, adjacent to foyer and administrative suite, across corridor from language arts and social studies wing
Book capacity: 15,000
School library quarters:
Total space: 6181 sq. ft.
Reading area, seats 156: 4877 sq. ft.
2 Conference rooms, each seats 8
224 sq. ft. each: 448 sq. ft.
Work-storage area: 494-384 sq. ft.
Office area: 130-240 sq. ft.
Audio-visual preview and storage room, including 2 listening booths, 18 1/3 sq. ft. each: 232 sq. ft.
Type of school: Senior high, grades 9-12
Type of community: The school serves primarily a suburban community. While evidence is somewhat inconclusive in the first year of operation, there is an indication of a slight bimodal economic distribution, with lower and upper middle economic groups having the heaviest representation. There are approximately 50,000 people in the area served by this institution.
Type of student: Students are predominantly average, with large navy facilities creating a rather sizable transient group.
Type of curriculum: The curriculum is being developed and evaluated with particular emphasis on general education with both commercial and academic programs growing out of this basic course of study.
School philosophy: The faculty feels that its basic responsibility is to accept each student as an individual, provide for him opportunities for satisfactory learning experiences, and challenge him to accomplish as much as possible. The faculty desires that each student become increasingly competent at weighing alternatives involved and at making intelligent decisions in light of these alternatives.
Relation of library to school program: The library must serve as an integral part of the institution's instructional program, providing both resource materials and the laboratory for the development of social science research skills.
Community library resources: The community has access to the services of the city library which is somewhat limited in its facilities and resources.
Special comment: Audio-visual materials and equipment are circulated from the library as are printed materials.

Comments

Good features

1. Good location (see plan).
2. Reading room provides fairly adequate seating for 10 per cent of the enrollment of 1900. Width gives spacious atmosphere and permits attractive arrangement of furniture and special areas.
3. Shelving capacity will house approximately 8 books per pupil. Additional shelving space is available if more is needed.
4. Location of charging desk serves both entrances, is close to office and workroom, will encourage efficient administration, and commands view of whole library for easy supervision.
5. Grouping together of office, workroom, A-V rooms, and charging area expedites service and supervision.
6. Two browsing areas with informal furniture add to pleasant atmosphere.
7. Jalousie windows between library and conference rooms and office help with ventilation in all areas.
8. Map and screen storage arrangement is efficient.
9. Desk counter in workroom most practical.
10. Folding doors for conference rooms help to meet need for two small groups or one large group.

Suggestions for improvement

1. Omission of library classroom reduces opportunities for class instruction with easy access to library facilities to practice use under guidance. The library will be limited in performing a dual function of helping a class to learn how to use library facilities at the same time individual students are in library during study hall periods, etc.
2. Storage for back issues of magazines inadequate for a senior high school this size, particularly if this school operates as a materials center. The cabinets provided in the workroom must also provide space for new books in process, books for rebinding, supplies, etc.
3. Entrance to A-V preview room is not readily accessible via the library reading room.

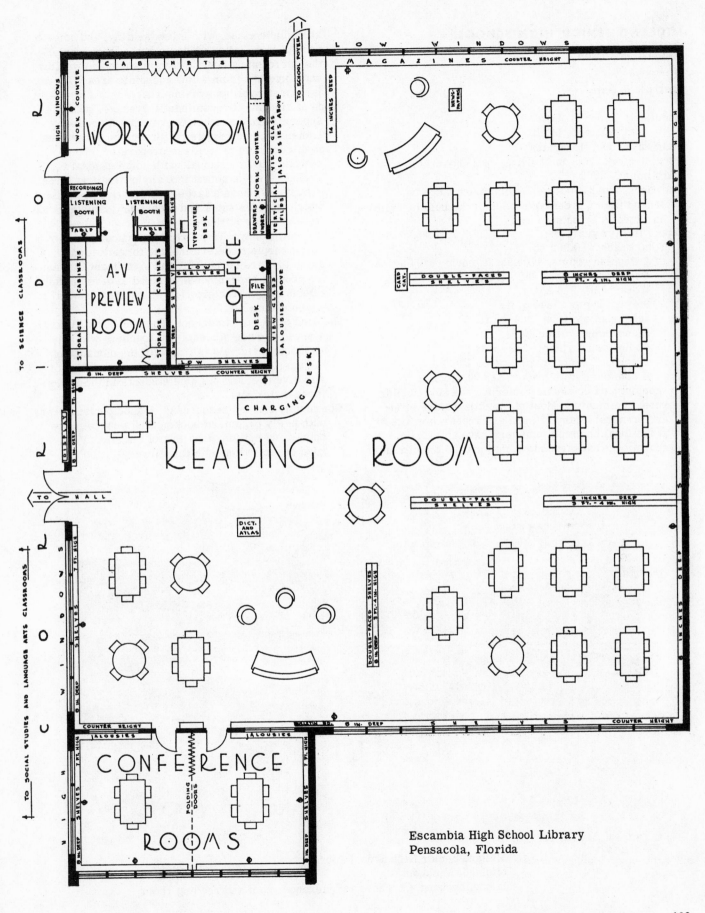

Escambia High School Library
Pensacola, Florida

MIDLAND SENIOR HIGH SCHOOL

Midland, Michigan

Statistical Data

Architect: Alden B. Dow
          Midland, Mich.
Staff: 2 trained librarians
      2 clerks (co-op students—half-day each)
Enrollment: 2000
Location: Third-floor center (main entrance on
   second floor), a center section of the building with
   no windows or outside walls
School library quarters:
   Total space: 10,962 sq. ft.
      2 Reading rooms, 4704 sq. ft. each: 9408 sq. ft.
      Conference room: 240 sq. ft.
      Workroom: 385 sq. ft.
      Storage room: 784 sq. ft.
      Librarian's office: 280 sq. ft.
      Classroom: 784 sq. ft.
      Audio-visual room: 385 sq. ft.
Type of school: Senior high, grades 10-12
Type of community: A town of 31,500 which is the
   shopping and economic center for the surrounding
   rural community. Most of the citizens are property owners. Many of them are research workers
   at the local chemical plant and have an excellent
   educational background. A majority of the citizens

are middle class, with a few wealthy, and some
very poor. Tuition students come from most of
the surrounding county. Again some are wealthy,
and some are from a low economic area. There
is no metropolitan area nearby.
Type of student: Predominantly average, with a few
   superior and some below average. Very few
   transients, and very few with foreign background.
Type of curriculum: College preparatory, commercial, and vocational, with some general for
   students who do not fit into any of the first three
   groups. We have a large co-operative program
   which includes sales and laboratory assistants as
   well as office workers.
School philosophy: To provide opportunities for
   young people to determine and to work toward
   goals that are purposeful and significant to them.
   To provide experiences designed to develop their
   talents and characteristics which are essential to
   a wholesome life.
Relation of library to school program: The library
   aims to provide students and teachers with enrichment materials in line with the demands of
   the curriculum, to organize these materials for
   effective use, and to guide students in the use of
   these materials.
Community library resources: A good public library
   with newly organized bookmobile service to the
   county and outlying sections of the city. Very
   good co-operation with this library. Also can

Midland Senior High School Library
Midland, Michigan
Lobby, showing entrances to reference room and reading room

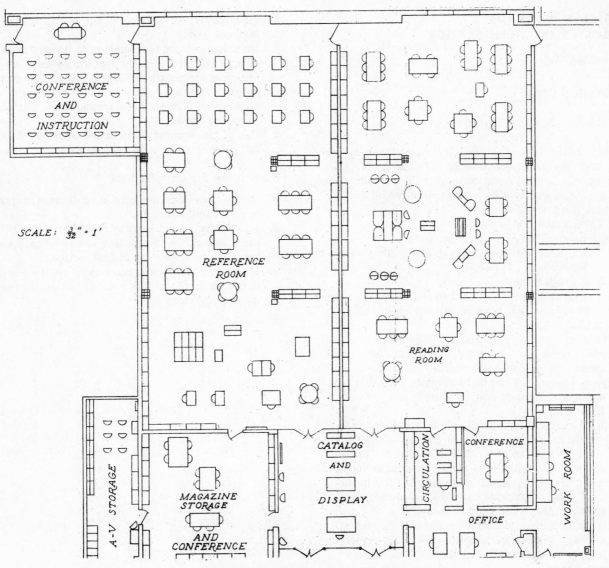

SCALE: $\frac{3}{32}$" = 1'

CONFERENCE AND INSTRUCTION

REFERENCE ROOM

READING ROOM

A-V STORAGE

MAGAZINE STORAGE AND CONFERENCE

CATALOG AND DISPLAY

CIRCULATION

CONFERENCE

OFFICE

WORK ROOM

Midland Senior High School Library
Midland, Michigan

borrow from the state library and from the extension service department of the state university library, and get good service from both.

Comments

Good features

1. Extensive quarters for serving as a reading center and a materials center.
2. Attractive in color and spacing.
3. An architect thinks that for a library without windows it has been planned well to give a feeling of light and spaciousness, achieved through the use of glass in dividing areas, pleasing colors, a floor covering without patterns, and an effective ceiling illumination.
4. Use of brick brings in another material in place of plaster for some walls in special areas. This

gives variety and relief, makes the area attractive and interesting, and shows imagination.
5. Grouping office, workroom, conference, and circulation areas at entrance expedites service and reduces footwork for library personnel.
6. Attractive informal area around magazine shelving should encourage recreational reading.

Suggestions for improvement

1. More librarians are needed to serve students using this much space.
2. How are exits for conference and instruction room and rear of reading room controlled?
3. Are closed metal cabinets the most satisfactory way for storing back issues of magazines? Are these cabinets old equipment? Open storage shelving and magazine filing boxes would provide easier access to magazines.

WILLIAM E. GRADY
VOCATIONAL HIGH SCHOOL

Brooklyn, New York

Statistical Data

Architect: Joseph Blumenkranz
     New York, N. Y.
Staff: 2 trained librarians full time; 1 three days a
 week while library is being organized
Location: Central location on third floor near class-
 rooms, directly above administrative offices
School library quarters:
 Total space: 4457 sq. ft.
  Reading room, seats 102: 3144 sq. ft.
  2 Conference rooms, each seats 20: 336 sq. ft.
  Workroom: 247 sq. ft.
  Storage room: 540 sq. ft.
  Librarian's office: 190 sq. ft.
Type of school: All boys vocational senior high,
 grades 9-12
Type of community: Half are middle class and half
 come from a low socioeconomic level in a large
 urban city of 7,900,000 people.
Type of student: Terminal education for most stu-
 dents who already hold part-time jobs. Average
 IQ is 90.
Type of curriculum: Emphasis on technical and
 vocational training. Half of day is devoted to shop
 subjects and the other half to academic (English
 and social studies) and related technical subjects.
School philosophy: To provide training for industrial jobs, to provide for personal development,
 and to prepare for good citizenship.
Relation of school to library program: Serves all
 areas of the school program and helps students
 to become independent in their use of library
 resources.
Community library resources: Good co-operation
 between public and school library. Students use
 public libraries near their homes.
Special comment: Library serves all areas of the
 school program with an especially strong book
 and pamphlet collection in the trade areas. Excellent co-operation among administration, subject departments, and library strengthens the
 active program in library instruction in which
 both academic and trade departments participate.

Comments

Good features

1. Width, greater than classroom width, gives a
   more spacious appearance (see plan).
2. Library classroom encourages instruction in
   use of library without competing with individual
   use. Dual use as visual instruction room advantageous use of space.
3. Separate enclosed space for briefcases and

students' books decreases use of library for
textbook study.
4. Planning recognizes function of library in modern
   educational program by providing space for conferences for small and large groups (accordion
   doors), work space, separate storage room, and
   librarian's office. Also arrangement provides
   browsing area.
5. Use of glass curtains in office provides means
   for privacy when it is necessary.

Suggestions for improvement

1. Third-floor location may have disadvantages for
   use by some students.
2. No entrance from library classroom into library
   for easy access to practice use of library under
   guidance as follow-up of instruction.
3. Is it important in a large city to restrict access
   to stackroom? Is this related to special need
   for supervision?

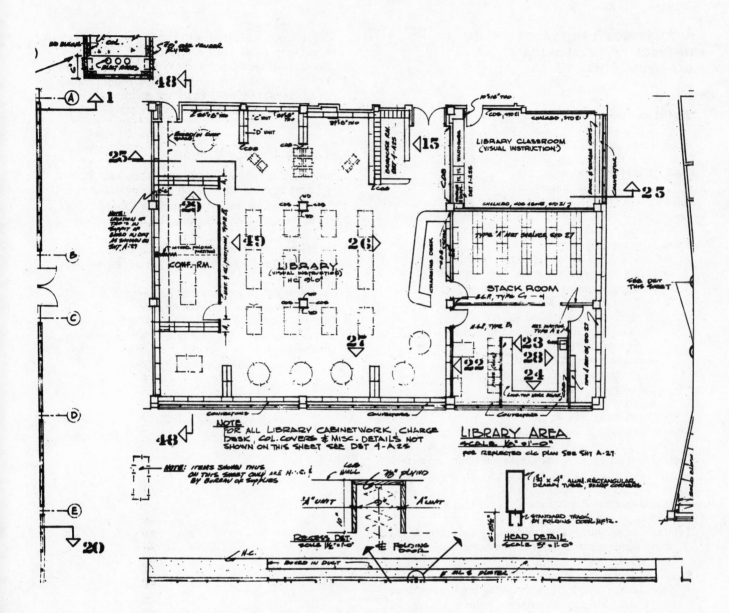

William E. Grady Vocational High School Library
Brooklyn, New York

P. K. YONGE LABORATORY SCHOOL
UNIVERSITY OF FLORIDA
Gainesville, Florida

Statistical Data

Architect: Goin & Moore
    Gainesville, Fla.
Staff: 2 trained librarians
   2 college assistants (paid)
Enrollment: 960 (420 elem., 540 sec.)
Location: Single building centrally located between
 elementary and secondary classrooms
School library quarters:
 Total space: 6164 sq. ft. (rest room, janitor's
  closet, and closet in office not included below)
  Reading room or rooms: 1446 sq. ft. in elem.;
   2150 sq. ft. in sec.
  Conference room: 550 sq. ft.
  Workroom: 200 sq. ft.; combined with li-
   brarian's office
  Storage room: 230 sq. ft.
  Librarian's office: see Workroom
  Classroom: none
  Audio-visual facilities: 690 sq. ft.
  Corridors: 386 sq. ft.
Type of school: A department of the College of
 Education, University of Florida, grades K-12
Type of community: Urban, upper middle, univer-
 sity town in an agricultural area; 50,000 popula-
 tion including 12,000 university students.
Type of student: Predominantly average; some
 foreign students.
Type of curriculum: Comprehensive (academic,
 home economics, industrial arts, business education, and music).
School philosophy: To provide the best education
 possible for children by fostering pupil growth in
 skills and abilities, knowledge, values, health,
 creativeness, and self-direction.
Relation of library to school program: An integral
 part of the school, providing many materials of
 instruction for the implementation of the curriculum and for service to students and faculty.
Community library resources: Public library, one
 bookmobile, state extension division, university
 library with 10 branches.
Special services or comments: Students are permitted to use the facilities of the university
 library and its branches.

Comments

Good features

1. Central location. Attractive decoration, including
 expanse of glass on outside wall, creates inviting
 appearance.
2. Planning of two separate areas for use of elementary and secondary students with dual use of

circulation facilities, work area, and audio-visual
areas practical and economical.
3. Good consideration for all types of audio-visual
 needs including previewing, dark room, maps,
 projectors, storage, and work counter. Also
 personnel assigned to this phase of service important.

Suggestions for improvement

1. Need for more cabinet space along wall in A-V
 center, since audio-visual equipment and use
 seem to be an important service in this school.
2. Is there sufficient shelving for books in both
 rooms?
3. Is there sufficient glass paneling between work
 areas and reading rooms to permit easy supervision?
4. Is there space for housing projectors and audio-
 visual machines in A-V center?
5. Should provision be made for faculty areas in
 these quarters? Is this done elsewhere on the
 campus?

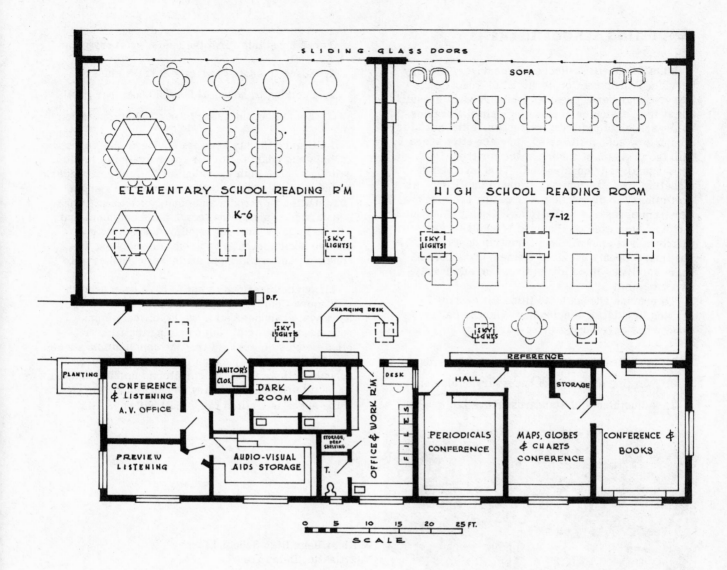

P. K. Yonge Laboratory School Library
University of Florida
Gainesville, Florida

REMODELING SCHOOL LIBRARIES

Miss Elizabeth D. Hodges, supervisor, Library Service, Baltimore County Board of Education, Towson, Maryland, presided and served as consultant at the session on remodeling school libraries.

As school administrators recognize the need for elementary school libraries, they are often faced with the problem of finding space for them in buildings already constructed. This involves remodeling space to achieve adequate facilities. As a preliminary to discussing remodeling problems, a filmstrip developed by Baltimore County, Maryland, for the Committee on Planning School Library Quarters was shown. This filmstrip describes how Baltimore County provided elementary school library facilities in buildings five, ten, and twenty-five years old.

To provide adequate facilities for central libraries in existing elementary schools, Baltimore County has developed a three-part plan:

1. Specifications to meet national standards

2. Working drawings of necessary equipment

3. Adjustments of standards to available space

Three constants form the basis for every plan:

1. Space to seat *at least* the largest class

2. Shelving to house *at least* 5 books per pupil

3. Equipment necessary for efficient operation

Baltimore County uses its standard plan for new schools and adapts it to the space available in old buildings. The plan provides for 25 feet per reader. Included in the standard plan are a library and a combination workroom and conference area. The standard plan shows the location of equipment that will be built in, such as regular, magazine, and picture book shelving; cabinets for supplies, recordings, and filmstrips; and a work counter with sink.

Many combinations of space have been used in Baltimore County—classrooms, storage rooms, hallways, abandoned stair wells, offices, cloakrooms, and so forth. In explaining the filmstrip Miss Hodges pointed out that the *combination* should provide minimum space as indicated above even for schools with as small an enrollment as 250, and that a functioning school library cannot render service if the space is limited to a small hallway. Blue-

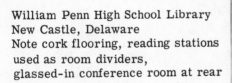

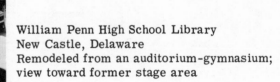

William Penn High School Library
New Castle, Delaware
Remodeled from an auditorium-gymnasium;
view toward former stage area

William Penn High School Library
New Castle, Delaware
Note cork flooring, reading stations
used as room dividers,
glassed-in conference room at rear

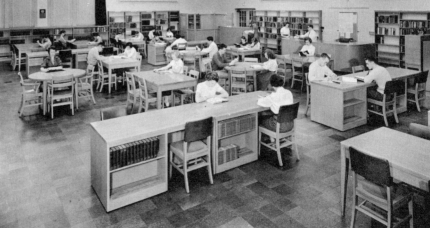

Renton Junior-Senior High School Library
Renton, Washington
Remodeled from a gymnasium

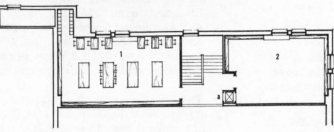

1 FACULTY STUDY
2 LIBRARY CLASS ROOM

MEZZANINE

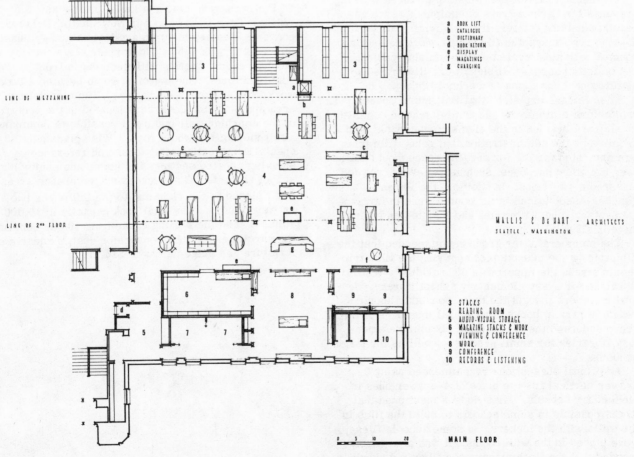

a BOOK LIFT
b CATALOGUE
c DICTIONARY
d BOOK RETURN
e DISPLAY
f MAGAZINES
g CHARGING

LINE OF MEZZANINE

LINE OF 2ND FLOOR

MALLIS & De HART - ARCHITECTS
SEATTLE , WASHINGTON

3 STACKS
4 READING ROOM
5 AUDIO-VISUAL STORAGE
6 MAGAZINE STACKS & WORK
7 VIEWING & CONFERENCE
8 WORK
9 CONFERENCE
10 RECORDS & LISTENING

0   5   10   20   MAIN FLOOR

Renton Junior-Senior High School Library
Renton, Washington

prints and pictures to illustrate the plan in action were shown.

1. One school utilized a stair well for a workroom, and converted a classroom and cloakroom into a reading room.

2. Another school removed the cloakroom partition to create an adequate library reading room with a work space in one corner.

3. A large primary classroom became a library in another school.

4. One school combined two storage rooms and part of a corridor to provide an attractive library.

5. A small office, a cloakroom, and a classroom were combined in one school to form the reading room and library workroom.

6. Another school combined a classroom and conference room to form a library, used the corridor for a display case, and utilized space opposite the corridor for a workroom.

7. By creating a 6-foot archway between two classrooms adequate space was obtained for a library and work space.

The second part of the filmstrip pictured working drawings for various types of equipment, such as regular shelving, picture book shelving, cabinet for housing recordings and filmstrips, work cabinet and counter with sink, coat cupboard, display cabinet, and bulletin boards. All plans were illustrated with pictures of these items in a school library.

Miss Hodges explained that Baltimore County had two factors in its favor: an administration committed to central libraries in the elementary schools, and a promise by the administration that once a librarian was appointed for the library, the space would not be used for other purposes, such as relieving crowded classroom situations. In addition, the Parent-Teacher Associations in the county were in favor of elementary school libraries and insisted on having them in all schools.

The members of the group recommended that the filmstrip or the manual accompanying the filmstrip should stress the importance of providing a trained librarian for every elementary school library. Several members thought the three constants should read: librarian, books, space. All members of the group endorsed the necessity of obtaining elementary libraries for small schools as well as for large schools.

Additional suggestions recommended using 3-drawer vertical files in place of 4-drawer ones in elementary schools. Miss Hodges mentioned that it was possible in some schools to build the files in the walls with the lockers. In some schools files were placed in the workrooms. It was also recommended that the floor plans in the filmstrip should include the area dimensions.

Though time did not permit discussion of secondary remodeling, pictures and blueprints of remodeled libraries were displayed in the meeting room and examined by the Institute participants. The Renton Junior-Senior High School, Renton, Washington, was remodeled from a gymnasium. The blueprint and pictures showed that good planning resulted in an attractive library. The following library facilities were available to 2200 students:

Reading room: 77' x 68'
Library classroom: 20' x 29' (on mezzanine)
Conference room: 19' x 12'
Workroom: 22' x 24'
Periodical room: 24' x 16'
Preview room: 20' x 12'
Listening rooms: 2' x 8'
A-V storage and repair: 13' x 16'
Record storage: 2' x 8'
Faculty study: 20' x 25' (on mezzanine)
Corridor space for storing some equipment

The librarian noted in remarks accompanying the plan that a booklift from the main floor to the mezzanine made it easy to send books to students and faculty using mezzanine rooms. Two librarians and one clerk consider this a successful remodeling situation.

Pictures were also available to show how the William Penn High School in New Castle, Delaware, converted the combination auditorium and gymnasium into a library in 1955. The former stage became a faculty reading section with shelving in front of the stage platform. One dressing room became a large workroom and one a stack area. The circulation area and charging desk were located in the center of the corridor wall making it possible to command a full view of the whole room. Wise placement of special combination study desk and reference shelving created sections for junior and senior high school students. Glass-enclosed conference areas were placed to the right and to the left of the two entrance doors. The total book capacity is 10,000 volumes, and the seating capacity is 10 per cent of the enrollment. Total conversion cost, exclusive of furniture and stage unit, was $16,314.

AN OUTLINE

SOL LEVIN
Assistant Superintendent for Business Affairs
Rampo School District No. 2
Spring Valley, New York

I. Basic preliminary considerations
   A. Know what you want to buy and why
      1. Determine what is needed to do the job satisfactorily *under the circumstances in which it will function*
         a. In general terms (a charging desk)
         b. In detail (which units)
         c. In fine detail (what dimensions, what specific design and construction). How fine? To the point where it makes a difference to a good librarian who knows her tools of trade
   B. Know what is available and from what sources
      1. Catalogs
      2. Salesmen
      3. Viewing samples and what others have
      4. Sharing experiences with colleagues
      5. Professional literature
   C. Reconcile your needs with available materials or pioneer into the fields of made-to-order or do-it-yourself
   D. Be practical
      1. In order to be prepared for the inevitable compromise with the ideal, you must first know what is the best (a measure of professional competence); and the minimum of acceptability should be crystal-clear (a measure of a good, realistic, practical librarian)
      2. Consider your needs as a part of an over-all need in which you are entitled only to your just share

II. Translation of needs into written specs
   A. Classification of specs
      1. Open spec—a description is given of the item without reference to a brand name
      2. Brand name spec—a brand name is used to describe the item, usually accompanied by a catalog number
      3. Modified brand name spec—a brand name is used, accompanied by a supplementary description of certain special features ordinarily not included with the standard item
   B. Preliminary research (the process of learning the fine points)
      1. Try to find the desired item in *recent* catalogs
      2. Check several sources
      3. Read descriptive material carefully—be skeptical
      4. Look for facts (sizes, specific features)
      5. "Ask the man who owns one." There is no substitute for personal inspection of an item
      6. Ask the salesman for detailed construction specs. He can get them for you and they are good to have, even if you don't understand some of them
      7. Learn all you can about the item. The more preliminary research, the less difficulties encountered in making an award later
      8. Get a "budget estimate," but make clear that you are not asking for a bid price at this time
      9. Make up your mind, with an objective, defensible basis. Know exactly what you want and why!
   C. Writing good specs—making your exact wants exactly clear
      1. General description heading (for quick identification)—example: Stand, dictionary, floor model
      2. Body of spec
         a. Use concise statements and brief paragraphs without unnecessary words
         b. Make sure dimensions and catalog numbers are accurate
         c. Remember the use of "shall be" implies mandatory requirement
      3. Use of general specs as word savers (see examples following)
      4. Brand name spec (see example)
         a. Clearly indicates the type of item wanted and establishes a standard of quality
         b. Is the simplest and often the most effective type, especially suited for the purchaser without much technical background and with a minimum of testing facilities at his disposal
      5. Modifying a brand name spec (see example)
         a. First make certain the manufacturer will make the modification and at what cost

6. Open spec (see example)
    a. Generally used when an item is made to order
    b. Is unfair to purchaser and bidder unless it is complete and clear in every detail
    c. Generally requires technical knowledge and may require testing facilities to determine compliance
    d. Should not be used when a brand name will suffice
7. Inherent hazards of combining partial open spec with brand name spec (see examples)
    a. Unnecessary wordage
    b. Can be interpreted to mean that only the descriptive part of the spec is the essential requirement of the particular brand name item
D. General conditions or stipulations
    1. State determination of equivalence as the prerogative of the purchaser, but do not be arbitrary
    2. Prescribe requirement for furnishing samples, etc., when bidding on alternates
    3. Include a "true intent" clause to protect against errors in specs
    4. Reserve right to reject all bids and to increase or decrease quantities
III. Miscellaneous suggestions
    A. Work closely with your purchasing agent and business office in preparing your specs
    B. Do not attempt to be an amateur engineer, designer, or lawyer in writing lengthy and ambiguous specs. You won't fool anyone!
    C. Spend public funds with the same shrewdness as you would spend your own
    D. Seek competition; do not try to avoid it
    E. Anticipate who will bid on your requirements and what each bidder will intend to furnish. Decide which of these are acceptable, and write your specs accordingly
    F. Do not rely on a transparent technicality in your specs as a basis for disqualifying certain products. This can be interpreted as an arbitrary act. If you do not have a sound basis, then you really do not know the difference. Do further digging and you'll find the answer!

EXAMPLES

No. 1. Brand name specs

BOOK TRUCK, Small
Shall be Library Bureau 7607, Myrtle 630BT, or Sjostrom 173.

No. 2. Modified brand name specs

BOOK TRUCK, Small
Shall be equipped with rubber bumpers along entire length of outside corners of both end members. Shall be furnished in dark walnut finish to match existing furniture; successful bidder shall furnish sample color and finish panels for the approval of the librarian before proceeding.

Shall be Library Bureau 7607RB, Myrtle 630BT, or Sjostrom 173 with exceptions, if any, as herein specified.

No. 3. Open specs (very inadequate example; provides for bare minimum quality)

BOOK TRUCK, Small
Shall be constructed of birch or maple, with natural finish, 2 intermediate shelves, and a bottom shelf. Shelves shall be securely fastened to end members. Shall be equipped with 4 rubber-tired casters.

No. 4. Open specs (very complete example)

BOOK TRUCK, Small

Standard of quality
The general specs described below are intended to establish a standard of quality consistent with usual practices in industry for furniture and equipment of this character. No departure from the construction and finish is acceptable by the Department of Education as equal or superior to the specs.

Lumber
The wood used for all items of school furniture, unless otherwise specified, shall be sugar maple (acer saccharum) or birch (betula lenta and lutea), selected for favorable appearance of grain and well-matched color. The stock shall be clear and sound, free from any imperfections affecting the strength and appearance of the wood.

It shall be thoroughly air-seasoned and then kiln-dried to a moisture content not exceeding 7 per cent, and shall be stress free. After drying, the lumber shall be allowed to temper in controlled atmosphere for not less than three days before being milled. Stock selected for all steambent parts shall be air-seasoned only to moisture content of approximately 30 per cent before bending, and kiln-drying shall be effected after bending in suitable forms or shackles to insure permanence of form.

Glue and glue joining
In all joints where glue is employed (dowel, mortise and tenon, butt joints, etc.) all parts and surfaces constituting the joint shall be thoroughly and completely covered with glue. The glued joints shall be so strongly formed that they cannot be pried open with damaging or breaking the dowels, tenons, or other parts of the joints.

Finish
Finish block showing quality of finish required and color blocks showing allowable limits of color are available for inspection of bidders at the Department of Education, Business Office, 3 East 25th St., Baltimore 18, Md.

Finishing materials and their application: Unless the specs under an individual item stipulate explicitly a different finish, the finish that shall be applied shall consist of 3 full wet coats of the highest grade lacquer O'Neil Duro #32231 (gloss) and #32232 (Semi-Gloss) or equal.

Construction
Shall be 30" long x 14" wide x 35" high, over-all. Shall consist of 2 end members 14" x 35" x 1" thick, 2 shelves 13" x 28" x 13/16" thick with a bottom consisting of a double thickness of boards of the same dimensions as the shelves. Shelves and bottom shall be grooved, glued, and screwed into the ends, with screws concealed. Space between shelves shall be 10". Casters shall be 5" diameter, 2 swivel and 2 rigid, wrought steel, with semisoft rubber tires. Casters shall be bolted to bottom with nuts and lock washers. Casters shall be Bassick No.1.

No. 5. Combination open spec and brand name spec

BOOK TRUCK, 30"
Shall be 30" long x 14" wide x 35" high with bottom and 2 shelves secured into 1" ends. Truck shall be equipped with 2 swivel and 2 stationary casters. Shall be Library Bureau 7607, or equal. (This type of spec has a built-in hazard; it may be interpreted to mean that the only important features to you of Library Bureau 7607 are the ones specifically noted in the spec. If the intent is the equivalent of Library Bureau 7607 with *all* of its features, subject to your interpretation of equivalence, the brand name and catalog number suffice.)

No. 6. Illustrates importance of preliminary research before preparing specs. Variations in dimensions and other features between similar products of several manufacturers should be known.

DICTIONARY STAND, Floor type

Mfg.	Wide	Deep	High	Back	Standard Finish
LB	24	$14\frac{1}{2}$	$43\frac{1}{2}$-41	yes	Maple, several available
SJ	22	16	44-42	yes	Maple, natural or tinted
SD	22	16	44-41	yes	Mellow oak color (tan)
M	24	$14\frac{1}{2}$	$43\frac{1}{2}$-40	no	Maple, natural, gray tint

If the above dimensional differences are of no consequence, then the use of the various brand names and catalog numbers would be sufficient. If the back is important, then "M" would be omitted from the specs. If a specific finish or color is desired, it should be included in the specs, otherwise you could be required to take any the manufacturer cares to furnish, particularly if he has several to offer.

See example No. 2 which illustrates a method of specifying standard products, but with certain exceptions applicable to some manufacturers.

TO REMODEL
OR NOT TO REMODEL
FROM THE POINT OF VIEW
OF THE LIBRARIAN

HARRY N. PETERSON
Librarian, District of Columbia Public Library
Washington, D.C.

It seems to me that librarians have been faced with the question of whether to remodel or not to remodel ever since King Assurbanipal of Assyria founded the first great library of ancient times. At any rate, it's been going on for quite a while. And there's no doubt in my mind that this question will continue to vex generations of librarians yet unborn.

There are several reasons why a librarian has to consider the possibility of remodeling. These include aesthetic considerations, repairs to buildings or mechanical equipment, the need for more space, and the desire to improve services or to increase efficiency and reduce operating costs. All of these are worthy objectives. However, I shall ignore the first two items mentioned, for obvious reasons. As I am sure that you will agree, it is utterly impossible to generalize regarding aesthetic considerations. Individual solutions have to be found for each problem. The same is true with respect to repairs to buildings and mechanical equipment. Manifestly, needed repairs have to be accomplished. However, if there is any prospect of getting a new building, it is unwise to waste money on extensive repairs.

I should like to use the time allotted to me to discuss what can be done when the lack of space becomes a problem or when there is a need to improve service and increase efficiency. Incidentally, while my remarks are primarily concerned with the public library, and specifically central library buildings, the same basic principles apply to other situations.

At the outset I should like to say that before a librarian concludes that he needs more space, he should make sure that the need really exists. This may seem obvious, but it is often the obvious that escapes us. A thorough analysis should be made. In this connection it is fundamental that the librarian re-examine his objectives. Next, he should see that his staff organization and his service plan are capable of accomplishing those objectives in the most effective and efficient manner possible. Finally, the building should be examined to see if, with modifications, it can continue to meet the needs of the public, not only at the present time but for at least twenty years ahead.

Consultant and Architect

Librarians who have not had experience in remodeling or in planning new buildings should obtain the services of a library consultant—preferably one who has had such experience and has demonstrated competence in developing solutions to organizational and service problems. When the time comes, and long before any decisions regarding remodeling or building are reached, an architect should also be engaged as a consultant. It is not wise to have just a library consultant or just an architect. Both points of view are necessary if effective results are to be obtained. This is as true in remodeling as it is in planning a new building.

Any number of illustrations can be given, but perhaps one or two simple examples will serve to emphasize the point. We found in the District of Columbia Public Library that three staff members were required to man a subject division in the central library. However, if two related divisions were juxtaposed, the combined units could be staffed with five instead of six people. Administratively it seemed sensible to place the literature division next to fiction. Unfortunately a wall divided the available area in two, thus making it impossible to carry out the plan. However, the superintendent of buildings and grounds pointed out that the wall was nonbearing and could be removed. This was confirmed by the municipal architect. Incidentally, it cost approximately $3000 to take the wall down, but that one-time outlay has resulted in a personnel saving of over $4000 a year.

The collaboration between the librarian and the municipal architect in developing a proposed large, "U"-shaped extension to the old and outgrown central library building offers a better illustration. However, this project is too extensive to discuss in the limited time available. Always keep in mind that consultants' fees will be repaid many times over by the savings gained from their advice. They will protect you against making expensive mistakes which, once made, may never be rectified.

It is recommended that the yardsticks developed by Wheeler and Githens, and published in *The American Public Library Building*,[1] be used to determine the

1. J. L. Wheeler and A. M. Githens, *The American Public Library Building* (Chicago: A.L.A., 1941).

present and future requirements for central public library buildings. Manifestly the need for a new building should be questioned if the present library is in a good location that is in or near the center of retail shopping, and if the square footage measures up to the yardstick based on anticipated population for at least twenty years.

Finding Simple Solutions

Before getting involved in extensive remodeling a librarian should make every effort to find simple solutions to space and other difficulties. Is the building being used to the best advantage? Maybe a meeting room should be converted to a subject division or some other public service and meetings held elsewhere. Is space improperly utilized or wasted? Perhaps it is possible to move a function which is, in effect, a separate entity from the central library to another building without impairing service. As an example, the District of Columbia Public Library schools division was shifted from the central to a branch building, thus providing badly needed space for central services.

Is your problem book storage? Possibly bound newspapers and magazines can be replaced with microfilm or microprint editions. This may take care of the situation for many years to come. Do you lack space for a growing collection? I hesitate to mention it, but maybe weeding is the answer. Too often that simple expedient is overlooked. Perhaps extra shelves can be installed in existing cases. A growing collection can sometimes be exchanged with a static one to obtain room for expansion. A similar solution may provide additional space for readers.

If you find one aspect of the service which has declined in use occupying a larger area than is needed, move it to smaller quarters and make the space available for a service which is continuing to expand. Look into the possibility of reorganizing operations to utilize space to better advantage and to improve services. Again, with the District of Columbia Public Library for an illustration, the central building used to be operated on a closed shelf basis. About ten years ago services were completely reorganized on the open shelf, subject divisional plan. Where readers had once been concentrated in the general reference room and the technology division, the reorganization helped distribute them throughout the building, thus utilizing space which previously had had only limited use. That services were greatly improved by the reorganization goes without saying. The changes also had the added advantage of increasing the capacity for books on open shelves from 35,000 to 150,000 volumes.

Even if a new building is needed, there is no point in deferring administrative improvements until construction is completed. On the contrary, it is a good idea to improve facilities wherever possible *before* planning a new building, so that the final design will include the latest and, presumably, best thinking. Changes of the kind mentioned have the advantage of bringing about service improvements more promptly than would otherwise be possible. However, if a new building is in the offing, expensive remodeling should obviously not be undertaken.

Consideration of New Construction

If the investigation suggested indicates that reorganization is at best only a partial solution to the problem, then we are in a better position to decide whether to remodel the old or build a new library. If the present building is too small to meet immediate requirements—not to mention future needs—obviously something more than a rearrangement of facilities will have to be accomplished.

First, let us review the circumstances under which new construction should be considered. If the library is in a poor location, removed from retail shopping activities, then every effort should be made to obtain another site and funds to erect a larger building. If the location is good but the lot is too small for lateral extensions to the existing structure, and the library cannot be extended vertically, a new building is also indicated. If the site is not large enough to erect an adequate new library and the adjoining property cannot be acquired, then another site must be obtained. If remodeling and extensions are possible, but only at a cost that is prohibitive or in excess of new construction, then certainly another building is the only logical answer.

Unfortunately decisions cannot always be made on the basis of logic. For instance, if the voters or the appropriating body do not regard with favor the proposal to erect a new library, and there is no prospect of getting construction funds in the near future, remodeling may be the only way to relieve the situation, even though a new building is the best solution to the problem. Ordinarily, under such circumstances renovations should be held to a minimum.

On the other hand, if there is likely to be a long delay before a new building can be erected, and the cost of renovations can be amortized in improved service over a period of years, the possibility of extensive renovations should not be ruled out. As a check on the cost of remodeling, compare it with the cost of renting space equal to that gained by renovation for the length of time the renovated building will have to be used. To sum up, the factors to consider in determining the need for a new building are the size, location, and condition of the old one; whether or not it lends itself to remodeling and enlargement; the cost of new construction versus renovation; and, finally, the availability of funds.

Despite what may be said to the contrary, it is not invariably better to build than to remodel. This has been demonstrated time and again in the business world. In this connection, if you are not already familiar with it, you may be interested in examining a book entitled *Modernizing Buildings for*

Profit[2] by Kenneth Kingsley Stowell, a member of the American Institute of Architects and a former editor of *The Architectural Forum*. While this volume is primarily concerned with modernizing commercial buildings of all kinds, it contains ideas that may also be applied to remodeling libraries.

If the present building is inadequate in size according to the Wheeler and Githens formula but of sound construction and in a good location, if it can be remodeled or extended at reasonable cost, and if the site is large enough, it is quite possible that remodeling or an extension may provide a very satisfactory solution to space and other requirements. In any event, the advice of a library consultant should be obtained and, after his evaluation of the situation, an architect should be engaged to see if the administrative ideas developed by the library consultant are sound from the architectural and engineering points of view. The architect will not only furnish the technical knowledge needed but will also be familiar with building codes and other pertinent regulations.

Examples of Remodeling

At this point (which, I must confess, is a little belated) I am beginning to wonder if the title of this talk should not have been "Remodeling Can Be Fun!" In any event, I think it goes without saying that, at least so far as the librarian is concerned, remodeling an old building requires much more imagination and ingenuity than planning a new structure. Each building represents an individual challenge. Manifestly the possibilities are almost limitless. While they cannot be enumerated here, a few examples should be noted.

First, of course, unused space should be investigated. Storerooms and large closets can often be utilized to excellent advantage. Basements may be converted into public service areas or workrooms. If they are not properly ventilated, possibly air conditioning can make them habitable. Nonbearing walls can be removed to create large service areas. Rooms can also be increased in size by eliminating unused closets or, as happened in the District of Columbia Public Library, an old spiral stairway. If necessary, walls can be built or double-faced bookcases set up to divide large areas into smaller units. Bookstacks can be installed or stack wings added. A building can be extended to provide more reading rooms and workrooms. When ceilings are high enough, mezzanines can provide space for readers and books, or offices. The installation of an elevator may make the basement and upper floors better suited for public service. Even straightening out winding stairways can yield useful space.

Incidentally, when we wanted to do that to the monumental stairs in the central library, objection

was raised because the 44 square feet saved in each stair well did not justify the cost of approximately $5600 for the alteration. However, it was pointed out that the change would modify the traffic pattern so that, in effect, 2000 square feet of virtually lost space would become available. Since this amounted to less than $3 a square foot, everyone concerned agreed that the cost, far from being excessive, was actually a bargain.

In renovating an old building, the basic approach should be to simplify. A good test of a proposed renovation is this: When a building is remodeled or enlarged, the final result should look as if it could have been included in the original design. Generally speaking, when an old building is extended it should, if possible, be a complete entity—not merely an old building with a nondescript addition. However, an exception should be made if plans call for the ultimate removal of the old library.

Naturally there are hazards in remodeling, and librarians should not be unmindful of them. Aside from the suggestions offered, it is a good idea to alter as little as possible to get the desired result. Extensive structural changes can be costly. Before embarking on such a program it is a good idea to have the architect prepare tentative plans and a rough estimate. Compare this figure with the cost of constructing a new building of comparable size. Such cost comparisons aid in making sound decisions. It is best to develop an over-all plan. This can be carried out in stages, if funds are not available to have all the work done at one time. But it is vital that the matter be thought through before any action is taken. Once mistakes are made, it is difficult, if not impossible, to correct them. Common sense and a well-developed plan are the best guarantees against regrets and excessive cost.

2. Kenneth Kingsley Stowell, *Modernizing Buildings for Profit* (New York: Prentice-Hall, 1935). O.P.

TO REMODEL
OR NOT TO REMODEL
FROM THE POINT OF VIEW
OF THE ARCHITECT

J. RUSSELL BAILEY
Architect, Orange, Virginia

Restorations, alterations and additions, or re-modeling of buildings have a prominent place in architectural history. I suppose it should be considered a mark of distinction if a building is re-modeled and additions are made to it throughout the years. At least there are outstanding examples which indicate this to be so. St. Peter's Cathedral in Rome was 161 years in the process of going through alterations and additions. There were twelve architects and artists who had a part in the long history of alterations to that cathedral. Bramonte, Sangallo—in fact, two Sangallos—Raphael, Michelangelo, Vignola, and Bernini are some of the architects who contributed to this changing, growing monument.

Our United States Capitol building is another notable example of restoration, alteration, and addition. Our White House has had major alterations. Many presidents and many architects have had a hand in its development and growth. Our country is so young we can hardly appreciate the time it has taken to create the famous architecture of antiquity. If we take 161 years off our history—the time it took to build St. Peter's—we would place ourselves back at the beginning of our Capitol building construction. Our forefathers had been working on the Capitol building just five years in 1798. It took about twenty-six years to complete our Capitol in its major con-struction. That is a long time by today's standards. There is a new multimillion dollar shopping center being built here in the District of Columbia area that is scheduled to take just seventy days from start to finish.

The point of mentioning St. Peter's, the Capitol, and White House as examples in the history of re-modeling work is simply to have us recall how com-mon a practice remodeling really has been and is in our day. And if we are to learn anything from the past about library buildings, it seems we should learn that it pays to design a library so that the building can be added to and, thus, made to function over a long period of time. We cannot pay today for all the buildings which will be needed twenty years from now. The coming generations are going to need more than we can provide, so let's be kind to them and give some thought to growth when planning new library buildings. And remember that many magnificent buildings are magnificent because space and thought were given to growth.

It is easy to resolve the problem of whether or not to add to a library building if there is space enough, if that space is in just the right location, if the library is a grand and much-loved architectural gem, and if the public would consider nothing but keeping it and making it work at any cost. It is easy to decide what to do if a library building is poorly located and there is not enough land, and if the character of the building is not pleasing and its structure not sound. But it is not easy to make a decision when the conditions are halfway between these two extremes as is more often the case. What do we do then? What are the things to check? How do we start?

Why not begin by making a check list of questions and then fill in the answers to them with facts? A check list can easily be made, but obtaining facts to answer properly all the questions on the list is more difficult. Then what do we do? Follow a do-it-yourself plan, or call in an experienced, talented person to help evaluate the conditions and make a sound recommendation? The answers to these questions should be made on the basis of a balanced consideration of costs for outside, expert advice and for quality of talent among those interested in the library, including both staff and board members. The check list and its answers can then be worked into a statement of program similar to that pre-pared for a new building. It will comprise the needs for the library. In this area the librarian is expert.

Needs

Librarians are particularly well qualified to de-velop a creative list of needs. Creative list means a list born of knowledge, experience, and imagina-tion. Such a list would recognize the need for space for books and readers, and space for staff. Require-ments would show a desire to develop the library's collection, to create a general interest in the use of the library with all its services, and to develop interest in all means of communicating knowledge and wisdom. A librarian would be quick to recog-nize needs in making more efficient use of the library staff. The statement of needs would show comprehension of the problem. Through it a deci-sion on whether to remodel or to build a new building would begin to come into focus.

Site

About site, there is a wide gap in the thinking of library consultants. Location, topography, size, and technical or subsoil considerations are some of the elements of this problem. About location, there are many opinions also. There is no hard and fast rule or set of rules for deciding on the location of a new library building or on deciding whether the existing building is in the correct location. For example, the ideal decision today may not be ideal for the future. Cities change so drastically that a logical decision made ten years ago may be an unfortunate one today. A new shopping center in a suburban area may completely change the pattern of the pedestrian center of what seemed to be the fixed and permanent center of a community.

There are important principles of good site selection, however. In cities that are growing fast the library staff and board must be careful to select a site with understanding as to the likelihood of area growth. The private automobile has a much larger part in library site selection now than it had even ten years ago. In some suburban areas the family car enters into site selection more than the bus line. This is not the time to go into detail on site selection, but we should consider the value of an existing library building partly in relation to the effectiveness of the site—as it has application to space for services, present and future—and for convenience to library patrons, present and future. Public and private transportation and pedestrian traffic must all be considered since service to library patrons is our real objective. The site may make the difference in whether to remodel or build anew.

The Building

Is it structurally sound? Does it meet the requirements of fire safety regulations or of a reasonable code? Is it air conditioned? Can air conditioning be installed with a reasonable degree of economy? Are the other mechanical services in compliance with reasonable building codes? This last question relates to electric wiring and lighting, plumbing, elevators, heating, ventilation, communication systems, and so forth. Are the books and other reading materials properly housed? Are the shelves adequate? If there is a multitier stack, does it prevent a functional addition and alteration? Is the arrangement of the library efficient? How can it be improved? Has the library fallen into a general state of disrepair? Are the floors, the lights, the walls, the furnishings in need of refurbishing? Is the atmosphere of the library one that is inviting, pleasant, and stimulating? And—the big question—is the building planned for efficient use by the staff?

This is a most interesting question for the librarian, but it is equally interesting to the administrator, the trustee, the library board, the city or county council. If the staff is not working efficiently because of building handicaps, then money is being poorly used. "It's not the heat; it's the humidity," we say in Washington. In libraries it's not the building cost; it's the staff cost. Furthermore, if the staff is not as efficient as it could be because of building inadequacy, then library service suffers. Keep the library staff happy, and new readers will use the library. It is knowledge and information and wisdom and understanding we need. If the old library building can't do the job, remodel it so it will, or build a new one that will help in getting library resources in the hands of patrons.

Money

An ample supply of money is what is needed today for remodeling or for rebuilding. Generally, it costs more to remodel than to construct a new building—square foot for square foot. There are exceptions, however. Why does it usually cost more to remodel and make an addition? The cost of demolition is high in labor, in dirt, in inconvenience, in damage to books, and so on. It is difficult to obtain a fixed contract for such work without paying a premium price. Also, it is more difficult work for the architect. Because it cost him more to do his job, he must add to the cost of his services. As there are many unknowns in remodeling, a large contingency budget must be provided. There are structural risks and dangers involved in many alteration projects. Contractors and architects do not like to take these risks. And some library administrators and boards never quite recover from a full-scale remodeling project!

The brighter side of the subject is this: Remodeling is justifiable if the results are satisfactory and if the reasoning was correct in deciding whether or not to remodel. For example, if a city had to wait a long time for a bond issue to pass to get a new building, the cause of the public library might be largely lost for many years. Remodeling may be the wise thing to do even though it costs more—square foot for square foot.

Opinion

Public opinion can be molded. (This statement must be made with reservations.) If the community has the potential and if remodeling is the correct procedure, then *sell it* and convince people they are going to have a fine library, the best library for the conditions, the best for the community. Remodeling does not have to be a second best. It can be the best. We who work on libraries like to think our new library buildings are going to be worthy of remodeling. We like to think we could do a fine job on them if we were called back to remodel our own designs. We like to think we have planned for additions. There should be no stigma attached to remodeling.

I would like to give here two or three illustrations which are variations of opinion on remodeling. Opinion and decision on this subject can be based on sentiment, or expediency, or can be calculated. Your colleague and library buildings expert, Mr. Keyes Metcalf, supplied me with these examples at breakfast the other morning. A perfect use of sentimentality is found on the Delaware State College campus. At this school the library was developed from an old slave quarters' building. Here there was no question. The building was to be remodeled at whatever cost would be required.

The donors of Harvard's Widener Library building stipulated that no additions were to be made to the building and that the courts were not to be filled in. This calculated bit of foresight is unusual and perhaps unique in the history of library buildings.

For the Belmont (Massachusetts) Public Library the donors of the land stipulated that a library building must always be on the land or the land ownership would revert to the family. There was much love for the site and the building. It was expedient, to say the least, not to break the will by using the land for another purpose or by allowing a new library to be built on another more appropriate site where parking and other building problems could have been solved more readily.

From these illustrations it seems wise to appreciate the real limitations set by opinion.

Proposal

A proposal should lead to a commitment and a commitment to a completed project. The proposal is first made to the representatives of the community, and then it may have to be voted on by the public. At any rate, the proposal to remodel must be clearly and enthusiastically stated, it must be positive, and it must be convincing. Librarian and architect and board must be convinced themselves that the alteration and addition are the best answer at the moment and that the moment is right to go all out for the project.

Conclusion

In recapitulation, let's agree to the following:

1. It is usually not easy to decide whether or not to remodel; therefore it is necessary to question the procedure with a carefully prepared and answered check list of questions.

2. A remodeling project should never be rushed into just because it has always seemed the best thing to do. It may be better to use the existing library for some other function and to construct a new library building.

3. It usually costs more to remodel than to build new construction, which is a good reason for pause.

4. If the needs for enlargement are great, perhaps a new building is the real answer.

5. The site may dictate whether to rebuild or to remodel. A fine building in a poor location would be unfortunate. An unsatisfactory building in the right location perhaps should be remodeled.

6. Giving money for remodeling is not as glamorous as giving money for new construction. But if remodeling is the correct thing to do, make a convincing proposal—and sell the idea wholeheartedly!